IN THE BALANCE

A 15,000 KM VOYAGE
OF THE SEAS OF EUROPE

JONO DUNNETT

First Published 2022

ISBN: 978-0-9957782-4-5

Copyright © 2022 Jonathan Dunnett

A CIP catalogue record for this title is available from the British Library.

Maps: Author's own based on shapes from the following sources:
* https://www.eea.europa.eu/data-and-maps/data/eea-coastline-for-analysis-1/gis-data/europe-coastline-shapefile
* https://www.eea.europa.eu/data-and-maps/data/wise-large-rivers-and-large-lakes
* International Hydrographic Organization, IHO; Sieger, Rainer (2012): Limits of oceans and seas in digitized, machine readable form. Alfred Wegener Institute, Helmholtz Centre for Polar and Marine Research https://doi.org/10.1594/PANGAEA.777975

Photographs: Author's own unless stated
Cover (front): Gamvik, Norway (71°3'48"N, 28°15'59"E)
Cover (back): Atlantic coast of Portugal (40°18'13"N, 8°53'17"W)
Cover (back, inset): Viana do Costelo, photo by Monica Vicente-Arche
Cover designs: Author's own

To Alba and Rafa. You had little to do with the writing of this book, but everything to do with why I wrote it.

Contents

CONTENTS I

FOREWORD 1

BOOK STRUCTURE: THE SEAS 2

THE WORLD OCEAN 4

EUROPE 5

1.   BARENTS SEA 6

        GRENSE JAKOBSELV 8
        EXPEDITION LIFE 12
        VARANGERHALVØYA 14
        SVAERHOLT 18

2.   NORWEGIAN SEA 24

        TROMSØ 27
        LUNDØYA AND MANNSHAUSEN 30
        THE ARCTIC CIRCLE 32
        RE-ENCOUNTER WITH MS NORDLYS 34
        ISLAND HOPPING 36
        STADLANDET 38
        SAILING WITH VIKINGS 41

3.   NORTH SEA – PART ONE 44

        EIGERØYA 47
        EIKVÅG 49

4.   SKAGERRAK SEA 52

        STAVERN, AND TØNSBERG 54
        OUR CHOICES MATTER 57

5.   KATTEGAT SEA 58

        LÆSØ 60

6.   LIMFJORDEN 64

        THE EAST SEA TO THE WEST SEA 66

7.   NORTH SEA – PART TWO 70

THORSMINDE...72
ESBJERG 74
HELGOLAND 76
THE WADDEN SEA 79
SCHEVENINGEN 83
GATEWAYS TO EUROPE 87

8.   ENGLISH CHANNEL 90

BLIGHTY 93
DIEPPE 95
CONTACTS..98
BAIE DE LA SEINE 99
RAZ BLANCHARD (THE ALDERNEY RACE) 100
THE BAY OF LE MONT-SAINT-MICHEL..102
NORTH BRITTANY 104

9.   CELTIC SEA 106

FINDING A WAY 108
RAZ DE SEIN 110

10.   BAY OF BISCAY 114

CHARLIE..116
STORM OPHELIA 118
SIX HOPS TO LA ROCHELLE 120
REPAIRS..123
LA GIRONDE 124
AQUITAINE COAST 127
BIENVENIDO A ESPAÑA 131
SAN SEBASTIÁN 132
BILBAO 134
ALFONSO 135
WINTER...138
CABO DE ESTACA DE BARES 142

11.   NORTH ATLANTIC OCEAN 144

IN THE BALANCE – CARIÑO TO CEDEIRO 147
LA CORUÑA 151
MALPICA, AND BASECAMP MUXÍA..154
FINISTERRE TO THE ISLES CIES..156
THE TRADES 159
NAZARÉ...162
MY DOLPHIN TEACHERS 163
NATURAL PARK OF THE SOUTHWEST 164
ALGARVE COAST – PORTUGAL FINAL DAYS 168
CABO TRAFALGAR..169

Contents   iii

12.   MEDITERRANEAN SEAS AND STRAITS 170

13.   STRAIT OF GIBRALTAR 172

    CONSCIOUS PILOTS 175

14.   ALBORAN SEA..178

    LA ATUNARA 180
    THE SEA OF POLYTHENE... 184

15.   MEDITERRANEAN SEA PROPER – PART ONE 186

    CARTAGENA 188
    MAR MENOR... 189
    THE OTHER NICK 190

16.   BALEARIC SEA..192

    THE ALIEN AND THE ASTRONOMER 194
    DELTA DEL EBRO... 197
    NERVES THAT HAVE A NAME 201
    TARRAGONA, SITGES, BLANES.. 204

17.   MEDITERRANEAN SEA PROPER – PART TWO 206

    COSTA BRAVA.. 208
    THE SOUTH OF FRANCE... 210
    CAPTAIN PABLO 212

18.   LIGURIAN SEA..216

    THE HOBIE CAT BROTHERS... 218
    NOLL, GENOA AND MONEGLIA.. 219
    CINQUE TERRE 221

19.   TYRRHENIAN SEA 222

    MATT.. 224
    CHRIS.. 225
    CIVITAVECCHIA.. 226
    BAIA DI NAPOLI 228
    ILENIA 230
    A LOOK BACK FROM SCILLA 232

20.   IONIAN SEA – PART ONE...236

    STRETTO DI MESSINA 238
    CALABRIA... 241
    BRUNELLA AND CATALDO 244
    PREPARATION FOR A CROSSING... 246

21.   ADRIATIC SEA **248**

THE CROSSING 250

ALBANIA 255

22.   IONIAN SEA – PART TWO **258**

CORFU TO KEFALONIA 260

PYLOS 262

THE MANI PENINSULA AND CAPE MATAPAN 264

CAPE MALEAS...268

23.   AEGEAN SEA **270**

LIFE'S GENEROSITY 273

THE SARONIC GULF...275

BEDTIME STORIES...277

NICKOLAS OF CHALKIDA 278

THE VOLOS PENINSULA..279

THESSALONIKI 281

HALKIDIKI AND MOUNT ATHOS 283

ELEFTHERON..287

ALEXANDROUPOLIS 288

ENEZ..290

24.   MARMARA SEA **292**

GELIBOLU (GALLIPOLI) PENINSULA..................................294

PICKING YOUR BATTLES...297

TO ISTANBUL 299

WINTER PAUSE 301

A PLAN TO CLOSE THE LOOP 302

THE BOSPHORUS 303

25.   BLACK SEA **306**

LAUNCH, SAIL, LAND, REPEAT..309

A LEGAL ALIEN IN EREGLI 310

ZONGULDAK 311

AMASRA, SINOP, SAMSUN 312

REFLECTIONS ON THE *KARADENIZ* 314

THE THREE AMIGOS..317

ARRIVAL GEORGIA 318

ODESSA..321

DANUBE DELTA – PART ONE 324

DANUBE DELTA – PART TWO 326

ROMANIA – SOUTHERN PART 328

BULGARIA – THE END OF THE VOYAGE 332

ALL CHANGE AT BURGAS...334

Contents

26.   BIKING FROM THE BLACK SEA **336**

NORTHWARD 336

27.   BALTIC SEA **340**

THE BALTIC STATES 343

FINLAND 345

28.   BIKING TO THE BARENTS SEA **346**

BETWEEN SEAS 346

THE LOOP CLOSED 349

EPILOGUE **351**

APPENDIX 1 – THANKYOUS **352**

APPENDIX 2 – DATA AND TRACK **356**

Foreword

It all began with a long standing ambition to solo windsurf round Britain. The concept was simple: a normal windsurf board with a barrel on the back to carry luggage; sailing by day, alone at sea; and nights spent ashore – either sheltering under the sail, or as a grateful recipient of hospitality. The circumnavigation was completed in 98 days, and became the foundation for this much longer voyage.

Long distance windsurfers are a rare breed. We have access to the shore like a sea kayaker, yet punch through the waves like an ocean going sailboat. Or at least that is what we may think until a gale comes in. We balance on an unstable plank: with no cabin, no engine, and no crewmate.

Next time you glimpse open water – perhaps from a ferry or through binoculars – imagine being out there. Put yourself far from land, alone, on a log with a handkerchief for a sail. You will sense our vulnerability, but also our freedom.

This book captures real adventure. Accuracy is prioritised in the telling of the stories. My intention was to provide an honest record of this voyage round Europe. The book is also – in part – an essay on the seas, so that for the reader they become more than simply blue on a map.

Additionally, this book is an acknowledgment of – and a thankyou for – the help received. For everyone who I met, it is a way to tell the stories that I was too tired to tell at the time, or that would unfold later in the voyage. Having lived this story, it was my duty – and is my privilege – to share it.

And, finally, this book is an invitation to us all to care more deeply for nature. I have seen our coastline close up. Every river, wetland, forest, rocky shore, reef and estuary can be counted. If we do not protect nature there will come a day when – for those who come next – it has gone.

It is a book of gratitude and wonder, nerves and fear. These are my years as a long distance windsurfer.

Book Structure: The Seas

Throughout this voyage, the coastline being sailed mattered more than the language spoken back on land. Borders are invisible at sea. And – either side of them – people talk in different tongues of the same sea. Mariners also tell stories of other seas that contrast with their own. Those who set sail know that the sea would drown them: that there is the sea and its final embrace, or the salvation of a safe return to land. The challenges ashore are of secondary concern.

Accordingly, the divisions of World Ocean are used as structure for this book. Within each chapter – each "sea" – are accounts of three types:

Log entries (blog posts) were written soon after the experiences of which they tell, when the emotions were still fresh, the eyes were stinging of salt, and my mind was offshore. Many log entries remain online, and a subset of the better ones – tidied up – are included here.

Retrospective accounts recall other noteworthy passages, and give completeness to the story. They highlight the challenges of particular seas; and provide detail about tactics and strategy.

The glue for these accounts are sections with informative or more reflective writing. These give context, relate to my state of mind at various stages, and perhaps point to an evolution in my own outlook.

Before launching into the chilly Barents Sea there is an introduction to the World Ocean, and a note about what is meant by Europe.

The introductions to the seas are short and not essential to the storyline. Those who do not share my fascination with the maritime may experience them as heavy weather. The choice lies with the reader whether to battle through or skip these sections.

The Seas of Europe[1]

[1] Reference: International Hydrographic Organization (1953) *Limits of Oceans and Seas*. 3rd ed.
[2] The "Inner Seas off the West Coast of Scotland".

4

The World Ocean

At the level of our planet, there is a single contiguous World Ocean. This is partially divided by continental plates: slabs of rock that wander according to convection in the Earth's mantle. Since the breakup of the supercontinent Pangaea the plates have drifted to create three major divisions of World Ocean. These are the Pacific, Indian, and Atlantic Oceans. The major oceans are all linked to – and delimited by – water in circulation round Antarctica, which is usually referred to as the Southern Ocean. A mental image of the three-petalled Yellow Iris flower would be somewhat accurate. The petal representing the Pacific should be imagined as twice the size of its neighbours – and it alone corresponds to an area of the planet more expansive than all land combined. The calyx – the green, outermost whorl of the flower – would be the Southern Ocean.

Missing from this model is the Arctic Ocean. Accounting for less than 5 percent of the World Ocean by area, this is the shallowest and smallest ocean, and also the coldest. It is linked to the World Ocean principally by connection with the much warmer Atlantic, and is often considered a sea or estuary of the latter. Circulation of water with the Atlantic Ocean, both in and out, is measured in millions of cubic metres per second. Consider that, to understand that the oceans are the heat pumps of our planet.

Within oceans, are seas. An uncontroversial definition of a sea is as a large division of the World Ocean. To what extent gulfs, bights, bays and straits are eligible is essentially a matter of taste. As official arbiter of the seas sailed on my journey, I have closely followed boundaries defined by the (currently applicable) 3rd edition of the International Hydrographic Organization's *Limits of Oceans and Seas* (1953). Deviations from this reference are flagged.[1]

Following the logic of how seas are described, it becomes evident that all of Europe's seas are part of the World Ocean; and all are also part of either the Arctic or Atlantic Ocean; and many are also part of some further subdivision.

---

[1] Note: The IHO *Limits* (1953) are from a time when less was known about the oceans and their currents, and the polar regions were of relative unimportance. For example – according to the 3rd edition – the major oceans extend south to Antarctica such that there is no Southern Ocean. An updated edition of *Limits* was drafted in 2002 – and does include the Southern Ocean – but disagreement between IHO member states prevents its publication.

Europe

I decided to windsurf round Europe. That had a ring to it. And a logic too. I had already windsurfed round Britain: as a way to "know" my country. It takes a wander round a home to really know it. But after that, what? Slippers and Netflix? Not yet. There was the neighbourhood to see: the continent to know.

My assumption then was that the continents were real things, corresponding strictly to continental plates. In fact, though geology may instruct their identification, the definitions are more arbitrary. Based on geology alone, Europe is at most a subcontinent. We share a continental plate with most of Asia. In a geological sense Europeans are Eurasian, and populate the Eurasian continent.

300 million years ago, and long before the land mass that we now identify as Eurasia came to take a recognisable form, a sea was pinched, and a mountain range – that we now call the Ural Mountains – pushed skywards. The plate boundaries that formed these ancient mountains fused, and the Urals were left behind – like a scar – across the newly formed Eurasian plate.

The ancient Greeks first distinguished Europe from Asia, presumably as a way to make sense of their world. The dividing line has since been fluid, influenced by history and culture. The modern definition is for a boundary that traverses the Ural Mountains – from the Russian Arctic to Kazakhstan. Tidying up southward of here, it then meanders along the Ural River to the Caspian Sea; then heads west over the Great Caucasus to reach the Black Sea; and then bisects Istanbul on its way to the Aegean Sea.

A start from deep within Russia was never on my radar, and would in any case have taken years to organise. From the outset, therefore, the project developed as a plan to windsurf "round" Europe as understood in a narrower political sense.

1. Barents Sea

The roof of Europe is often taken to be Nordkapp, in Norway. Observers are drawn to this point, and most spend a few moments gazing north from the cliff edge. They are looking out over the Barents Sea.

This is the Arctic Ocean. Nordkapp itself is a little over 2000 km from the North Pole. The northern limits of the Barents Sea are defined by locations within the Svalbard (Norway) and Franz-Josef Land (Russia) archipelagos. Novaya Zemlya (Russia) – an archipelago that may be considered an extension of the Ural Mountains – separates Barents from Kara Sea, and has the dubious distinction of having been used as the test site for the most powerful nuclear weapon ever detonated.

Winter sea ice is a feature of the bounding archipelagos, providing habitat for polar bears. The southern waters are relatively warmer – maintained ice-free year-round by the North Atlantic Current, an extension of the Gulf Stream.

The Barents Sea is strategically important for reasons relating to natural resource, access to them, and access to other parts of the globe. This includes to the Arctic more generally – that is becoming increasingly accessible as technology advances and sea ice retreats.

Commercial fishing focusses upon cod, capelin and red king crab. King crab were introduced by Russia in the 1960s and have expanded their range westward such that Norway now considers them an invasive species – albeit an economically useful one.

Gas and oil fields have been exploited by both Norway and Russia – at great economic cost due to remoteness and latitude.

For Russia, the Barents Sea is important for the direct access it offers to the North Atlantic. Russia also controls the Northeast Passage – a potentially important trade route that links Atlantic and Pacific through the Arctic Ocean, and that is now ice-free in the summer.

For these reasons, Russian naval operations in the Barents Sea are continual and high profile. Norway and NATO allies respond in similar fashion, to remind of their own presence.

From the roof of Europe, the Norwegian coastline bends to the south and to the east. After about 300 km it reaches the border with Russia. It is with the assistance of the Norwegian military that I reach this point: The edge of Europe. The start of my journey.

Barents Sea
extent and track

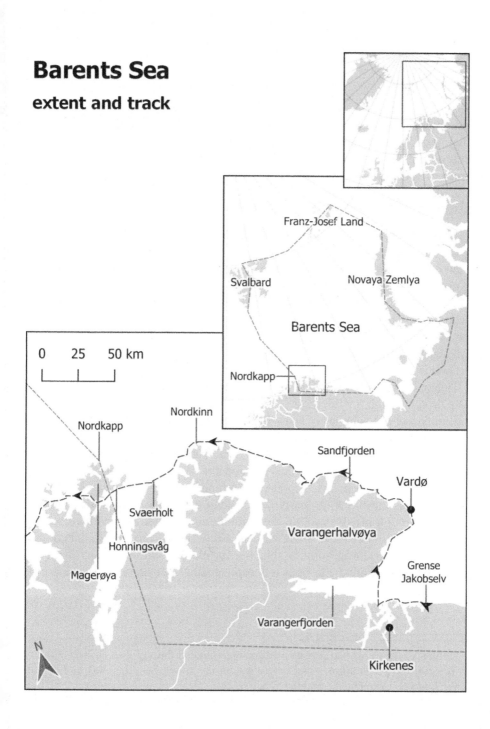

Grense Jakobselv

September 2016 and May 2017

Those who have lived by the sea will understand its pull. A seaward gaze becomes an invitation to be accepted or declined. Deprived the possibility of that gaze, contentment seems at best transitory, or requiring of mental contortion. Landlocked time is subtly depleting. A lungful of sea air is relief from suffocation. At least, that is my experience.

Eight months previous

I have been in Kirkenes, Norway for five days – researching an idea to windsurf round Europe. Kind people have offered their time and advice: Helene, my outward-bound Airbnb host; Dag, who has kayaked much of Norway's northern coastline; and the masters and crew of a solitary sailboat.[2] Much has been seen and learned. But Kirkenes is far inside a fjord where real waves do not reach. The sea that would have to be sailed is yet to be observed, though I feel its pull. I would like to eyeball reality at Grense Jakobselv, a tiny hamlet situated on the Norwegian side of the Norway-Russia border.

Helene – who is more wonderful with each passing day – suggests a trip. We drive through a wilderness landscape formed of rock that is nearly three-billion years old. The latter stage of the journey is on a road that is blocked by snow for half the year. Finally, we drop down into a valley, and follow the river Jakobs northward, towards the sea. Russia is just across the river.[3]

The floor of the valley widens over the next 5 km. At 1 km from the sea we pass a small but intensely pretty church, and then – in this land of rock – beach comes into view. I survey the launching options. Nervous excitement courses through me. It is a cold day with a colder wind, and there are waves enough to qualify as surf. Black heads – a few seals – are fishing the choppy waters. They appear at home in this, but for me it would be a risky launch. I run off to and around the next outcrop, sensing that there will be a better option there, and there is.

---

[2] Sailing Yacht *Cérès* had just arrived having voyaged through Russia. Her journey – years in the preparation – had been through the Baltic Sea, the Gulf of Finland, Lake Ladoga, Lake Onega, and the White Sea.

[3] "*Grense*" means border in Norwegian, and "*elv*" means river, so Grense Jakobselv means "border at the Jakobs river".

There is something about this place that already has me captivated. Also notable is the sense of being observed: by the Russian and Norwegian forces who are surely aware of our presence. Each military has a fortress, upon a ridgetop, and these face each other across the border, and they are out of bounds for even my camera lens.

The sea appears cold and empty, but also familiar. It is just sea. I would follow the coastline eastward, rather than attempting to cross Varangerfjorden, which at this point is still over 50 km wide. That would be an unnecessarily ambitious leap for day one. The near coastline is black, fringed with white foam, and appears steep enough to prevent landing at most places. Would there be landing options? In summer, there would be no night. I would just continue until one is found. My imagination does the sailing and cold hands dig deeper into their pockets.

May 2017

After arriving in Kirkenes, I hear that the road to Grense Jakobselv is still blocked by winter snows. Some days later I receive a message from Dag – the local adventurer with whom I had consulted previously. The army are clearing a way through the snow, and thanks to Dag's intervention, they will take me and my gear to the coastal hamlet in three days' time.

The drive to Grense Jakobselv with the Norwegian army

Journey's Start

Today is 20 May 2017. It is not restful in the back of the army jeep. The engine is loud. The suspension bucks and bounces. The wheels slide and occasionally become stuck in deeper snow. Our number are ten, between two vehicles. Towed behind one vehicle is a trailer stuffed tight with snow-clearing gear, backpacks and skis. Above all this is strapped a strikingly-visible pink and blue windsurf board.

The journey from the border station takes an hour, and it is too noisy for conversation. Through the windscreen it can be observed that the snow level is at times above the height of our jeep. I fail to suppress a grin. Dag has been in touch again. He suggested – based on the weather forecast – that I might want to hold back a few more days. My take was that the wind looks suitable. It will be cold, but I can cope with cold. And perfect rarely happens, so good enough will do. Now, it is just a case of avoiding screw-ups; hope that the board survives this journey; hope against a day one showstopper.

We pile out at Grense Jakobselv. The sea looks familiar, and conditions not challenging, despite some flecks of snow. Final preparation is a little hurried because the army teams are waiting to wave me off. A nice coincidence is that mine is not today's only expedition departure: two of the soldiers are kitted out in white fatigues and will be making their return journey by ski, towing sleds with their gear. It is a happy atmosphere. We gather for a group picture of big smiles.

Smiles at the start with Helene and the Norwegian army (with the skiers back left)

The soldiers help to move the gear to beyond the rocky outcrop, to the sheltered corner of beach. Then I struggle the final metres to the water unaided. The board is almost too heavy to lift. Once afloat, I clamber on for an inelegant but reliable getaway.

Puffing heavily from the exertion of the launch, I swing hips inboard to hook into the harness line that hangs from the boom. The metal hook of the harness bar engages, then pulls away, because it is unsecured. That makes for an unimpressive start. There is no alternative but to drop the sail: to free-up hands that will properly fasten the hook. The onlookers may have assumed me to be competent, but it surely does not seem that way now.

On second attempt the line takes my weight. The board lifts up onto a rail and begins slicing through the Barents Sea wind chop. When I look back, the figures on the beach are small, already too distant to hear my *tusen takk* – a thousand thanks – farewell.

***

It is a relief to be sailing. The stress of getting to this point has been considerable. I am thankful again to Helene, who has provided a haven during these last few days of preparation.

And I am thankful to Dag, who in his quiet and thoughtful way arranged to deliver me here – to a place that is more theirs than mine. I would have liked to linger longer at Grense Jakobselv; to say goodbye, because I do not expect to return. There are places where one senses a belonging, and – strangely – it was felt there.

The beginning of the voyage. Photo: Helene Erlandsen

Expedition Life

Welcome aboard for a tour of my ship. Up front we have a spray deck, sewn from orange PVC, with a transparent top pocket for a solar charger. Beneath this is a waterproof backpack stuffed with lighter, bulkier items including sleeping gear. Stuffed up front are also 20 freeze-dried expedition meals, two reserve gas cannisters, and a pair of Crocs. The spray deck has a shallow angle at the front so that it is not torn away by oncoming waves, and elastics pull it tight at the back.

On the back of the board is my barrel, which has previously accompanied me round Britain. It is strapped to a support over the rear footstraps, then strapped again to the footstrap fixings themselves. The barrel is filled with food including a three-weeks' supply of expedition porridge, cooking gear, clothes, repair gear, tracker and sundry essentials. The support itself also holds a thermos flask, fishing line, and a system for balancing the sail when in paddling mode.

On my back is a smaller backpack, that it would be nice to keep light but ends up feeling heavy. Inside are the things that might be needed on the water, including: VHF radio, gloves, hat, snacks of nuts and chocolate, water in a bladder with a tube for drinking while sailing, spare rope, a knife, sun cream and the like.

Both backpacks seal as rolltop drybags. In contrast to the barrel, these are not 100% waterproof when submerged, so additional drybag layers are essential for watertightness. Inside my smaller pack, wrapped within two extra drybags, I also carry a small laptop computer.

When sailing, under my drysuit I wear a woollen thermal base layer, and synthetic layering on top. A fleece-lined waterproof hat paired with ski goggles keep my head and face warm. Open-palm mitts are the best solution I have found to combat cold hands. Regardless, cold hands are a daily challenge. In my pockets are more snacks, my phone in a waterproof case, a waterproof camera, and a Personal Locator Beacon.

The sail itself is a 9.2 square metre Severne Turbo GT, but custom built with stronger laminate films. It is set up to be fully adjustable while sailing. An unusual modification are the "pogies" on the boom. These are more usually fitted to kayak paddles and help to reduce windchill on the hands. Also clipped onto the boom is a basic GPS unit.

The gear carrying modifications were conceived and built with my friend John – aka "Q" – at his forest hideaway on the island of Menorca. The board, unloaded and without the rig, weighs about 18 kilos. Loaded weight probably exceeds 40 kilos. A single-bladed SUP paddle is stowed with the blade under the spray deck and the shaft strapped to the deck.

The expedition board in full flight. Photo: Monica Vicente-Arche

The additional weight makes launching and landing difficult. However, once afloat the board feels the same as a normal windsurfer in most situations. The negatives of the extra gear are mostly felt at low speeds – instability; and at high speed when the shape of the spray deck can force the board deeper underwater when it nosedives.

The upside of carrying gear is autonomy. Provided there is fresh water – which might be snow – then in theory and practice it is easy to go days at a time without finding civilisation. Shelter for the night – although there is no night up here at this time of year – is provided by the sail, which is propped up by the paddle. Provided the orientation is correct, the wind pins the sail in place and beneath it there is escape from wind, rain and snow. If the wind is from a reliable direction it makes for a cosy home. Swirly winds are more problematic and can cause the roof to flip. It is often necessary to reorientate in the early hours.

At this latitude, all time under the sail is spent inside my sleeping bag. The bag has a generous fill of down and is protected by a waterproof and breathable outer shell. An inflatable mattress smooths out the stones and insulates from the cold ground. I have an additional set of wool thermals for use on land, a pair of trousers, woollen socks and mitts, a down jacket, and a synthetic jacket. Fully clothed in the sleeping bag, with all the drawstrings pulled tight, means that I am snug even when temperatures are below zero.

Home cooking is achieved with a Jetboil stove. These are fast and efficient at boiling water. At this stage of the journey all my cooking is simply reconstituting foods by adding hot water. I start, end, and punctuate the day with coffee. Proper filter coffee. That's important.

Varangerhalvøya

25 May 2017

In Norway an *-øya* is an island; and a *-halvøya* – a half island – is a peninsula.

After three days waiting out harsh weather at Vardø – Norway's easternmost town, on the island of Vardøya – I am sailing again. Conditions are amenable for good progress now, and allow the mind to wander. As I will come to appreciate, the delays should be cherished – rather than considered bad luck or an inconvenience. Neither dawdle, nor be in too much of a hurry, I remind myself.

One of several notable experiences in Vardø had been a conversation with the director of the Pomor Museum. We had met in the North Pole Bar and he had at first thought I was a birdwatcher sheltering from the snow. In centuries past, the Pomors, from Russia's north, traded by sea in fish and corn with the northern Norwegians, to the extent that they developed a pidgin language: Russenorsk. I had seen the museum building earlier, and had indeed spent some time watching the kittiwakes nesting on the sills under its eaves.

The director has a history of expeditions, and a deep knowledge of Svalbard. And then he bowls an unexpected, intentionally challenging, question. Do I think it is right that humans can go wherever they choose? On his mind is probably the trajectory of Svalbard – now in some regard a tourist destination, with cruise ships, and the infrastructure that these require and encourage. The wildness that brings the tourists is being gradually undermined by their coming.

My response at the time is based on the notion of whether the traveller can reach these places independently, which I take as a proxy for low impact. By this yardstick we should be free to walk where we choose, but not to fly.

There is a self-justification in my reasoning of course. I consider my lone windsurfer to be low impact, and exempt. I choose not to count the air and boat travel that got me to Kirkenes, the equipment manufactured on the other side of our planet, and the satellites in the sky that guide me.

Fundamentally, I now realise, my objection to the loss of wilderness is as a human animal. For us to thrive, the natural world must thrive; and for the natural world to thrive it requires that we act as humble custodians rather than reckless exploiters. Nature needs space. Yes, we can conquer the world, but it is folly to continue to do so.

I round the headland off Hamningberg, which is as far as the summer-only road from Vardø reaches. Beyond here, it is truly wild.

***

The board tracks parallel to the shore. Satellite imagery had suggested I may find some beaches. But reality brings dustbin-sized boulders that would only encourage a landing on a day of complete calm. Snow is held in frozen waves that curl from the cliff top, and elsewhere spills through gullies to the rocks below. Snow falls gently into the sea now. I regularly give each arm thirty shakes to move warming blood to the fingers. A snug-fitting hat makes it a silent experience, gliding through this wonderland.

In Varangerfjorden I had seen many sea eagles, and eider ducks; here there are razorbills. Note that I am using Norwegian spelling for fjord names. The *-en* suffix is like the definite article in English. An anglicised Varangerfjorden would be The Varanger Fjord.

Later in the day, which in the context of no darkness has little meaning, I am approaching the entrance to Sandfjorden. A few-hundred metres ahead a fin surfaces. The initial sighting appears to be an upright fin, suggestive of an orca. As I draw nearer, the sightings are of a more curved fin, more indicative of a minke whale. The tiredness I had been feeling evaporates, replaced by a hint of trepidation as I gently sail into the fishing ground. Sandfjorden is comfortingly diminutive and has no strong currents to contend with. Instead I can simply wait as a medium-sized minke whale goes about feeding, seemingly unperturbed by my presence.

I spend perhaps an hour floating above where presumably is a rich stock of fish. I lose the animal for minutes at a time, and wonder if it has moved on; but then each time am rewarded by an extravagant exhale as it surfaces nearby. Other times I am genuinely centred over the action, revealed by a jacuzzi of bubbles rising from the depths.

The animal comes up a few metres away, and through the clear water is visible an intense pink colouration. At the time I wonder if am seeing into the whale's mouth. Now, I understand that the pink is caused by blood flow diverted to the throat folds, so that overheating does not occur during the exertions of feeding.

Eventually, the animal becomes curious of the object in its vicinity. It passes by just a few feet away, rolled over on its side for an unobstructed view. Behind that eye is an intelligence. Either of us could be the author of this thought. The animal moves with precision and grace, suggestive of an utmost mindfulness. The interaction triggers calm rather than fear.

I pull myself away, perhaps thinking I will see more whales in coming days. In fact, I do not. On reliving this experience later in the journey – after meeting people who still eat these animals – I promise to the cetaceans that I will never eat their flesh.

It is late now, and I am tired. Perhaps it would have been wiser to head into Sandfjorden which – if the name is to be believed – promises an easy landing. Instead, I opted to continue. The breeze is now dying and the next good landings are many hours away. I spy a nook in the rocks on the east side of Sandfjorden – another of my so-called "beaches" – and decide to head there to camp before reaching more exposed coast.

Despite the calm sea, the rocks make it difficult to get the gear out of the water. I am aware it might be a tricky launch tomorrow, but am too tired to care.

***

Once ashore, changed into double thermals, double jacket and double socks, and with a sausage on the go in the camp-stove pan, I love this spot. The correct terminology for the first course of today's meal is a "*ventepølse*" – a waiting sausage – the Norwegian equivalent of an appetizer. It is cooked in abundant butter. Food, in the cold, travels and keeps well. And as for water, there is snow everywhere.

This is an inaccessible spot. Perhaps Dag has been here. Not many will have been. Decades-worth of timber is piled-up bizarrely far inland – evidence of winter storms that must be ferocious. Close to where my board lays – at a tide line denoted by more regular storms – is a rusted, dented, spike-covered mine. And all along this contour – amongst the boulders and smaller pieces of timber – are battered, brightly coloured fishing buoys, and scraps of net.

Wind and snow is forecast. The sail is positioned in such a way that it forms a shelter. If its orientation is correct, the wind will pin the sail in place, rather than flip it over. There is a comfortable bed of heather upon which my inflated camp mattress is rested. I pull tight the sleeping bag's drawcord, and succumb to sleep.

***

By morning a weather front is passing over. The wind direction is steady, and the pinned sail flexes in the gusts, as if breathing. Small flecks of snow become more substantial flakes, that build on the sail, until its panels sag under the weight, and require a double-legged sleeping bag kick to clear. Conditions have decided that these are hours to rest up.

Peacefully, from within my feather-lined cocoon, I observe the softly falling snow. Calories are lazily replenished through expedition porridge, coffee, chocolate and nuts. A while after returning to gentle observation, there is a visit from a small white bird – a snow bunting. The sail that shelters me is shelter for the bird too. The bird has curiosity that is so evident. Whereas I found the whale; it is this little bird that has found me. If I had to choose a favourite experience of my journey, it is perhaps this face to face encounter with a snow bunting that I would choose.

Sail shelter covered in snow at the mouth of Sandfjorden

***

Late that day, with clear skies and fresh wind, I assess that it is fair for sailing. Significant waves complicate the launch. They could easily snap the mast and thereby cripple my vessel. I study the waves and mentally rehearse every move of the getaway. And then I wait, and I wait, and then I have gone, and I am swimming with the urgency of being chased by an alligator. That gets me past the shorebreak, but the heist is not complete until I have uphauled the sail and found deeper water. Only when that is done do I notice the explosive energy expended, the gasping for air and my pounding heart.

There is a headwind, and a sizeable sea that the board thumps into. To make progress along open coast I must sail a zigzag course, sometimes heading far to seaward. On one foray offshore I pass close by a boat, the first I have seen. Upon closer inspection it is a ship. The bow of the vessel falls into the waves to part them in a whooshing divide of white. I am momentarily taken back to childhood, and the memory of television advertisements for fishfingers.

Svaerholt

31 May 2017

The most challenging sail of the Barents Sea is the last one, from Svaerholt – a remote peninsula jutting out between two immense fjords.

To the east of Svaerholt lies Nordkinn: the most northerly point of mainland Europe. To its west lies the island of Magerøya. *Mager* is Norwegian for "big"; øya – the reader may remember – means "island". Magerøya is therefore "big island".

Nordkapp is a peninsula on Magerøya. It has a globe sculpture and visitor centre to celebrate and reap dividend from its far north location. In reality, the Nordkapp peninsula is outflanked by an adjacent one. And – if we are being picky – neither is Magerøya Europe's most northerly island. The Svalbard and Franz-Josef Land archipelagos – both arguably European – are ten degrees of latitude further north.

Headwinds and snow have made for staccato progress towards Nordkinn. After three nights in the town of Berlevag – two of which were made comfortable by the local café owner who insisted I must not "sleep like a dog" – comes a day with a light to moderate north-easterly wind. It is an opportunity to push on. By early evening I am a kilometre or so off Nordkinn. High cliffs and an unforgiving coastline give little option other than to continue into Laksefjorden. There is a stiff current flowing out of the fjord, being squeezed on its way past the roof of Europe, and running against the direction of the Barents Sea swell. The current holds up the opposing swell and together they combine into standing waves. The board travels fast down the faces, but it is like sailing on a treadmill. Progress is slow. From here it is a 20 nm ($\approx$37 km) sail to cross the fjord's mouth.[4]

After about 8 nm I have mostly escaped the conveyer belt of moving water. The wind has moderated to a light breeze. Svaerholt peninsula is approached around midnight. The low sun briefly breaks through the clouds to register as a memory. Off the headland, the current spills past rejuvenated.

From previous inspection of satellite imagery, I know there is a landing option on each side of the anvil-shaped promontory. The westernmost one is preferable: to have the headland behind me, and to have a clear view of the

---

[4] Nautical units are the nautical mile (nm) for distance and the knot for speed.
1 nm = 1852 metres and is equal to 1/60 of a degree of latitude.
1 degree of latitude is therefore about 60 nm.
1 knot = 1 nautical mile per hour.

Descending, from the north, upon Svaerholt peninsula

next expanse of sea. The beach, when it arrives, is comprised of boulders rather than sand. Judicious timing delivers a safe landing with a wave that surges up the rounded stones.

Shattered. But what a reward! This epic amphitheatre, teetering at the end of a deserted 70 km outcrop, surrounded by lonely sea. And to the east and west – rising from beyond the maritime horizon – are distant cliffs supporting snow-covered plateaus.

I set up camp under the sail; change to dry and less odorous land clothing: double thermals, down jacket, synthetic jacket. All my remaining clothes! Water from a meltwater stream is heated by Jetboil, then used to rehydrate a Drytech meal. And soon after comes wonderful sleep: cocooned in sleeping bag, immersed in wildness.

***

I wake again mid-morning, still damn shattered! Despite the remoteness of this location, mobile signal is strong. The forecast is for weather conditions to deteriorate: more snow flurries, wind strong enough to build a sizeable sea. It would be better to cross Porsangerfjorden early, but unwise to attempt when still so fatigued. I defer a decision; and after breakfast set out to explore – for it would be criminal not to.

I gently pick my way over clumps of vegetation to the east facing bay, accompanied by the haunting *hwoo! hwoo!* of Golden Plover. To my ears there is nothing more beautiful than nature at rest. Reindeer are grazing, some with calves.

Quite recently, this was a wilderness shared with man. There are abandoned houses, made of wood, and one grander barn that would have made a comfortable sleeping place. I seek high ground next, for the vantage point it offers. The small mountain at the tip of the peninsula – viewed from above like the head of an anvil – is boulder-strewn and soilless. At its highest point are the sharp concrete lines of a now broken-up gun emplacement. The buildings nearer to sea level presumably housed soldiers. And the rusted barbed wire I stepped over earlier would have been to protect them from surprise attack.

It is predictable where humans choose to set up camp: dictated by geography. The Germans were here. And probably much earlier settlers too. Indeed, on Magerøya there is archaeological evidence of habitation that has been dated to 10,000 BC.

***

Come the afternoon I surprise myself by thinking about sailing. Although I will forever want to return to Svaerholt, the urge to push on now is strong. If I complete this crossing there is protection from the islands beyond, and the weather there will not hit as hard. But I am nervous too. The wind is strong. And being cold it carries more weight, making it more powerful for a given strength. Sail now, or wait – possibly for days?

Svaerholt peninsula, west facing side

A decision can come later. For now, autopilot takes over: practical and mental preparations for battle, to keep the option open. Land is visible, though which part to head for cannot be discerned. I will need to sail deep downwind [with the wind very much from behind]. As deep as possible. Provided I can maintain a roughly appropriate course, then shelter will be found. My friend Helene calls at this moment. It is all I can do to hold back tears. The mix of fear and awe is close to overwhelming.

This is another high stakes launch. Waves surge and retreat and barely pause for breath. The shoreline is awash with foam. Boulders are tumbled; and the spaces between them form crevasses that are hungry to swallow a leg.

To make the board lighter, I remove the backpack that is normally stowed under the spray deck, and carry it instead on my shoulders, piggy-backed over the smaller backpack. The double backpack method means that I can lift board and sail together. Once again, I wait my opportunity to leap with the gear from the boulders, and then swim furiously to get away from the churning shorebreak, and then climb aboard and sail away before more meaningful waves arrive. Adrenaline flows. It could so easily go wrong, but it doesn't. Once again, my heart jumps out of my chest.

Before the open sea proper I stop to correctly stow the second backpack. Then I haul the sail up again and proceed to where the wind blows with full force.

***

The board is 3.8 metres long. My feet are jammed hard into the footstraps of its rearmost metre. The sea is white horse streaked and the board races through it. Full attention is required. I seek a line that limits the tendency of the nose to spear the waves. Even so, spearing is inevitable and frequent. The ride is extremely wet. Occasionally, lumps of water rear up to exact a thumping body blow. A few minutes in, to assess progress, I snatch a glimpse back. A line of wake flies out from underneath the board, remaining narrow until lost in the distance. Svaerholt already appears small. That safety is lost.

I am controlling the sailing. The sail – well tensioned to exhaust the excess power – is coping well. But my course line is too high. It is safer to sail high – there is less danger of a crash – but there is no landing on the other side, where mature sea meets the hard rock of Nordkapp. I must force myself to sail deeper. Much deeper, toward the protected water of the strait between Magerøya and the mainland.

The wave height is now in excess of two metres. This is sailing with the accelerator jammed down. When a route opens up to go deep, I follow, switching lanes like a manic joyrider. And when a lump rears-up in front, and there is no way round – or over – I go through. And the water in that moment is hard and unforgiving. There is an explosion of spray. Sinews strain to hold board and sail in alignment. If I keep the rig locked down, and the nose comes clear, I come out the other side and blink away the dripping sea.

It is only a matter of time before the nose submarines irretrievably. Deceleration from twenty-something knots to nothing in a few tenths of a second. Instinctive reactions transform what would otherwise be an ugly mast-breaking catapult fall into a less impactful crumple, but I cannot avoid being flipped and rolled in the process, and am now under the sail, itself underwater. Though I am concerned for the board, in case it has broken free of the rig, in which case it would already be being carried away downwind, I know better than to rush. There is a peace underwater to be used wisely: ensure that none of the control lines or equipment tethers are going to impede exit, then feel a route out to the surface. Once there, I grab a lungful of air, and – reassuringly – the footstraps of the board, which has also flipped upside-down, and now resists the downward pull of the submerged rig.

Once back on deck, the fall is an opportunity to catch my breath, take a mouthful of nuts and chocolate, and assess progress. Eating and navigational checks are impossible whilst sailing so totally on the limit. My position is still too high, too north, but for the moment this tack is getting me closest to land from where it will be easier to navigate by sight.[5] I further depower the sail – haul on the downhaul [a sail adjustment] until there is not a millimetre left to be hauled – and return to the objective of going deep downwind.

There are several more falls. Sooner or later the nose spears at an angle it will not recover from. Partly, this is simple probability: the big lumps are out there to be found. And likely it is fatigue related too, since by the time of each fall at least a few more kilometres have been achieved. The effort expended means that the cold is not problematic. Even my extremities are warm. Most unpleasant is a fall when I remain hooked in and am hauled along under the sail by a breaking crest. But the principal danger is to the equipment. My objection to crashing, and determination to try to avoid the falls, is to safeguard the gear.

Nearer to land the effort of having gone deep is rewarded. I am sufficiently far south to receive partial shelter from Mageroya's easternmost peninsula. The sea flattens off. It remains very windy a kilometre off, but compared to mid-fjord it feels safe. The adrenaline ebbs away and tiredness sets in as I zigzag downwind along the flank of Big Island. I hook round the corner and

---

[5] The word "tack" has a number of meanings. In this case it is used to distinguish starboard tack (wind from the right) and port tack (wind from the left).

there is Honningsvåg. Flat water now. And a moderate, gusty breeze. A different world.

***

Wow! That was a wild one. I am in a daze – too spaced out to care much where to make for land. There are some houses before reaching the harbour, with gardens that back down to the sea. There will do.

From one of the houses emerges Per, who hears my story but gives little away through facial expression. That is typically Norwegian. But yes, I may camp on the grass. A few minutes later Per upgrades me to an ice-fishing tent. I am then ushered inside to take a hot shower, during which time the tent is erected, and heating installed.

Reaching Honningsvåg is a huge landmark. A deep satisfaction fills me as I relax into the warm air inside the tent. Fifteen minutes later comes a delivery from Per's wife: burger and chips that surpass any I have tasted anywhere, and a cool beer that is like heaven for my throat.

Honningsvåg

2. Norwegian Sea

IHO *Limits* (1953) locates the Norwegian Sea within the Arctic Ocean, and has it bisected by the Arctic Circle.

Its north-south range is from Nordkapp to latitude 61° north, which meets the Norwegian mainland near to its most westerly point.

From 61° on the mainland, the limits of the Sea extend westward to a position about 10 nm north of Shetland. From here, they extend to the Faroes, and then to Iceland. From Iceland, they head north-eastward – via the island of Jan Mayen – to Svalbard, then back to Nordkapp via Bear Island. The maritime limits correspond in an approximate way to subsea geography that describes the Norwegian Sea as a basin.

The majority of the Norwegian Sea lies beyond the continental shelf and is extremely deep. It descends to 4000 metres at its deepest, and is about 2000 metres deep on average. This is vastly deeper than the Barents Sea to its north, and the North Sea to its south, both of which are underlain by continental shelf.

Coastal waters are shallower, and are warmed by the northeast flowing North Atlantic Current that exerts a moderating influence on Norway's climate. The seabed here is striated from the same glaciation events that carved the fjords. These subsea valleys are the most important spawning grounds for herring in the North Atlantic. The herring eggs are washed to the Barents Sea, where the young fish hatch, and feed on abundant summer plankton, before returning to the Norwegian Sea to participate in the next annual spawning event. Other species – such as whiting – spawn further south and release eggs that are carried *to* the Norwegian sea. Whitefish species such as cod, pollack and haddock are also abundant.

Fishing has always been important to Norway, but it is the oil and natural gas under its seas that made it rich. Offshore exploration and drilling are ongoing in all shelf waters except those around Lofoten, where it is banned. A beneficiary of this protection is the Røst reef – the most extensive deep-water coral reef yet discovered.

In recent years salmon farming has become commercially important. In the shelter of the fjords, cold water helps to keep the fish in good condition by reducing the incidence of lice.

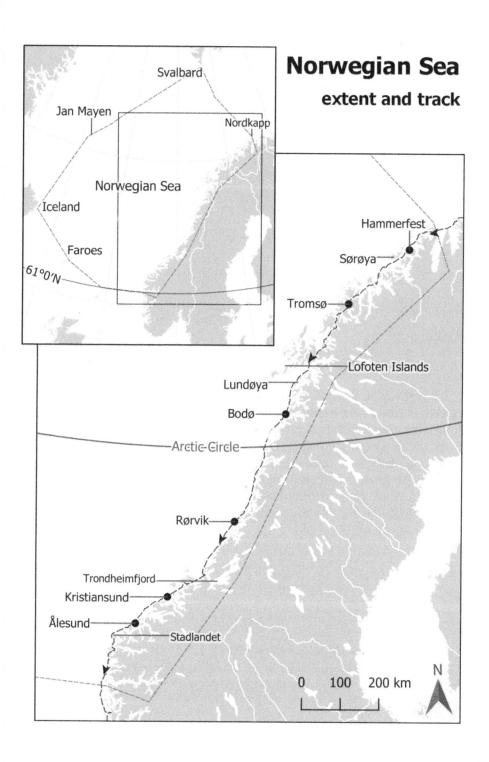

Norwegian Sea
extent and track

Protection from swell behind the islands of the Norwegian Sea

The Norwegian Sea mainland coast lies behind a patchwork of islands that extend its entire length. Between these is a network of connected fjords and straits, forming the basis of transport routes that are in most places protected from ocean swells and storms. Ships from Norway's Hurtigruten fleet operate a daily service along the "coastal express" route. The voyage between Bergen and Kirkenes requires seven days and spans three seas.

I owe a thank you to Hurtigruten, since it was with their help, and aboard the ship MS *Nordlys* that my four-metre-long craft and I reached Kirkenes, and friendships were forged.[6]

---

[6] MS is a standard abbreviation for Motor Ship. The MS *Nordlys* picked me up from Bergen and the voyage to Kirkenes was a wonderful experience. Captain Lars and crew welcomed me to the bridge, and the ship's "Adventure Team" were particularly supportive. Other passengers on board were also kind and generous, and some offered sage advice that I keep present to this day.

Tromsø

11 June 2017

Heading south there are any number of days that could speak of the sailing. But there is never monotony. Each day is a puzzle to be solved. The game is simple now: get south, get food, get sleep. And stay in good enough condition to keep going.

It is difficult to reconcile my memory of the landscape during the voyage north with that being observed now. Aboard MS *Nordlys*, to cross a fjord was effortless, and at a constant pace. To sail the same water, there are a dozen winds to contend with. Or no wind; or waves pushed by wind from a tributary fjord; or tremendous gusts that spill off a headland. All these things. Wind moves as a liquid, and like a mountain stream it rushes through some parts, is turbulent in others, and elsewhere forms calm pools. And when I am through the calm, or past the headland that was a struggle, I look back, and cannot know for sure if what-has-been-come-through is still there. The weather may have changed. And perhaps – as only witness – my testimony is unreliable.

When interactions with people are few, those that do happen can brighten a day. On a crossing from Masøya to Havøysund I come within hailing distance of a fishing vessel at work. I have cold hands, and am tired of the concentration required to maintain balance in the sloppy following sea. Suddenly, there is a bellow in my ear from a loudspeaker. I jump six inches, then register the friendliest of greetings: "Halloo, halloo, halloo! Don't look back! There's a shark behind you!" I laugh out loud, risk a half-second thumbs up, and pass the boat with a smile that stays fixed for the rest of the crossing.

I arrive at Hammerfest chilled to my core, having sailed the last hours of a long, grey, heat-sapping day. Fortunately, there is an offer of a place to stay nearby with family of Helene. The final part of today's sail was inside an island occupied by a huge natural gas processing site. Landfall was made outside a large building originally intended to accommodate gas plant employees, but that now houses migrants – mostly Syrians and Afghans who entered Norway through the northern border route from Russia. A kindly fellow named Bjørn – who has a friend who once rowed here in a dinghy from Oslo – provides a place for the windsurf gear to sleep.

28

Sørøysundet

From Hammerfest there is an impressive two-day sail down the mighty Sørøysundet – literally the Sound of Sørøya.[7] Conditions are rarely comfortable. Though the air remains still, the land each side has many fjords that spit-out a steep and tightly-packed wind chop. The waves are not the work of mischievous trolls, but the result of katabatic winds spilling down from the cold, snow-covered mountains into the tributary fjords. The winds have typically faded before they reach me, and I experience only the choppy sea they have lifted. Sometimes the winds *do* reach further out into the Sound. Where the wind has legs, the board lifts onto a plane – so that it is skimming over the surface of the water – and the sailing is joyous.

Camping locations are memorable. I search out easy landings with calm water, flat land, a stream, and a strategic view: the oases in this land of hard rock. At some, the evidence of previous German occupation is rusting away. Or there are boulders configured in a way that is suggestive of human intent. Of course, regardless of epoch, all seafarers would seek out such places.

Tromsø is reached in an explosion of green. Vegetation growth at sea level is now almost perceptible in real time. Arctic terns fill the clear air.

---

[7] A sound (and also a strait – the terms are synonyms) is a relatively narrow body of water that opens at each end to a relatively larger body of water.

Continual daylight means there is no shortage of hours to sail or paddle. Rest is more difficult. It would be more physically depleting were it not for the good food, solid shelter and easy companionship of strangers. Sometimes the strangers are contacts who know of my journey; other times, not: it is purely coincidental that we meet. Regardless, bonds form quickly. It does not feel that we are strangers for long. Help comes from Laila; and then Siri, who also nurses me through a migraine; and then two Estonian brothers. One brother is eager to show me his island, so we go sightseeing even though it is 3am. And later that day, as I prepare to sail, he earnestly delivers a two-week supply of corned beef. The cargo of tins makes the board too heavy to lift, but that matters little, because the landings are gentle now that there is protection from swell.

The Estonian brothers at Dyrøyhamn. Salmon farm workers on Dyrøya were also friendly and gave me a tour of their floating workplace.

Lundøya and Mannshausen

21 June 2017, from log entry

Yesterday, with just over a month of progress behind me, I had a first day of feeling uninspired. It was cold, grey, and not difficult, but a bit of a slog to make progress. And the many cabins made for an almost suburban feel compared to the wilds of Finnmark. And despite there being more people, cars, and cabins – I felt lonely. Also, the shaft of the paddle had a split and was slowly filling with water. A minor thing, but it sloshed and played on the mind. I decided to head for the town of Lødingen, and daydreamed of pizza.

That was a good call, or a "smart move" as the Norwegians would say. Lødingen has a pizza restaurant. The Turkish owner does an excellent pizza and was understanding when my bag flooded the floor. The marina facility has showers too. Hoorah! When I returned to my sail for sleep I was both cleaner and happier.

This morning I discovered a chandlery. They lent me a drill to drain the paddle, and sold me a pack of resin impregnated cloth for repairing the cracked tube. The paddle now has a repair to be proud of.

The day then went from good to great! Northerly winds: ideal for making miles! The inner route through the Lofoten chain – through which I have just passed – had been cold, but it is warmer now that I am back on the proper sea. And the landscape is back to being awesome! The final 10 nm of the day – past Hamarøya, to Lundøya – were just breathtaking. My fixed, awe-struck expression has returned!

With occasional pulses of ocean swell noted, I wondered how far it would be to find a landing, and then a sheltered beach came into view. I set camp: on the bend of a stream, beneath a towering mountain, behind a curl of coral sand. On the scale of great camp spots this redefines *perfect*.

***

The onward sail through shallow archipelagos is breathtaking: Islands topped with soft meadows; chilled but turquoise waters; wilderness and wild peaks as the near shore; the snow-capped arm of Lofoten as a distant backdrop. I stop at some capsule-like glass-fronted cabins on Mannshausen island, and meet Børge Ousland – proprietor and celebrated polar explorer. He arranges for the resident chef to cook me some fish, and is interested in my journey. He seems to approve of it – apart from the Black Sea part – which I suspect he considers may be an uninspiring slog. "Why do you want to go there?" he asks. I don't have an answer, or particularly want to go to the Black Sea. It just happens to be part of the route.

With Børge Ousland (left) on Mannshausen

The Arctic Circle

26 June 2017

The Arctic Circle is an imaginary line of latitude in the northern hemisphere. At this distance from the pole, on the longest day of the year, the centre of the sun does not dip below the horizon. Conversely, on the shortest day of the year, the centre of the sun does not rise above the horizon. To the south of this division is the Northern Temperate Zone; to the north is the Arctic.

The Arctic Circle is indicated in Norway by an elegant, metallic, frame of a globe, placed on a tiny island. On the northward journey, aboard MS *Nordlys*, I joined with other passengers to gawp as we glided past, and it felt significant.

On the southward journey, I have navigated mostly by sight, with reference to the maps and charts on the five-inch screen of a smartphone. The phone fits inside a waterproof pouch that is secured by an elastic to a pocket of my drysuit. On a sunny day, when it is possible to stay dry, it is usually easy to determine where to go. If there is continual splash or spray or rain; or fingers are cold, wet and prune-like – then the phone becomes inoperable. Under these conditions, and when well prepared for an ambitious passage, I rely upon a small GPS unit that has physical buttons. This works well for A to B navigation, but is hopeless for determining what is at B, or what might be found in between. By combining the strengths of each system, and with awareness of their limitations, navigation of Norwegian coastal waters is relatively straightforward.

Five weeks after setting out, threading my way between islands, the possible outline of a distant globe is observed, and later confirmed. It comes as a surprise. I had been unaware of approaching 66° 33' latitude where I presume the circle line to reside. A GPS fix reports that in fact the island is south of the circle. That detail I clear up later. The latitude of the Arctic Circle fluctuates according to the tilt of the earth on its axis. Currently it is drifting north by about 15 metres per year.

The little island has a rocky bay with perfectly flat water that makes for a simple landing. Regardless of its positional exactitude, for me this is another significant milestone. One that brings tears of gratitude. And of loss – for there is something magical and romantic about the Arctic that I am leaving behind. It also allows buried fears to surface – about parts of the journey that had previously been too distant to cause concern.

The fears are both specific and vague; known and unknown. I know that the Atlantic will be the most challenging coastline to sail. That now seems imminent and scary. The latter stages of the journey, beyond the familiarity of the European Union, prod at a different type of concern: about alien cultures, isolation through difference, and my own security when on land. I worry that I will be vulnerable when dislocated from my own.

When the goodbye is said, I resolve to source a beer in recognition of progress. It is rare to see other craft, but a yacht has showed up and is lingering by the island with the globe. I sail over to them and during a brief conversation learn of a nearby island that has a little town and even a bar. That seems fateful enough to determine where I should head for next.

When I reach the bar it is closed. And the small settlement has no shop. And there are no people about. I wander the empty street, then return to the jungle of rampant shoreside vegetation.

Three more days of sailing are required before a resupply is possible. Then I sail a little further – to Torget island, from which rises the distinctive Torghatten mountain, which has a hole straight through it from one side to the other.

Though I am now south of the Arctic Circle, there is still no night. Instead, the day briefly dims, and then return to its full summer splendour. Dinner is leisurely. Every drop of the cool beer is savoured. Then a midnight walk through the mountain leaves me tired enough for bed.

Vikingen Island – home of the Arctic Circle globe – is not far off latitude 66°33'

Re-encounter with MS *Nordlys*

30 June 2017, from log entry

Today promises little. There is no wind through the morning, and a feeble breeze when I do set out, hoping to make a token few miles. My mind wanders elsewhere, barely registering the scenery going past. I wonder if I should push on for more miles, sail more hours? I could do that. The sailing inside these lower islands is mostly uncomplicated, and the wind direction usually favourable. It is difficult to know how hard to push. If I just power on – machine-like – does that make the experience almost... empty?

But if I take it too easy now, I may regret that later too. Bad weather or light winds will come at some time and make progress slow. And maybe a small delay will compound into a much larger one if I get stuck the wrong side of a difficult headland or crossing.

I know the answer already: to "make hay when the sun shines" – and if there is lots of sun that means lots of hay too. No deliberate slowing up. But also, be ready to accept opportunities to connect with people, and welcome a bit of randomness whatever that may be.

My mind moves back to the day. Sailing through rocks, skerries, small islands. Almost all are home for birds and their defenceless young. The birds' fish diet returns a favour to their island homes. Guano is nature's fertilizer. Rocks that barely protrude above the sea are topped by a thick meadow of vegetation, ideal for ground-nesting birds. Nature has it all worked out.

Some gusts come and allow the board to plane a few hundred metres. I miss a turning between islands, harden up [make a turn towards the wind] to correct, and feel a pleasantly cool breeze on my face, now enjoying the day.

Midway through a narrower channel, a few cabins are nestled closely together above a gently-shelved pebble beach. Two children play in the water and there are people on a balcony. People! I drink fast to deplete my water supply, then stop and ask the adults for a top-up.

The day has more miles, so it will only be a quick stop, but these nice people volunteer coffee, pancakes, and a beer for later. I wonder if this is the mainland and learn that it isn't, a boat is required for access. It is a lovely spot. I leave from the island refreshed. There is a good wind. It is a great day!

A text arrives from Diego, one of the MS *Nordlys* "Expedition Team". The *Nordlys* is the Hurtigruten ship that carried me to Kirkenes in May. Kari – another of the "Expedition Team" – who is a sailor and boatbuilder had gifted me some handwarmers. The ship is heading south, between Kvaløya and Leka. They may be close. I start a small open-water crossing, and then see the *Nordlys* about 3 nm away. Twelve minutes at their pace! I want to wave to my friends, get close enough to see their faces.

I pump the sail – repeatedly open the boom angle and then haul it shut – so that it generates more power. My hope is to reach mid channel in time to position myself on the bow of the ship, where the crew will see me. The foghorn sounds. I am sailing dead downwind when they pass. It is wobbly, and difficult to look up, but I see many passengers, and Kari, and on the bridge there is Kristian.

Thanks Captain Lars, and Diego. That was a nice manoeuvre we pulled off!

MS *Nordlys* after our rendezvous

36

Island Hopping

22 June - 10 July 2017

Countless islands punctuate each day. When I am tired, an islet with a gentle shelve of beach will catch my eye and persuade me to set camp. That is the case with Dypingen: 400 metres by 800 metres of paradise, and part of a close-knit archipelago of similar treasures. Coral-sand is backed by a meadow of soft grasses; shorter grasses and heathers occupy low lying rock; and numerous other flowering plants flourish. The air is cold and clear.

In the morning, I realise that I have camped next to a seagull's nest and the mother bird is nowhere to be seen. Even if she returns after I am gone the eggs will not have survived the "night", so I boil them up for breakfast. The eggs are of similar size and taste to chicken eggs, but with a definite trace of seafood. They are, in fact, delicious.

Dypingen islet and a more rugged backdrop

***

I pit-stop, fatigued, on Ystholmen. This islet is roughly circular and 300 metres across, with a small beach protected by a larger neighbouring island. I am stretched out, resting my legs, nursing a cup of hot coffee, when I notice the advance of a large animal with a dense white coat. Before I can react it is upon me. There is no time to ask myself how a Polar bear got here. I roll away but cannot avoid the big white head as its jaws bite down. And then I realise that the assailant is a sheep, and that my sandwich is a goner.

***

Civilisation arrives at Kristiansund. There had been a stiff headwind earlier, but then it became a day of intermittent paddling. Trial and error has at last enabled me to figure out how to balance the sail. A double tie-down system keeps the boom located on the blocks that support it. This improvement enables me to paddle across an opening with rolling swell, and to reach the island-city home of contacts Morten and Louise. My fatigue is semi-permanent, and I am grateful that one night of comfort becomes two. Happily, though we do not know it at this first meeting, we will meet up again in southern Norway.

The onward sail meets another stiff headwind in Bremsnesfjorden. I pass the semi-submersible drilling rig *Transocean Barents* – a goliath – and then head to open sea where conditions become more brutal. Strong wind, a rowdy sea, and outlying skerries make it a stressful sail, and I am grateful to find the shelter of a small inlet on the west side of Sveggøya. There are a few cabins but no signs of life at the anchorage. I stop on a rock. Perhaps, later, the wind will moderate. Somewhat dejected, I check my phone. There is a message from the tenant of my apartment that the washing machine has broken and caused a flood. "Can you fix it?" Great. At least there is internet. Maybe I can.

An hour later I see a person. Evidently, one of the cabins is occupied and they had seen me come in. And here I am stuck on a rock, and they wonder if I am in trouble. "What are you doing?" they ask. Wearily, I look up from my phone and tell them that I am trying to buy a washing machine. A brief pause as they consider this information, then a finger points towards the east. "Kristiansund. You'll find a washing machine there."

Stadlandet

14 July 2017

Stad – or Stadlandet – is a mountain plateau peninsula that juts out into the southern Norwegian Sea. At Stad there are no outlying islands to provide shelter, meaning that maritime traffic must navigate round it through open and sometimes dangerous waters. In 1834 a ship tunnel was first proposed that would cut through the headland. The latest version of the project has funds allocated and work is due to begin in 2022/2023.[8]

Significant headlands such as Stad are fully exposed to swell and waves. Tides or other currents flow at their strongest. Wind can be very disrupted, and localised wind acceleration is to be expected.

Headlands stand tall, proud, and remote. Part of their difficulty is access. There is frequently a long passage to reach the business end of an outcrop, and at the pinnacle is where the dangers are greatest. In my mind, I consider headlands as mountains, to be tackled in three stages: approach, summit and descent. For a fragile craft, safe navigation of these features requires fair weather.

Advice for tackling Stad comes from sailors Erlend and his father Harald. The forecast for tomorrow is that Stad will become a very unfriendly place. If possible, I should push all the way round today.

Whilst preparing to launch on a sunny field north of Ulsteinvik, a local journalist shows up for a few quotes and snaps. Then I set afloat in the direction indicated by Harald. I have new boots donated by Erlend, and notice that my feet that are oddly warm and comfortable – how nice!

The wind may be light, but the direction is good. Direction is everything. I head offshore, then free-off [adjust course away from the wind] to pass between a trio of islands connected by bridges. There is a weak but steady current of air, enough for progress whilst the sail remains upright. After 10 nm of supporting the sail the shelter of the islands is lost, and my back aches – in part because my backpack is so amply loaded with snacks today. It is a sunny day. The scenery is spectacular. Stad lies ahead.

I sail direct to the peninsula: further offshore than is my habit. A buoy is passed that tells of unseen rocks. Mind games too mindless to repeat help pass the time. Or maybe their use is to keep anxieties buried. A trickle of breeze rolls southward. The sea is calm in manner, but ruffled and constantly moving. I pump the sail though it delivers meagre power. The board splashes

---

[8] https://www.kystverket.no/en/news/2020/green-light-for-the-stad-ship-tunnel/

awkwardly, complainingly. Without the reassurance of GPS it would be easy to think that the task is too great.

The current of air – though gentle – is reliable. In time, Stad arrives. The sea undergoes some mild transformations where currents meet, and there is a small, lazy swell – but nothing of concern. This is a day when the beast slumbers. It is a fine day for a summit! The job – however – is not yet done. It is already late afternoon. The air will soon fall still, and there is a descent to make.

I allow a kilometre of sea room, which seems optimal to benefit from a slight wind acceleration off the tip of the headland. There are intriguing bays inshore, and probably landings too on a day like today. But to stop along this stretch would be to defer the task. And since tomorrow's forecast is unsettled it is best to push-on further.

The band of wind now peels away from the headland. With the sun already low in the sky it would be unwise to follow it. My preferred target – a distant island – is also a crossing too far. A partial descent is a safer option. There is a point – a headland upon the main headland – about 2 nm from my current location, beyond which there will be good shelter. Ninety-minutes of pumping are required to reach the outcrop. The wind has dropped to zero.

Beyond the headland there is no longer a sense of exposure. The prudent decision to change course is further rewarded when a gentle breeze fills-in alongside a line of high cliffs. It carries me past a hamlet: four houses clinging to a steep slope. It looks to be an awkward landing there. Further on, there is the slightly larger hamlet of Indre Fure. There is also a rock quay. Eyes have been watching the sea, and a man strolls out on to the quay as if this is his front garden, which it is. He indicates that the harbour is open. Beyond the wall is mirror-calm water, and a narrow strip of white sand that provides a blissfully easy landing.

The man's name is Kjell. He offers a warm greeting, as if he were expecting *another one* to be along soon. "Oh yes, they all stop here. Andrew was the last one, with his kayak." Kjell indicates homeward, towards a lush green lawn. "Come along, you are welcome, and we have a house book you must write a few words in."

Indre Fure is entrancing. The collection of houses is nestled in a relatively safe nook at the base of a four-hundred-metre-high cliff. Kjell is a fisherman and retired postmaster for Stadlandet. Mrs Kjell addresses my perceived malnourishment with a steady supply of fishcakes. At last light, Kjell and daughter zoom off in a lightweight boat. Fifteen minutes later they are back, bringing ashore whitefish and crab. I join with the extended family group, and we feast through the evening.

The following day there is a strong headwind. It is a relief to have Stad behind me – I would not wish to face it in such weather. The semi-enclosed waters here are a different prospect. From here, it will be an exhilarating sail towards greater shelter, but there is nothing to be fearful of.

I enjoy a few tranquil hours, and a roll on a bike along the carless road that goes no place beyond here. Then I leave my thoughts and thanks in the house book. I leaf back through the pages. There is an entry by Andrew North, who "found shelter from the storm" here with Kjell and family. Andrew's visit was in 1995. It may be true that we all stop here, but we are not yet a crowd.

Indre Fure in the night-time twilight of summer

Sailing with Vikings

Summer 2017

Many people have been in touch to volunteer themselves as safe ports. Those who make contact through the expedition website can also drop a pin on a map to indicate their location. Many of these "contacts" also leave a friendly message. I find it much easier to overcome the nerves of getting back in touch if there are a few encouraging lines. Most people have nerves about establishing social contact. At times mine are quite exaggerated.

Some of the most enthusiastically friendly messages are from fellow windsurfers. These contacts know that it is not possible to predict when or even if I will reach them, because "it depends upon the wind." They know I will be wet, tired and hungry. They know that the equipment will need a place to overnight.

It is motivating to be heading for a contact. Their location becomes a definite target for the day: the miles become a challenge, with reward if they are achieved. Frequently I push for more miles than I otherwise would. At the end of a hard day there is always a slight euphoria, and that is nice to share. The intention is almost always to stay just for a night, but often I end up staying two, or sometimes more.

My first windsurfer contacts are Håvard and Carlo, in Trondheimfjord, who are reached after sailing a personal best 58 nm (≈107 km). It is late in the evening when I see the two figures bounding across the field. They guide me in with ear to ear smiles and excited chatter, and before I am out of the water a Guinness is cracked open and delivered. I stay for two wonderful days and batteries receive a much-needed recharge.

Most windsurfers do not own Raceboard type gear, so rarely is it practical to sail together. An exception is Bjørn from Ålesund – a previous mayor of the city. In a rather surreal experience, we sail together from Ålesund to the Atlanterhavsparken Aquarium, where we are treated to a complementary guided tour. Bjørn seems very much at home in his wetsuit, but I wonder if we should be in the tank with the fish.

There is another Viking who stands out as a kindred spirit.

Before I have even met Tord, I have stayed in his house at Ulsteinvik; been ambushed into a most welcome drinking session at Rørvik by his ex-inlaw's sister and her irresistible troupe; and enjoyed fishing and lodgings with relatives Arve and Marit near Bergen. During this most recent stop, from a boat, Arve handed me the rod that caught a 6-foot ling that weighed nearly 40 kilos; and Tord finally showed up in person. The next day we sailed together to Bergen in almost no wind.

At Bergen we were met by Rob – who rowed out in a rubber dinghy to issue a proper welcome. Rob and I were both in Bodø about a month ago, where I had noticed his elegant sailing yacht *Tintin*, and observed that she was flying a Blue Ensign. I initiated a conversation and not so subtly wondered if a fellow countryman and sailor might have a berth available. When Rob stated that he knew me, I initially thought he was unhinged – until he pinned me down to a previous life working at Minorca Sailing. With that prompting I remembered Rob too, and it was a thoroughly pleasant stop.

Bergen is in fact bathed by the North Sea, but its fjord-indented coastline is thoroughly representative of the Norwegian Sea, so a mention of it here will have to be excused. A shared history with Rob has unfolded over two seas, or three if our meetings in Menorca are to count.

As for Tord, we'll find him again in the Skagerrak Sea section.

Top row (left to right): Tord, Avre, Marit

A welcome from Rob upon arrival at Bergen. Photo: Jo Withers

3. North Sea – Part One

South of parallel 61° is the North Sea.

This sea is partially enclosed by southwest Norway, west Denmark, Germany, the Netherlands, Belgium, northwest France and the east of Britain. It shares a border with the Skagerrak Sea along a limit between Norway and Denmark. To the south it meets the English Channel. To the north it opens into the Norwegian Sea, and in the northwest it meets the Atlantic Ocean proper.

The North Sea resides over continental shelf with an average depth of about 90 metres, though a much deeper trench runs parallel to the Norwegian coast. Over the last 2.5 million years, the North Sea has drained and filled many times, as sea levels have responded to the formation and loss of ice sheets.

At the time of the Last Glacial Maximum – about 20,000 years ago – northern Europe was covered in ice, and sea levels were about 120 metres lower than they are today. Over the following millennia of ice retreat, tundra was exposed that became home to animals including humans, and it would have been possible to walk from "Yorkshire" to "Denmark" crossing the Dogger Hills. The still-rising sea isolated the hills, that became first islands, until they were eventually lost beneath the waves about 8000 years ago. The Dogger Hills – now referred to as the Dogger Bank – are today a productive fishing ground. Occasionally, fishermen trawl evidence of human habitation of ancient Doggerland; and extraction of aggregate often leads to the discovery of animal remains including mammoth and rhinoceros.

The North Sea coastline is glaciated in the north; and generally lower and straighter – and more prone to erosion and flooding – in the south. Storm tide flooding in the late Middle Ages caused tens of thousands of deaths. In living memory, the North Sea Flood of 1953 claimed 2500 lives. In response to this latter tragedy storm surge barriers for major cities were constructed, and the dykes along vulnerable coasts were improved. 27 percent of the Netherlands lies below sea level.

North Sea
extent and part one of track

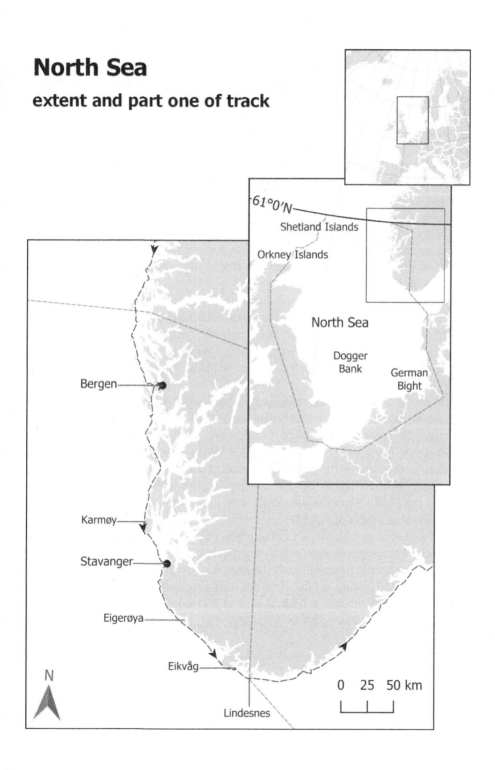

North Sea fish stocks, which are naturally abundant, have been depleted by overfishing. Trawling is the predominant fishing method, though it is destructive to seabed habitat, and leads to bycatch of non-target species. The original EU quota system – intended to protect stocks – implicitly encouraged the "discard" of bycatch, such that roughly a third of the total North Sea catch was dumped at sea, most of it either dead or dying. Recent changes to the Common Fisheries Policy have finally put an end to this practice.[9] There is now an obligation to land bycatch, most of which is processed into fishmeal for use by the agriculture and aquaculture sectors.

Commercial exploitation of the North Sea's oil and gas reserves began in the 1970s and peaked in 1999 at 6 million barrels per day. In early 2020 production was roughly one-third that figure. There are roughly 600 platforms in the North Sea, many of which are awaiting decommission. There is debate over the extent to which removal and clean-up is desirable. From an environmental perspective it would arguably be less damaging to leave them in place.

Most of Europe's offshore windfarms are in the North Sea. In 2020, the UK alone had 8.5 gigawatts of installed offshore capacity, mostly in the North Sea; and wind – onshore and offshore – accounted for 20 percent of UK electricity generation. Expansion is ongoing, and the 3.6 gigawatt Dogger Bank windfarm will be the world's largest when it becomes operational in 2025.

The North Sea witnessed major naval battles during WW1. The largest of these was the Battle of Jutland that led to the loss of 8500 lives. A mine barrage was positioned between Orkney and Norway during the war, after the success of a smaller barrage between England and France. The northern barrage is thought to have been responsible for the sinking of up to eight German U-boats. Clashes in WW2 were frequent, although smaller in scale. Today, the North Sea is strategically less important, since all the bordering nations are members of NATO.

To the Danes, the North Sea is their West Sea; to the old Scots it was their East Sea. The English name North Sea probably comes from the Dutch, for whom their word "*Nordzee*" has relational accuracy.

I grew up at Clacton on the East coast of England. The brown soup upon which I learned to sail, which then had an empty horizon and now has spinning turbines, was – simply – the sea.

---

[9] 2015, full implementation 2019.

Eigerøya

29 July 2017

South of Bergen I thread an inshore route. The weather is fine, and when there is a breeze the smaller channels are a delight to silently glide through. But I become tired: of being left becalmed, and of the steep sides of the islands that make it exhausting to haul the board from the water, and of sweating in my sleeping bag – because outside of its cocoon the insects would bite me to pieces. When I do dream, it is of an easy landing and a restful night.

The sense of tiredness and lack of inspiration are short-lived. I am happier where the channels open out into wider fjord. Finally some wind arrives – plenty to punch out onto open coast, and then race down to a curl of beach on the island of Karmøy. A slope of white sand comes into view as the sun sets. I have a contact here: Lorent. The board is safely nestled amongst the dunes. An enormous "late breakfast" of eggs and sausages makes for a perfect dinner, and soft sheets allow for a much needed full night's sleep.

The beaches and gentle landscape of Stavanger remind me of Northumberland. The empty sea offers good sailing. I sail a few miles with a local windsurfer, and end the day with some surfers who are camped at their favourite spot. Later the following day, beach gives way to boulders, and then rock. Having neglected my navigational homework, and with a freshly raucous sea state, I scrape my way round a small headland, then dive into the shelter of an inlet, that will be home for the next two nights.

There is a strategically-placed little harbour hooked round the inside of the tip of the headland. It is a perfect base camp location with an unobstructed close-up view of the open sea. Already, a stiff breeze locks my sail shelter down onto the cropped grass. Tomorrow it will blow a gale.

The obligation to take a rest day is welcome. There are no midges that can fly in this, and the temperature inside my sleeping bag is perfect. A boathouse dwelling appears to be occupied, and there I meet Ragnar and Hilde, who replenish my fresh water supply, and invite me to join them for a bowl of warming stew. They tell me about this island – Eigerøya – and its lighthouse, that was operated by Hilde's family. The ground floor of the boathouse is like a nautical museum, with many artefacts, including archaeological finds dredged from the little harbour.

In the low light of evening, I rest under a sail being bent low by savage gusts. A man and his daughter arrive with armfuls of army rations. He explains that these are courtesy of Norway's King Harald – by which he means the armed forces. The ration packs are a perfect gift. In the raging wind we then battle our way across barren rock to the mighty cast iron lighthouse from where Hilde's relatives had signalled to the ships. I am unable to remember the man's name, but will be forever grateful that he came to find me.

Eigerøya lighthouse

Eikvåg

31 July 2017

The sail from Eigerøya is no pushover. The wind that blows towards the land makes for an inhospitable lee shore. Waves are reflected off hard-edged rock and cliff. They rebound and head back out to sea, to add or subtract from the waves that are yet to arrive. The result is an unpredictable mess – a sea of rowdy crests. Though there is wind enough for the board to knife through the water, the movement of my craft is checked by jarring slaps.

At some distance from the coast – a kilometre, perhaps – the rebound is no longer a hindrance. The waves roll as a migrating herd.

To advance upwind I am obliged to sail a zigzag course: seaward, landward, seaward, landward... As the hours pass, the wind direction – and therefore the angles that can be sailed – are gradually shifted right. The zags of the zigzags become longer and more profitable. Eventually the zig is no longer necessary: it is possible to sail parallel to the coast, and even increase my separation from it. Helped also by a stiffening of the breeze, the board punches with confidence through a more noble sea.

I become aware of a fixed object beyond the horizon. Too steady for the mast of a yacht. Maybe a chimney, or a platform, or a lighthouse? Maps on my phone indicate that its bearing leads to land.

The miles to Lista Lighthouse are swiftly gobbled up. The granite tower sits on a corner of low-lying land: a shoreline that absorbs the waves rather than reflects them. There is shallow water around me now. Waves spill and break amongst a maze of skerries.

Progress so far is 28 nm – which is much further than anticipated for today – and as a result I am ignorant about what is coming up next. Now, beyond the lighthouse, comes fast downwind sailing in shallow water. There are skerries all around. It is all too hectic. From this perspective there is nothing on an unknown coast that seems friendly. I come across the manmade rock wall of a harbour. Neither is that friendly from this side. But there is a 50-metres-wide gap flanked either side by a green and a red pillar. Waves roll through the entrance, and without a second thought I accept the half invitation. The board bears away – changes course so that the wind comes more from behind, and accelerates down the faces and through the finish line.

Inside the harbour is a gentle summer's day. There is a beach of fine sand upon which to park. In this part of the North Sea the tidal range is just a few centimetres. There is still a current that alternates with the tide, but the vertical rise and fall is negligible.[10]

Over bread and cheese and a coffee it becomes apparent that I have contacts nearby. Geir had sent a welcoming invitation to call at Eikvåg:

"We can offer you a lovely guestroom, bathroom, food, drinks and almost true old stories from Eikvaag's proud past. It was the most important privateer cove in Norway during the Napoleonic War (1807-14) when Norway/Denmark unfortunately was at war with Great Britain. Welcome til Eikvaag!"

By late afternoon, the wind has moderated for the 8 nm dash to Eikvåg. Geir pilots a launch to intercept me, and then guides a way through the skerries and islands on the final approach. He and wife Bente are true to their word in every respect. The almost true stories are supplemented with real ones, including that of George Harbo and Frank Samuelsen, who were the first to row the Atlantic, from New York to the Scillies in 1896. Their story has a local connection and Geir presents me with a book about their voyage.

Eikvåg. Photo: Geir Heitmann

---

[10] On this section of coast I am near to an amphidromic point, or tidal node. See https://en.wikipedia.org/wiki/Amphidromic_point

Friends who show up include Harald-Dag – an Arctic historian and expeditioner. We met at a distance a while back – when a convoy of kayak-topped cars stopped to wave. Harald-Dag knows Dag from Finnmark. Many contacts are friends of friends. Now that I think about it, Geir probably heard of my voyage via Harald-Dag.

What is more certain is that Geir has a cannon trained on the island opposite. Apparently, it works and is occasionally fired, though during my stay the gunpowder is kept under wraps.

***

The following afternoon, it is time to say my thousand thankyous. Geir and Harald-Dag provide an escort to open water, and then I wobble to Lindesnes, the most southerly point of mainland Norway. A lighthouse sits upon barren rock, and – beside this – matchstick figures look out. One of the figures is waving in the photo I snap – which is the last of Norway's North Sea coast.

Lindesnes lighthouse

4. Skagerrak Sea

There is an arm of Atlantic Ocean that coils round the north of Denmark, then dives south of Sweden, before reaching up to Finland and Russia. The shoulder part of that arm – and a gateway to those sea areas beyond – is the Skagerrak Sea.

The land constraints of the Skagerrak Sea are Norway to the north, Sweden to the east, and Denmark to the south. Its longest maritime border is shared with the North Sea, on an imaginary line between Denmark (Hanstholm) and Norway (Lindesnes). There is a shorter maritime border where it meets the Kattegat Sea, on an imaginary line between Skagen (Denmark) and Paternoster Skær (a small island just off the Swedish coast).

The Danish Skagerrak coast is straight and sandy, and the sea is shallow. The north and east side of the sea is deeper – up to 700 metres deep in the Norwegian Trench, with a fjorded and island-studded coastline. Such variety of habitat makes it a biologically diverse sea. Around the Norway-Sweden border are cold-water coral reefs, where the source energy is sunlight – which is converted to organic matter by photosynthesis; and off the Danish coast are bubbling reefs, where the source of energy is methane – which is converted to organic matter by chemosynthesis.[11]

The Skagerrak sea is plankton-rich in the summer, and intensively fished. Target species include herring, mackerel, sprats, cod, and grey sole. Commercial shipping is an additional stress on the marine environment: in 2014 there were more than 10,000 ship transits. During the summer months the protected islets are cruising grounds for thousands of recreational craft.

The ecosystems of the Skagerrak – in common with those of many seas – are facing multiple pressures. These include pressures from local human activity, and also from our global impacts. In addition to becoming warmer, our seas are becoming more acidic as they absorb carbon dioxide. The rate of acidification is now a hundred times faster than at any time in the last 55 million years.[12]

---

[11] Chemosynthesis also occurs at hydrothermal vents, found at oceanic tectonic plate boundaries and other geologically active subsea regions. These vents support entire ecosystems at enormous depths where – prior to their discovery – it was assumed no life would be found.

[12] https://www.eea.europa.eu/ims/ocean-acidification

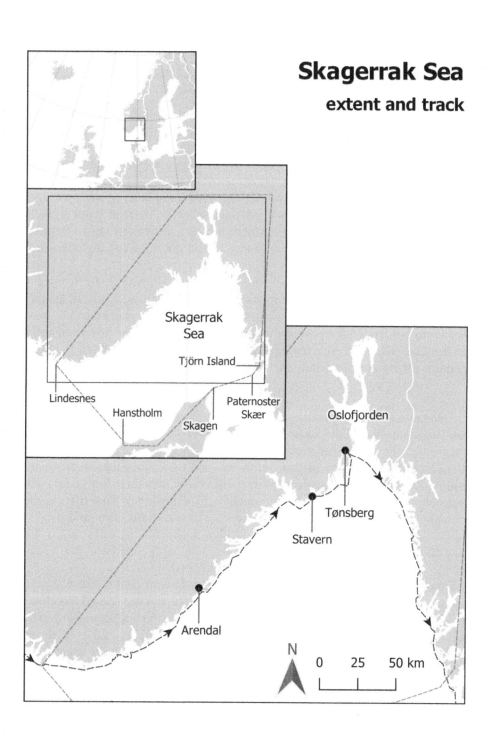

Skagerrak Sea
extent and track

Stavern, and Tønsberg

6-7 August 2017

This is southeast Norway. My pre-start plan had been to cross the Skagerrak Sea some days ago, when the distance from Norway to Denmark was less. But that plan changed. Perhaps fear played a part, because 65 nm of open sea is a challenging prospect. And there is – after all – an alternative route.

Part of me also counsels against falling into traps laid by my own ego. There is a great deal of intrinsic satisfaction to be derived from a well-executed act of daring. But there is nothing wise in taking risks to impress others. Knowing that the tracker is public should not influence my decisions, I remind myself.

Accordingly, a number of weeks ago, I decided to continue to Sweden – from where the crossing to Denmark is shorter. An added benefit of this route is that it will allow for the completion of the Norwegian coastline from border to border. To the best of my knowledge, I will be the first windsurfer to achieve this. I am sure my ego is complicit here too, but there is also a genuine affection – an affinity that has developed – for this rugged land.

***

The sail to Stavern is made noteworthy by an unexpected pulse of swell, and surprisingly shallow water. The combination of swell and shallow water means that the swell lines grow tall, even though I am kilometres from land. I am loath to detour any further out to sea, and the silent folds of ocean are rolling through at an angle that is perfect for catching free rides. An agreeable breeze provides power enough to effortlessly take-off on the downhill slopes. The board accelerates – travels light, fast and free – powered not by wind but by gravity – with a push from the wave that is felt like an invisible hand. Once hooked-up, it is like being on a train; but it may be the wrong train, because somewhere ahead lie skerries.

I stand on tip toes for a better view that is mostly restricted by the waves in front. This surf sailing is engrossing. When the skerries are sensed too close, it is time to alight and seek out deeper water before surfing shoreward once again. I lose myself and time. There is a sense of awareness for everything, on all sides, all at once: a flow state, in other words. Many waves later, and 8 nm from where I had taken the first of them, a clear route opens up and I sail through to a deeper water channel. Today the skerries go hungry.

The day's sail leaves me deeply satisfied. I fall into line with a few incoming yachts who have taken the long way round this area of shallows, and sail to the calm shelter of Stavern.

***

The following morning I am joined by Tord, who is keen to sail another leg, having joined me previously for the light wind drift to Bergen. Although I enjoy sailing alone, it is a real pleasure to have company, despite the added responsibility of looking out for two.

The Bergen sail demonstrated that Tord is a highly capable windsurfer. That is fortunate, because it is forecast windy today. We can both anticipate that conditions outside the fjord will be challenging. I double check the adjustment systems on my sail, and am nervous for both of us. We decide to head out for a look, with the option of heading back. If Tord hadn't made the journey over here I would be calling this a rest day.

Today there is solid wind. It gradually ratchets up as we head further out. I haul on maximum downhaul to leave the sail with extreme twist so that it releases air more easily. Tord's sail is not so easy to depower, and – somewhat concerningly – is held together with duct tape, but he has 100 kilos of Viking strength so is coping nonetheless. The wind blows at about 25 knots, or 12-13 metres per second in Norse units. We pelt-off downwind, and within a few minutes are already distant from each other, and too far committed to realistically consider heading back.

I am wary of the skerries, and take a more seaward course, hoping this will encourage Tord to follow. Despite the wind being much stronger today than it had been yesterday, the swell is smaller: blocked by low-lying islands and skerries further to seaward. A disadvantage of flatter water is that the nearby skerries are more difficult to spot, particularly as the sea is already awash with whitecaps.

The next moment I look round, Tord is on his backside being washed over a rock, his sail engulfed in white water. *Shit!* I have fears of this going downhill fast. I had been unwilling to gybe, but do so now, in a long drawn out arc with the wind ripping through the sail. The slightly upwind course back to the rock is more controlled. *Will Tord's sail have survived that?* I have a bad feeling. His sail suddenly comes upright, and Tord rises from the sea beneath it. *Yes!* Within seconds he is racing away, and I am struggling to turn my board to follow.

The "Invincible Viking" – which is Tord's email sign off – leads the charge to Sandesfjorden. He is blisteringly quick, and sails very open [with the wind very much from behind], positioned forward on the board and not using the footstraps. A Viking stance! It is unconventional, but the extreme directness of his course gobbles miles quickly, and it keeps us further inshore where the wind is perhaps a touch less strong. I give chase, with similar technique. The sea remains smaller than expected; those offshore skerries have helped us.

The wind – thankfully – moderates a little for the sail past the fjord entrance. I revert to a more conventional downwind planing technique: the mast-track positioned rearward and my feet in the back footstraps, The board goes faster, and it is a little bit more comfortable, but the zigzags of my course become more compressed, so ultimately it no quicker than the spinnaker method that Tord continues to use.

At Tønsbergfjorden it seems that Tord wants to go deeper into the fjord. I don't understand what he is up to, so obstinately push further out until Tord follows. When it is already too late, I see that we could have gone that route. Instead, we dive in a gap between the islands of Hvasser and Sando. This is now Oslofjorden, and the water between the islands on its western flank is totally flat. We stop on Hvasser, and thanks to a fluke of foresight I can produce hot coffee and nourishing supplies.

After the break, we enjoy a lightning quick downwinder between multiple island channels. It is desperately fun and inevitably competitive. I try hard to squeeze the extra tenths of a knot, find the strongest gusts, and use the full width of our racetrack.

Graunch! The sound is sickening. I have hit a submerged rock whilst going at full tilt. This is deeply unwise, and something I have managed to avoid until now. The tail kicks up as the fin scrapes over unforgiving granite. The bottom centimetres of fin are lost, which is a small price to pay for such an imprudence.

The downwinder into Oslofjorden delivers us to Tønsberg. It has been a truly memorable day already, and there is another highlight to come.

We make landfall at a house where we meet Kjell, a windsurfer friend of Tord. Hot water for a shower, and kilos of strawberries make for a quick recovery. By evening it is just Kjell and I. We take a boat over to Tønsberg centre. Kjell's tour through Norway's oldest city is as fascinating as it is unhurried.

It is the sailing that made this day memorable, but it is how it ended that now brings most gratitude. Many times on this journey people gave me their time. And time – as I sometimes have to remind myself – is the most precious of all gifts.

Our Choices Matter

3 August 2017, from log entry

As a kid, the forest at the end of our road seemed to stretch away forever, Scotland was remote and undiscovered. And beyond? Beyond required an imagination more fertile than the one I possessed. Britain – from my child's eye view – was too big to know; and the planet too big to comprehend.

In 2015 I windsurfed round Britain. That was a long-standing ambition, that later became a book. I set out in one direction and then – 98 days later – returned from the other. Far from being unknowably large, Britain was confirmed to be a *small island*, as author Bill Bryson has previously noted.

So, when my chronicle of that journey was nearing completion, and I began to wonder what would come next, it seemed reasonable to consider a challenge composed of multiple Britain-sized chunks. Russia's Baltic Sea border to Black Sea border was proposed by a friend. But my eye drifted to Scandinavia… To Russia's border with Norway… To Europe as a whole, in some contrived sense.

To sail the distance of Europe's mainland coast is equivalent to five times round Britain. Historically, that would have been a long distance for a human. But technology has shrunk our world, and changed it.

This "expedition" hopes to emphasise that our planet is smaller and more finely balanced than we are sometimes encouraged to believe; and that our choices regarding stewardship of the planet have never been more significant than at this moment.

The Arctic tern has brightened many of my days on this journey. These birds are great voyagers, and make annual migrations between the northern and southern polar regions. Their journeys demonstrate better than my own that our planet is shared, and that it does not stretch away forever.

The Earth is only 40,000 kilometres in circumference. Consider that a human-made satellite in low Earth orbit may take just 90 minutes to complete a circumnavigation. Surely that makes for a small earth (even though they are quite speedy).

We know that we are degrading and overwhelming our planetary home. It is easy and tempting to be defeatist about our ability to change that trajectory. But we *are* uniquely positioned: Like it or not, for the first time in history, we are at the wheel. That may not be a responsibility we wished for, but nonetheless it is "on us" to steer this ship.

5. Kattegat Sea

The Kattegat is a shallow sea between Denmark and Sweden. Its northern limit is where it meets the Skagerrak Sea, along a maritime border of approximately 35 nm. The southern limit is at the Sound and Belts of the Baltic Sea. The Sound and Belts are straits between mainland Denmark and Sweden.

The name Kattegat is derived from the Dutch for "cat's hole", which was a reference to the narrowness of the straits, that "even a cat would have difficulty squeezing through" – as someone may have once said. Today, the Great Belt has ample width to accommodate a busy shipping lane.

In the south, mainland Denmark and Sweden are connected by tunnels and bridges that cross the Sound and Belts. In the north, the connections are by ferry.

The Danish side is sandy; the Swedish side is sandy in the south, and rocky in the north, with many archipelagos.

The Kattegat has saline water, but there is mixing with the brackish water of the Baltic in the straits, contributing to habitat and species diversity.

In the 1970s, dead zones were first identified in the Kattegat Sea, and intensive agriculture has been recognised as a threat to marine life since then. Nitrate-rich waters encourage algal blooms that decay and suffocate other marine life. Various EU and nation-state action plans have been partially successful in reducing nitrate pollution.

One of the main islands of the Kattegat proper is Læsø, which lies 28 nm west of Sweden, and is a shorter hop from the Danish mainland.

Kattegat Sea
extent and track

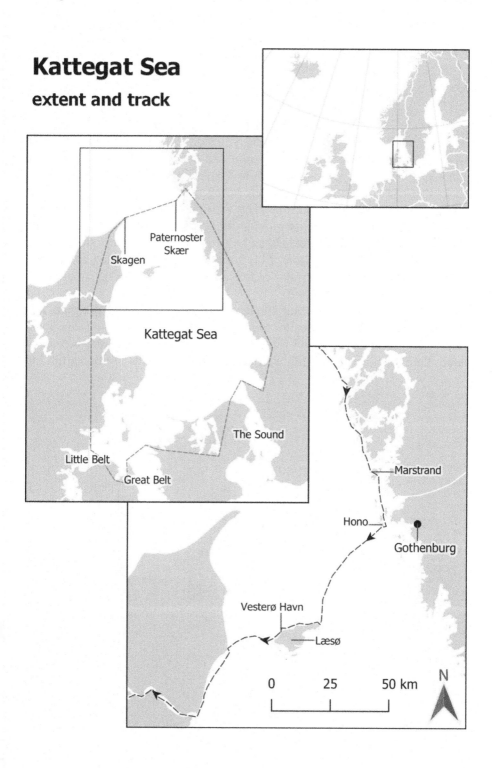

Læsø

13 August 2017

To sail the coast of Norway takes 81 days. I am then just 4 full days in Swedish waters. The sailing is mostly inside countless small rocks and islands. There is a day with driving rain and poor visibility, then 2 days of sun that everyone enjoys: Near the towns, people bask on lichen-painted rocks that rise steeply from the water. Away from human disturbance, seals do the same on favoured skerries. The well-marked channels provide total safety, and a parade of yachts provide a holiday feel. It is fun, social, and occasionally so easy that it feels like cheating. The people are as warm as the weather. There is amazing team-effort hospitality in picturesque Grundsund.

The transition from Skagerrak Sea to Kattegat goes unnoticed – there is no seam to be observed at this join.

I stop at Marstrand – a sailing hub that at this time is hosting a regatta that overflows with corporate wealth. Marstrand was once a free port. The town flourished during that period of questionable financial ethics, and perhaps it is not unrelated that it is doing well today too. The yachts are beautiful, but

An inside route in Swedish waters

their relationship to rampant capitalism – and the damage that does to our planet – makes it a tainted beauty.

My next stop is on Hono, arrived at in the rain. Some of my Spanish friends pronounce my name as Hono. That coincidence sealed my decision to head for the island. It seems to be an honest place, with a direct view and immediate access to the open sea. There is nothing hidden here.

A picnic table under an empty terrace becomes my bed. The sail is tied onto a pontoon to prevent it self-harming in a swirling and gusty wind. I try to rest, in preparation for crossing the Kattegat tomorrow.

***

Breakfast is at 7am, when the wind begins to moderate, as the forecast indicated it would. All forecast models agree that the weather will become more settled as the day progresses. That is reassuring.

My intention is to split the crossing by heading first for Læsø. With the wind blowing from the northwest, there should be a good angle for a fast reach [a sailing angle with the wind from the side, or slightly from behind] direct to the island. It is inevitable that the sea will be lumpy for the first part of the crossing, where the fetch – the distance of open water over which waves may build – is longest.

If anyone sees me launch, it is unlikely they guess I am sailing for Denmark.

There are the skerries to negotiate first. Today they are clearly defined by broken water. I sail slow and high [close to the wind], to push straight into the sea, rather than face it obliquely. Head-high waves lift the board with more muscle than coordination. It is a "rough ol' day" to be sailing an isolated and treacherous coast.

The wind blows at around 15 knots, occasionally 17, nudging a Beaufort force 5. The waves are steep and tightly packed, but by slowly nosing into them I am in control, and will reach safer water.

When confident that the skerries are behind me, I retract the daggerboard, pull the mast-track back, wiggle my feet securely into the footstraps, and bear away [adjust course away from the wind] until the board is planing. I sail on a beam reach, approximately 90 degrees from the wind. Any deeper and there would be a risk of the nose burying. A glance at the GPS – clipped onto the boom – informs me that my course is still somewhat north of the island. For now though it is fine – the priority is to get through this band of stronger wind and bigger waves.

The GPS is my guide. A compass in my drysuit pocket is backup. In these wet conditions the phone is too difficult to operate to be considered a reliable aid to navigation.

Away from land, the wind and sea gradually moderate. Conditions become enjoyable rather than intimidating. It is quite typical that the biggest

A ferry passes to leeward mid-crossing of the Kattegat Sea

challenge of the sailing is the initial launch and the final landing. The open water stuff in between may be relatively uneventful. I guard against complacency, but seemingly today is a case in point. The board sails more freely now, towards the island.

A ferry, presumably bound for Gothenburg, passes on the starboard [right-hand] side. A light aircraft is a more unexpected encounter. They bank over and circle a few times, presumably curious, before also continuing eastward. Blue sky has broken through.

Sea and the wind continue to drop. After two hours of good progress I take a few minutes to drink and eat, with the sail resting in the water.

Soon after comes the first sighting of the low-lying island. All tension dissolves and I sail a direct course to its eastern tip. An hour later I am landed on more sand than I have seen in months. It is a different world to the rocks of Sweden.

Læsø is a beautiful island of soft meadows. I take a proper break to brew coffee, eat lunch, and dry off. The exertions of the crossing have left the clothes beneath my drysuit sopping wet.

I suit up again for the afternoon sail, and proceed along the north coast of the island towards Vesterø Havn, until running aground on sand. Progress can be made by sailing the board on its side, but eventually it becomes too shallow even for that. In Norway I had dreamed of sand, and now there is too much of it. The obstacle is a barely submerged sand spit, the tip of which is 3 nm upwind of my position. I prefer to pull the board over it than sail round. A message comes in as I splash westward – an offer of a berth on the boat of Ingemar and Elizabeth. This gentle Swedish couple had been sailing in south Norway, and we overlapped in some places, so it is like meeting old friends when I do reach the little Havn.

Læsø is a very restful place, and it is easy to surrender the idea of more miles. The second stage of the crossing, a 10 nm hop to the Danish mainland, can wait until tomorrow.

6. Limfjorden

At various times in the past, and most recently in 1825, Denmark's West Sea (to us, North Sea) broke through its sand-dune barrier to establish a connection with an inlet of the East Sea (to us, the Kattegat). When this happened, the northern part of Denmark became an island, and the inlet – Limfjorden – became a channel.

The twisting 100-nm-long cut-through remains as a perfectly navigable waterway. Being a natural feature, it also fits my definition of an allowed route. I am strict with myself regarding allowed routes: only those that were available to the mariners of old are permitted.

Limfjorden falls outside the scope of any area defined by *Limits of Oceans and Seas*. That's a point for the record, not a concern. It is fun to be inventive with navigation. I imagine the route as like a wormhole, that instead of connecting different points in spacetime, tunnels between disconnected seas of the World Ocean.

Limfjorden: Seagrass calms the water and a navigable channel bends left

Limfjorden
track from Kattegat Sea
to North Sea

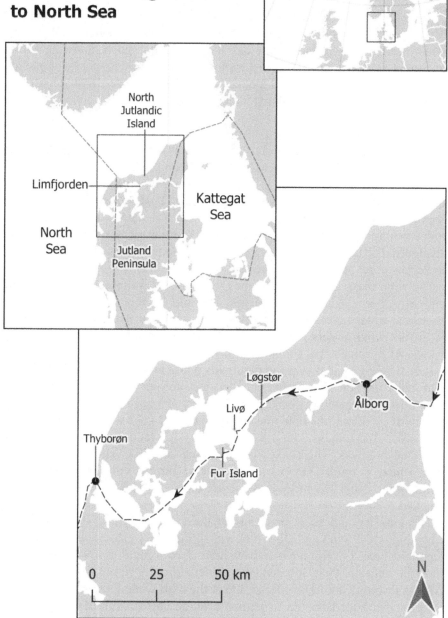

66

The East Sea to the West Sea

15-17 August 2017

The sail from Læsø to the "mainland" of the North Jutlandic Island had been against the wind. The only slight worry had been a rather feeble breeze mid-crossing. In fact, late in the day the wind came good, allowing for an overnight at Hou – just north of Limfjorden's eastern entrance. Completion of the Kattegat jump was celebrated with a Tuborg beer, and sleep came easily that night on the soft shoreside vegetation.

***

Today, there is a stiff easterly breeze. I am away and sailing before the onshore wind builds a shorebreak that would complicate the launch.

The entrance to Limfjorden is like a river estuary, with extensive shallows that are neither navigable sea nor habitable land. There is a "correct" approach – a deep channel that ships use – but it is narrow and begins many miles out to sea. I take a gamble on a shortcut across the white water shallows. The fin scrapes through sand for a kilometre or so before making it to deeper water and a lagoon-like sea.

The wind picks up and follows the twists of the Limfjorden, initially to the city of Ålborg. Were this open sea it would be too windy, but on such protected water I can zigzag downwind for 17 nm of flat-out broad reaching [with the wind largely, but not entirely, from behind]. The channel width varies. At its widest it is about a kilometre across.

It is difficult to predict if the day holds many miles or few. The variables, that make the hours profitable or otherwise, are uncertain or unknown. In a way it is like a game of Snakes and Ladders. To have a chance of progress you must go afloat: the dice must be rolled. If all goes well then some miles are made. And maybe – on a day like today – a ladder delivers better than expected progress. The snakes in this game could be harmful, but mostly their venom is mild. They bite as an adverse current, a headwind, too much wind, or too little. The miles they rob are the ones that had been prematurely counted.

The industry and taller buildings of the city are visible from far away. They block the wind and slow it down, so there is welcome rest when I am amongst them. Limfjorden is narrow here. Two bridges pass overhead. I dip the sail beneath their low-hanging underbellies, then make a landing at Ålborg Fishing Club. The gear is safe at the club while I grab a bite to eat in the city. An hour later the fisherman provide coffee, and interview me for their website. It seems a shame not to be a tourist for longer, but favourable wind beckons.

Limfjorden opens up to become 3 nm wide. I expect to sail near to the coast – the bank – but the bending channel stays central, and therefore so must I, because for the most part the area is covered in lush beds of seagrass too thick to sail through. The sheltering effect of the city lasts for 5 nm at least, after which there is solid wind for planing once again. But now the detached blades of seagrass clog behind the fin, soon slowing the board to a crawl. The weed is like a maritime gravel trap. Again, and again I catch sufficient to thatch a cottage. It is quite exhausting. A sprint becomes a crawl within a minute, and then I have to drop into the water to manually clear the weed from the fin, before waterstarting away [being lifted from the water by the sail] for the next brief dash.

I pass through another bridge-spanned narrow, then stop on a white beach at the pretty town of Løgstør. Not just here, but at all the places I have stopped, cleanliness and general good order is the norm. Løgstør public conveniences are spotless.

Today's ladder has catapulted me further forward than expected. Fur Island – where a contact has kindly offered to put me up in their hotel – is only 10 nm from here. I imagine the crisp smooth sheets, ignore the early evening storm clouds that are brewing, and head back out.

In the end, Fur is a hop too far. The clouds smother the wind and turn the sky black, and my concern becomes avoidance of electrocution by lightning strike. I decide upon a diversion to the diminutive island of Livø.

It becomes a very pleasant place to overnight, and had it not been for the torrential rain I would have explored more, and perhaps met some of the island's 10 full-time inhabitants, or tasted their local beer.

✳✳✳

Wind is forecast by the lazy turn of distant turbines. Soon after, ripples paint the water. Colours pop in the freshly rinsed air. The sail to Fur island – just 5 nm – represents a morning stroll.

From Livø extends a 3-km-long natural spit, topped with a thick layer of cockle shells. The dry part of the ridge is no more than a metre wide. This overlooked wonder of the natural world compels me to stop. I gather the shells in my cupped hands to feel and hear them.

Sailing is resumed on the other side of the spit. A strict reading of my own rules might consider that to be cheating. A more relaxed interpretation is that my rules are not precise. My rules allow that I can launch from whatever bit of beach seems most suitable. A spit is really just a long beach that doubles back on itself. Perhaps it is within my rules to walk across a spit to launch from the other side? Anyway, if there is anywhere that I did "cheat" on this journey, it was here.

My contact at the Fur Strand Hotel is away, but his son – Aron, running the show – is a kind and competent substitute.

The cockle-shell spit that extends from Livø island

***

Aron and some guests wave me off. Yesterday's short day had allowed for a good rest and a small explore. The island museum – majoring on local geology, palaeontology, and past evidence of volcanic ash clouds – had been an unexpectedly worthwhile visit.

The flat terrain is helpful in terms of wind. It allows today's southerly breeze to blow across the channel rather than be deflected into a headwind. The easy sailing allows for a meet, 20 nm from Fur, with a reporter from Danish TV. I haul the board onto the sand next to a road and rail bridge. A span of the bridge swings-up high into the air to let a yacht pass though in the moments before Christian arrives. He is friendly and interested and does a professional job.

My next break comes on a long and empty beach fed by crumbling sandy cliffs. It demands to be stopped on, and reminds me of East Anglia and home. The beach is covered in flint, like the beaches in Norfolk. The stones make a high pitched chink when knocked together, and spark, and form a good blade, just as they did when I was a kid. The North Sea is in reach, so I push on.

Another 20 nm further on is where the sea broke through, and now lies the town of Thyborøn. Limfjorden in this part is many miles across, and the most direct route situates me far from land. The approach to Thyborøn Channel is clogged by barely submerged sandbanks. They are like a maze. Satellite imagery is a helpful to locate the curling channels. Rain comes again, reducing the visibility to null. There is no lightning today, thankfully. The water is barely deep enough to drown in! At least I will not be hit by a ship.

The rain eases, and under a low sky I find deeper water to sail past the fortified wall of a major port. There is an easy landing in the Thyborøn Channel, before reaching North Sea proper, which is where today's ladder ends.

***

Thyborøn is a robust North Sea port. The dockside café does an excellent fish supper that compares favourably to the British gold standard (as established on my round Britain windsurf). There are two bars to choose from, and maybe I chose well, because the waitress from the café also chooses it at the end of her shift. Christian's filming has evidently been broadcast, because I am recognised, and – for a few moments – a celebrity.

But that all happens after a survey of the town, and a poignant wander through the dunes. Despite this being August, there are no people about. It is cold, and bleak. The dune area has been turned into a memorial to those who perished in the Battle of Jutland – the "largest naval battle in history" depending upon measure.[13] Granite slabs denote ships sunk. Surrounding each slab is a cluster of several – or a dozen, or more – ivory coloured pins. The pins, close-up, are seen as figures with faceless, bowed heads. Each pin stands for numerous men, and the groupings correspond to the loss of life from each ship. It is a particularly beautiful and moving memorial.

---

[13] In terms of "total displacement of ships involved."
https://en.wikipedia.org/wiki/Largest_naval_battle_in_history

7. North Sea – Part Two

The sail through Denmark, from east coast to west, is completed in 2 days. The only real peril of those inland waters had been possible ambush by electrical storm. The launches and landings had been trivially easy. That all changes after re-entering the North Sea, having emerged from Limfjorden.

Battle of Jutland memorial at Thyborøn

North Sea extent and part two of track

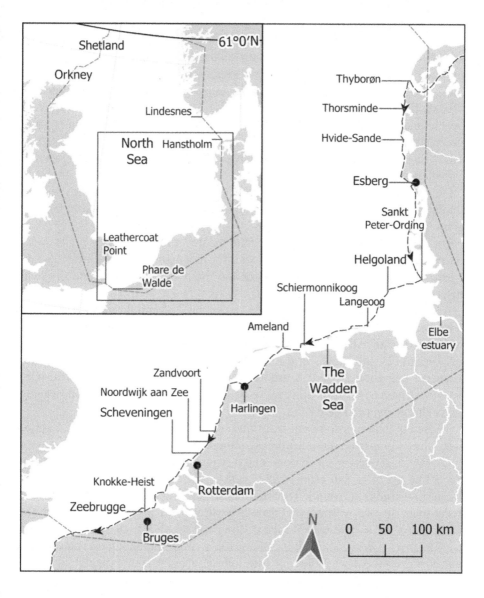

Thorsminde

18-21 August 2017

The west coast of the Jutland Peninsula is mostly uninterrupted beach. When that beach becomes a lee shore – which simply requires wind with a component of west – it is relentlessly scoured by waves. The waves patrol the route to shore like a pack of animals ready to fell and maul a straggler.

From Thyborøn I sail in upwind zigzags against a stiff south-westerly breeze. By the end of the day's run the sea has built sufficiently to make a beach landing unwise, but I have planned well, and sail between the red and green beacons that mark the opening to the port of Thorsminde. The next three days are waited out, under siege from the waves, with growing impatience.

On day two, I come within a whisker of sailing: suited up, board next to the water. But it is too windy and too lively, and the next acceptable landing is too distant.

On day three a retired fisherman, Ole, locates me and offers a night under proper cover. In fact he has been sending messages for days, after seeing Christian's TV report, but I have been too focussed on the sea, and my own discomfort, to attend to those things.

A sense of detachment from people has set in. Torrential rain; wet or wind-whipped sand; a sail shelter being laid low by gusts; mental indecision about whether to sail. All have played a part in undermining self-confidence and my becoming withdrawn. In this state I will be poor company, is the mental subtext. The thought that I am only doing this (journey round Europe) because I never really fit in, is more believed. A sense of being undeserving of kindness is more keenly felt.

These companions show up from time to time. I know them well. A lot of what they say is true, but untruths are slipped in too.

Ole swings open his car door and I know it is a good time to step in, accepting the offer that brings reconnection with humanity.

On my trudging round Thorsminde, I had noted a memorial to lost fishermen. In the warmth of Ole's bungalow, and prompted by a framed photograph of a pale-blue-hulled fishing vessel, I ask of the memorial's significance. Ole reaches to a shelf for a box that contains newspaper cuttings from the days following 14th February 1979, and explains:

It was not a particularly rough day, but it was cold. Most of the fleet were working. Then the wind turned to the east, and the problems began. Spray whipped from the sea hit the boats and instantly froze. Very soon the boats became completely covered under a weight of ice they could not carry. Ole was a lucky one, and a wise one – he took his boat onto the beach. The newspaper cutting and the picture on the wall show the same boat. But six vessels did not make it. They turned over and went down, drowning 15 men and boys.

The "great" Battle of Jutland... The lives cut short or left empty by the storm... These events put my petty frustrations into perspective. So too does Ole's now simple home and life; and his wife, and her work in the fish processing factory and a shift that starts at 6am. They seem content. I have been here just three days. It is ridiculous to be in a hurry.

I remind myself to stop striving... for miles, progress, achievement – even words on a page; and instead be content to just be.

A surfer plays in the waves at Thorsminde

Esbjerg

22 August 2017

Lumps of sea jostle the entrance of Thorsminde harbour-estuary. A rough start to the day. Current flowing out; wave upon wave piling in. A few tacks get me to the mouth, where I hang by the windward wall. Observe; be patient – is my self-counsel. The waves immediately outside the mouth – jacked up by the outflowing current – are steep, unsteady, and potentially dangerous. Observe. Be patient. Anticipate. Judge when the area just in front of the leeward wall will be between sets. And then commit!

Fishing boats can power straight through the crumbling froth, but I have neither the angle nor momentum to take on broken waves. Poor timing would mean being broadsided, entangled with the white water, and swept to the dangerous lee wall, where waves surge upon granite boulders and flood the cavities between them.

I climb seaward until outside the gap, riding the rise and fall, then bear off to sail low-and-fast, clearing the wall before bigger waves arrive. A track of unbroken water opens up to get properly clear of the coast. Prudent timing, and wind enough for a healthy turn of speed, have enabled the worst of the sea to be sidestepped.

The entire sea is moving southward after days of this north-westerly wind. The current now accompanies the waves, making for an orderly procession. Rounded swells carry the board on a continual plane. I stand middle of the board; mast-track central; sail depowered and floppy, swinging open. As much surfing as windsurfing. Only occasionally is a gybe necessary to creep back a little further inshore, and that allows for a rest of sorts as different muscles are called into action.

A time-out on land would be welcome, but crashing through the waves to the beach would be a one-way ticket, so I keep going, and 23 nm later reach the more generously proportioned port of Hvide-Sande. There is easy stopping here for a needed break, with coffee and a calorie binge.

A second hop of similar length delivers me to Blåvand, where a substantial square-based lighthouse marks a sharp angle in the coastline. From the corner, a spit extends seaward, forming a barrier to be hurdled or rounded. Conditions have moderated now, so I take a gamble to ride the waves all the way in, to where shallow water washes over the spit and it is easily crossed. In the lee of the sandbar it is like waves have not been invented.

After another stop – this time for tea – the board eventually glides into Esbjerg. A 65 nm day! I have a contact – Emil – who it turns out has volunteered his parents Klaus and Trine to offer support. They are lovely and become my new favourite people. Klaus teaches sailing, and when chatting with Trina one evening – and after being a bit curious that Klaus is still working at midnight – Trina explains that in the summer he takes on extra work driving combine-harvesters.

Blåvand lighthouse

Helgoland

26 August 2017

Coastal navigation of the German Bight is complicated by the delta of the river Elbe. When on land, the sea is often distant. When on the sea, it is unclear how to reach that which is reliably land. There are islands that might be reached at high tide, but which are inaccessible at low. The tide falls as if a plug has been pulled, revealing new islands of sand that grow to become desert-like expanses, remote from any green shore.

Occasionally, I stop on a sandbank. It feels other-worldly to be the only human. But also a privilege to experience such peace and isolation. There are birds on this one, and others are very popular with seals, but – mostly – there is just sand. My scraping footprints are a blemish next to the delicate brushings of the gulls and waders, but in a few short hours the marks will be gone, and the sandbank too.

Soon I will arrive at Sankt Peter-Ording, which is the last piece of accessible shore before crossing the sandbanks and shipping lanes of the delta. It is an unrealistically long passage to complete in one day, but the difficulty of reaching land complicates it being staged. Again, I recall that in Norway I had craved for sand. On occasion, when searching for a landing, I had pleaded for it. Now that there is sand everywhere, I lament that there is no deep water.

An interesting and simpler alternative to the desert route is to cross via the Helgoland archipelago.

***

I am waved-off from the sands of Sankt Peter-Ording by Sven and his son Jan. The whole family have very quietly ensured that I start the day well-nourished and well-rested. The touch of wildness to their garden – anarchic in contrast to the Germanic norm – had been nice to see. And I had very much enjoyed our cycle ride to the beach, despite being scandalised that payment was required to access it.

When I landed here yesterday, Manuel Vogel – the editor of *Surf Magazin* – arrived and offered greetings. Over coffee and cake many aspects of this project were discussed. The magazine will run a story. At the end of our interview Manuel asked if I would be interested in providing ongoing updates.

At the time, I imagined that nothing would come of that suggestion, but happily I was proved wrong. I contribute four articles a year for the remainder of the journey, and the income that follows is a central pillar of managing finances. A big thank you is due.

***

Helgoland is 26 nm offshore. Straight out, in the same direction the wind is going. The breeze now is painfully light, and it is forecast to stay that way, though it could disappear entirely, or go in circles. Local advice is to abort today's crossing attempt, but I am prepared to gamble, and perhaps paddle in the dark if necessary. If the wind comes up, then hopefully I will make it in the light; and if not, then at least the sea will be flat. Navigational due diligence has established that there are no sandbanks en route.

With the sail held upright and immobile the board drifts along at a speed of just over a knot, or about 2 kilometres per hour. That will make for a 24 hour crossing. Not good. But if the sail is continually pumped: fed forward and then swung back to take big scoops of air – then closer to 3 knots can be achieved, or about 5 kilometres per hour. A 10 hour crossing. Better. Though it is a good thing I started early.

I settle into a rhythm and keep swinging the sail – feeding it forward and rowing it back. The GPS dangles from the boom, usually turned off to conserve battery, but periodically brought to life to provide reassurance about direction and progress. The workout requires a pleasant twisting of my body; and is agreeably symmetrical, as both port tack [left hand forward] and starboard tack [right hand forward] help to close on the target. My mind double-checks the maths, monitors vital signs of weather and body, explains a gybe or another tactic that my muscles are already initiating, bounds off some place unbid for a while, comes back, re-does the maths... It becomes the mind of a distance runner.

The sea is an empty expanse on all sides. So why can I hear music? The beat is audible. Clearly audible. What the...!? I double check, but there are no boats; there is nothing that is not just sea that extends to a flat and empty horizon. The music comes and goes. I rip the battery from my phone, in case that is playing tricks. A hunt for a submarine also finds nothing. Hallucination is the best candidate at present, though it sits uneasy.

Some dolphins show up, those harbingers of good fortune. A proper sit down break is advised, though it lasts just a few minutes. Tired legs enjoy the caress of cool sea. Real food is chewed; and clean, fresh water imbibed with an appreciation that is usually overlooked.

The sky darkens. On the edge of the cloud there is light rain, and that brings wind for some easy miles. Uncertain hints of what could be land crystalize into a definite visual target. When the cloud is gone, the water is glassier than ever, and evening has arrived. 8 nm to go. Each haul on the sail is now a real effort.

I do not notice the ship until alerted by the low murmur of an engine. Then I ignore it. It follows astern, off my port quarter, like a creepy shadow.

Green and grey livery suggests it is a coastguard vessel. It halves the gap between us, but still no crew appear. All my effort goes into rowing the sail.

When the ship talks, it is in loudspeaker-amplified German. My only German is "Ich habe einen hamster." Even if it were still true that I have a hamster, that is hardly relevant. I skip a beat of rowing the sail to bawl back "English! Danke!" then return focus to air rowing.

Some minutes later a small craft is observed that sends spray out each side as it speeds in my direction. The boat and crew come close enough to talk. I explain my intention to reach Helgoland. The message is relayed to the mothership. The rowing of the sail punctuates our conversation, and fills the awkward silences.

"Where is your support boat?" Pump, pump, pump.

"No support boat." Pump, pump, pump. "But don't worry, I'll make it." That gets relayed back too.

"But you know darkness is coming?" The low sun is visible to all...

"Yes, that it why I am pumping."

I hope that a glimmer of a smile is detected.

Eventually, the instruction comes for the crew to return to their ship. There are just a few miles to go now. I pump hard through absolutely still air to round the tip of the first Helgoland island, where seals on the beach are performing a chorus of wailing, and then cross to the main island, expending the very last of my energy reserves to avoid being swept to sea by current flowing through the channel. Anywhere to land will do. An open lock gate in a concrete wall offers the quickest route out of the current. The board glides through, and another epic sail is complete.

***

Helgoland is a magical place, and the weather can rarely be balmier than this evening. Before I have touched land, some welcoming sailors invite me aboard their yacht. Before I have found the conveniences, the yacht club group beckon me towards their barbecue. I have a plate on the go with each party, and drink water like a camel. It is a very happy atmosphere.

The mystery of the music is resolved. There had been a beach cinema during the day, and the scores of the film must have carried all that distance.

The following morning, I walk to the cliff tops and am captivated by the many hundreds of gannets that fill both the sky and the precarious ledges just a few feet from the path. To observe these animals from so close up is mesmerizing.

The Wadden Sea

22-23 August, and 30 August - 1 September 2017

I had dipped into the Wadden Sea at Esbjerg, but have mostly sailed on the outside of the dashed line of islands and drying sands that defend it from the North Sea proper. The Wadden Sea is an intertidal zone – a huge beach really. Accordingly, it receives no mention in the *Limits of Oceans and Seas*. The islands of the Sea stretch from Denmark to the Netherlands.

When the tide drops, the Wadden Sea drains, so from a navigational perspective it is simpler to sail outside of the islands. From Helgoland I cross to Langeoog, missing out Wangerooge and Spiekeroog. Between the islands are strong currents. With a cycle of roughly 12 hours and 20 minutes a whole sea drains out and then floods back in.

Vegetation binds the sands of the islands together and prevents them being washed and blown away, and also makes them havens for wildlife. The long North Sea beaches are popular with tourists, but with few cars or tarmacked roads, a healthy balance is maintained between where people monopolise and where nature flourishes. Most people get around by bike.

It is easy to forget that land is sometimes an island. On Langeoog, I happen upon a railway station whilst supplies-shopping on a windless day-off. A friend in Hamburg has invited me to visit, so out of curiosity I ask about train times to the city, but the enquiry is met with a tired expression. Hmm. Sometimes people are put off by my shipwrecked appearance – perhaps a shave is overdue. Then an undersized train rolls up to the platform. "Choo! Choo!" it peeps. It dawns on me that this is an island trainset rather than a connected transport hub. Clean shaven or otherwise, there are no trains to Hamburg.

The islands of Baltrum and Nordeney come next. It is hot and sunny, and my offshore attire makes me stand out more than normal upon landing on a beach full of people, and then departure is delayed until the local paper have made their scoop. Then it is on to Juist. A friend-of-a-friend bounds over and is keen to offer a place to stay. He makes some phone calls, and then – visibly pained – must explain that his father-in-law – whose house I would be staying in – has vetoed the offer. The poor guy. It makes no odds to me, since plan A – the default, sleeping under the sail – can be reverted to. The father in law doesn't like my project, or has other reasons to say no, all of which are of course fine, but it is sad that the rejection will be most keenly felt by his own family. Then some kitesurfers offer a plan C, and I end up sleeping in a yurt.

Next day is forecast windy later in the day. I start early, briefly stop to enjoy the desolate and desert-like Rottumerplaat island – inhabited by birds,

Becalmed, though conditions will soon become wild

and a single observation tower – and then am becalmed off the island of Schiermonnikoog. The sea is eerie. Clouds hang low and reflect off a glassy-smooth sheen of water that begins flat but is soon undulating with swell. After half an hour the first gusts arrive, darting haphazardly as if joyful to be the first to lay ripples on the water. Soon after they find a coherent direction, and reveal the steely intent of a soon to arrive Beaufort force 6.

My strategy is to reach the end of the island and duck inside to the Wadden Sea, where the North Sea waves do not reach. There are 8 nm to cover, and then a complicated entrance between the islands. It is a race. In this wind, on this coast, I must get round quickly or accept that I will not get round at all.

Most of the distance is sailed in full preservation mode: mast-track just forward of middle, sail ragdoll floppy, harness lines twisted away to prevent accidental hook-ins, gunning as broad as possible. The previously smooth sea now has steps, drop-offs, and pits. The waves on the sandbars of the entrance are head high, and the wind desperately overpowering. The board careers off a step and is airborne for a moment. My feet are too light. The nose hits first, then digs in and slows in an instant. I am launched forward, face-scrape over the sail, and hit the water somewhere beyond the mast tip.

Litres of water have been pressure-forced into my drysuit, but that isn't the immediate concern. The mast and sail must be protected from the steep and crumbling waves. That priority allows a few moments of recovery time. After the restart I hold it together until inshore of the waves.

I am now on the Wadden Sea. Visibility is extremely poor, because it is chucking it down too, but the sea state is like that of any shallow harbour – and reminds me of similar conditions experienced when sailing at Walton Backwaters as a kid. The most significant danger is of being run down by an unseen and unseeing ferry. Wow! That was an intense 30 minutes.

A flooding [rising] tide is good fortune. It means there is water to sail on. Some hours later I reach Nes harbour, on the inside of Ameland island, and make landfall between whistling masts and clanging shrouds.

There is a disconnect between mind and body after a bruising sail. The body attends to the details: finds shelter, puts dry clothes on, rinses drysuit; but the mind is still at sea. It is perhaps akin to a mild form of shellshock. It seems that people are sensitive to this state. They tend to respond either by keeping their distance, or by engaging in a humanitarian way. The cause of my dazed stupor – a somewhat harrowing sail – is easily guessed, and it is common for people to enquire about my wellbeing. The effect is interesting. I wonder if people would engage were I to be less obviously a shipwreck case. I think not. "Odd" behaviour is perceived as threatening, and sometimes our fears override our humanity.

On this journey, time and again, the positive aspects of human nature come to the fore. I am shivering cold when I land – thermals soaking from that flushing of seawater earlier in the day. The harbour master loads the showers with tokens for limitless hot water, and waives the camping charge.

***

I am reading *The Riddle of the Sands*, penned by Erskine Childers in 1903. The book is a fictional spy novel set in and around the drying sands and mudflats of the Wadden Sea, and is exceptional for its accurate detail based on the author's obvious knowledge of seamanship and of the area. There is a passage where the main character – Davis – is led to near certain shipwrecking by a sinister yacht, leaving poor Davis against the shoals on a lee shore in a near gale. There is a degree of overlap in that description and of my experience today. The shoals will have shifted since Childers' time, but the dangers they pose are the same.

***

There are overlaps in the following days too. Inside the islands, even for a craft with such a shallow draft as mine, the channels must be kept to. Any wandering and the fin soon grounds, and scrapes against mud-dwelling molluscs. The watersheds that Davis talked of are still awkward to cross.

The North Sea floods into the Wadden Sea on each side of its many islands. Currents of rising tide flow in behind each as a pincer movement.

The waters behind each island meet at the watershed. Later, when the tide ebbs [goes out], the sea drains away from each side of these watersheds.

To cross a watershed, one must find a channel to approach it on a flood tide, link it to a channel beyond when the current is slack and the water deepest, and then ride the ebb downstream to more navigable water. That is how I reach the mainland town of Harlingen. The passage is made after setting off in the afternoon, well-fuelled by a hearty lunch provided by Rodney and Anita – contacts who are friends of friends in Norway. The board grounds-out hundreds of times on its approach, and I seem destined to be caught somewhere near the watershed on a falling tide, before finally breaking through. Davis had been fascinated by the maze of channels, and had navigated them by feel and sight, rather than electronic aid. In my case, the online resource OpenSeaMap helps to get me through.

The lunar cycle dictates that the tides become later each day. The tidal highs and lows trail those of the preceding day by about 50 minutes. This explains my late afternoon departure from Harlingen: there had been no water earlier upon which to sail. The traditional sailing craft that ply these waters are flat bottomed, and routinely wait out low tide rested upon the muddy sands. I sail close to one for a better view, and the friendly skipper lobs me a beer.

Today's sail is alongside the Afsluitdijk – a keyboard tantrum mix of letters. The literal translation is "shut-off-dyke". Constructed in 1932, this 32 kilometre-long barrier divides what was once the Zuiderzee (South Sea) from the Wadden Sea. On the other side of the dam is now the freshwater Ijsselmeer (Lake Ijssel). The province of Flevoland, now home to nearly half a million people, was also reclaimed from the Zuiderzee. A motorway sits atop the Afsluitdijk.

My evening commute ends in darkness at Den Oever. The night sailing was fun on this occasion, because the breeze had been gentle and the water calm. By contrast, windsurfing "blind" on a lumpy sea I know to be spirit-crushingly difficult. Balance has a strong reliance upon visual cues. Likewise, although the actual wind can be felt, to anticipate gusts and lulls it is necessary to see and "read" the water. It takes the loss of a sense to fully appreciate its contribution.

A beam from my headtorch picks a way through the yacht harbour. The arrival of a windsurfer brings about a minor commotion that results in a comfortable night aboard a fast catamaran, guest of Jelle and Obe.

Tomorrow, after dodging the ferries between mainland Den Helder and the island of Texel, and fighting against the flooding tide, it will be back to open coast and North Sea waves.

Scheveningen

7 September 2017

The sea often produces foam in windy and wavy conditions, but on 11th May 2020 the foam was freakishly abundant. The sea also moves about, that is just what it does. But on the day in question, the combination of current and foam was fatal. The five surfers were swept to a corner where foam lay deep on the water's surface. The men were all strong, fit, healthy and experienced; most were surfers by profession: instructors or lifeguards; but they were suffocated by the foam. It was a tragic, freak occurrence.

The beautiful Dutch people make every stop along their coast special. But this chapter is titled Scheveningen in memory of their loss.

***

My trivial troubles heading south are headwinds, foul current and breakages.

It is demoralizing that I can barely keep pace with a tubby yacht on the upwind zigzags. Ultimately, the relentless progress of the sailboat makes it an unfair match.

A calm evening allows for a few extra kilometres to be added by paddle, until a snapped shaft determines exactly where the day will end. Perhaps that is part of the plan, or the simulation, or whatever version of reality keeps throwing these happy coincidences my way, because the breakage occurs in front of the Hargen aan Zee lifeguard station. Jens and friends are excellent company. They are relentlessly positive and provide a broom handle for a repair attempt, a treatment room to overnight in, and pancakes. Their team also carry the gear to the water's edge the following morning. In terms of energy saved, that is equivalent to a five mile slog.

A colleague of theirs says hello when I pause on the beach at Ijmuiden, before dodging the shipping of the North Sea Canal. The man's name escapes me, but he has worked the same beach for 60 years, and is Holland's longest serving lifeguard. He sees no reason to retire. I agree with him that age is an overrated metric.

To the south of the canal, beam trawlers scrape metal plates across the seabed, their nets held wide open by goose-winged booms. Fisheries monitors observe from a nearby RIB ["Rigid Inflatable Boat"] as a reminder to fish by the rules.

Another morning, my coffee brewing routine is interrupted by a glistening, goosepimple-skinned swimmer. The mind of a sailor who has been a long time at sea is reviewing the encounter when she returns shortly after with a bag of food, and settles down close enough for the trickle of water from wet hair over bare shoulder to be admired. Then her friend shows up, wondering where his breakfast is, and the daydream ends as the embers of a fire are smothered by the sea.

At Zandvoort, support comes from The Spot beachclub, and I am hosted by Vincent, who is an all-round good egg. Vincent is quite inspiring in an unshowy way. He enjoys "streamlining processes" – making things work better – and seems to apply this to every aspect of his life, and appears to do so very successfully. He has windsurfed to the offshore windfarms too. We meet on the water for a departure farewell. Next time I sail from Southwold on the Suffolk coast, due west from here, I will wave and think fondly of our brief overlap.

A hard fight against tide and wind delivers just 9 nm total the following day, and camping options in Noordwijk aan Zee are far from optimal. There is no good grass to be had; ironic, given proximity to Amsterdam; only sand, and that gets everywhere. The town is too public, and moving the gear any distance is too difficult. When tiredness overcomes my hope of finding something better, I return to the beach, pitch the sail shelter against the building wind, and turn in.

I breathe and eat sand until 3am, when I can take no more. The sand finds its way into every opening: hair, eyes, ears, nose, mouth, and phone. It builds-up over the sleeping bag like a dune, and cupfuls find their way inside. It was a miserable night, but – with reference to the beginning of this chapter – how can any of us claim to have endured bad luck? I finish the night in a tube on a kids' playground climbing frame, though am turfed out early morning to "make way for the kids" – who we both know will not be coming in the howling wind and driving rain.

An angel arrives to lift my spirits. It is fantastic to see friend and one-time colleague Emma Brown. She has become native to Den Bosch, but for me puts on her proper Barnsley accent, and brings profiteroles and *Stroopwafel*, and recent arrival baby Noa.

Emma is probably keen to see me sail, and I am not keen for another night being buried, so determine to give it a go, though the onshore wind and waves will make for a tricky launch. I comprehensively fail to get beyond the waves, and am washed several-hundred-metres down the beach, before giving up. The day is recorded as the first with negative progress! A broken batten is not serious damage, and the fishing club balcony at the top of this part of the beach suggests itself as a place to sleep. Overall, an excellent result, and Emma is still here! The extra hours are a blessing. We take a car ride to a chandlery to buy Sikaflex – an extra strong glue for repairs, then Emma drops me off to begin her long journey home. Dear Noa has barely stirred.

A snap for the album with Emma and Noa, before my swim

I work into the night to clean up and properly stick the rubber seal on the underside of the board, the semi-detachment of which is at least partly responsible for my miserable pace. The floodlit balcony is an ideal workshop, and the club open the storeroom so that I have somewhere protected to sleep.

Another 10 nm upwind is Scheveningen. I sail double that distance in zigzags, and beach in the shelter of the wall, where a few surfers are taking waves. The happy mood of those enjoying the water is self-evident. My contact Mimi, and the Jump Team surf station, provide storage and hospitality.

Mimi, and partner Didi, are great hosts and big fans of Ireland. Every year, for week 39, they head to Dingle with friends for waves and Guinness. Although novel to me, I like the idea of numbered weeks. A group of us enjoy some Guinness in Mimi's local, and week 39 goes in my diary.

The following day is clearly too windy to sail, but I treat myself to some boardshorts in premature anticipation of Mediterranean waters. And Bram, the board and foil maker of the brand Woody Cookie, invites me into his den for a fascinating tour. The guy creates masterpieces from carbon fibre. Oh, and he has also fixed my batten.

Bizarrely, I see fit to have a go at sailing in the afternoon. It is an easier launch from Scheveningen beach, but within moments of departure the wind picks up to well over 30 knots. I am sailing upwind, and can hold the heavily downhauled and flattened sail, but the board barely advances, and instead crabs sideways. Fortunately, such negligible progress means that turning back is an option. I make it back – just – and the muscle burn is so intense that afterwards I wonder if I have done myself real damage.

Mimi has other visitors but makes room once again. A place at the table is added to share in an evening meal of mince, banana, baked beans and cabbage: all mixed together. It is a kick-ass combination.

Gateways to Europe

9 and 15 September 2017

It is unusual for a windsurfer to sail past the major ports. Sometimes there are laws that forbid it for small craft that are not universally considered vessels. But there is usually enough ambiguity in my case to be considered a sailing yacht, and where that is in doubt, ignorance is bliss.

Rotterdam

Rotterdam is the largest port in Europe. In 2018 it recorded nearly 30,000 sea ship arrivals, and processed a difficult to comprehend 14.5 million containers, and approximately half a billion tonnes of cargo.

On my approach to the canal-entrance to the port, ships descend upon the opening from multiple trajectories. There is a steady stream – a ship every few minutes – mostly incoming. I sail upwind to the farthest out buoy of the narrower part of the channel, where there is good wind to cross, and the angle to do so is reasonably square. There is safety in the vicinity of the buoy, and from here I radio Rotterdam Harbour Coordination Centre, on the assumption that I am already seen, and that it would be best to give notice before a dash between ships. Normally, the handheld VHF stays unloved at the bottom of my backpack, so this is a special occasion. The first call goes unanswered, but there are so many ships, and they move so fast, that I persevere.

The second radio attempt elicits a reply. The nature of my call is repeated back to me, and I confirm the correctness of its reception. There is a pause during which time the coordination centre verify my location. It is interesting to hear that I do not show up on their radar. Some high-powered optics presumably pick me out. Then I am told to use a different VHF channel, and communicate directly with Harbour Entrance Control.

Again, communication is professional and to the point. The instruction comes to "cross at my own discretion". There is a gap between the next two incoming ships – not a wide gap – but it seems to be the one they are expecting me to go for. With the seemingly reliable wind there should be time to squeeze through. The distance to the other side of the channel is about 1 kilometre.

I sail at speed as if on a mission to be mown down by the first ship, but it is long passed by the time its turbulent water off its stern is crossed. The next ship is already bearing down. The radio comes to life a few times: it is reassuring to know that someone is monitoring this... The wind holds steady; sufficient to keep the board on its rail the whole way across. The safety of the green channel marker is reached. Before my heart rate has subsided, the second ship is mid-channel where I had been a few moments earlier. A final radio call to thank the port controllers, and that is job done.

Zeebrugge

Rotterdam had been a quick dash. No great detour had been required, and immediately beyond the channel had been sand. Zeebrugge harbour – 50 nm further along the coast, in neighbouring Belgium, is less busy but more problematic.

The harbour is formed by two rock and concrete arms that extend out to sea and bend round towards each other. Each arm – technical term "mole", from the (roughly translated) Latin for "pile of rocks" – is over 2 nm long. The route round the harbour, allowing for some sea room from the unfriendly moles, is about 6 nm.

Bad weather has me pinned for 5 days at Knokke-Heist, to the north of the harbour. Robby from the Royal Belgium Sailing Club has been my saviour here. There are hundreds of catamarans literally dug into the sand, and the wind has been whistling through their shrouds the whole time. My gear and I have our own little shed that Robby's wife Pascuale has made more comfortable with some cushions. The ten-storey buildings that line the long seafront are an indication of land value, and scarcity, and paucity of camping options. Thanks Robby.

Belgium windsurfers Johann and Kristoff, and their families, are proactive in seeking me out, and ensure that the enforced rest is culturally and gastronomically rewarding. They take me for a particularly memorable tour of Bruges. It is a huge privilege to have local guides. We sample local beers and chocolates.

My contacts are also concerned about Zeebrugge. Apparently, various authorities have become aware of my intention to windsurf past the port, and have said that this is prohibited. I prefer to remain ignorant, rather than seek clarification or attempt to argue the point. As usual, I will just sail the obstacle in a seamanlike manner.

By the time the wind finally abates, we have a plan. Kristoff and Thomas will also sail, but they will launch from Zeebrugge west beach. If they attract attention all the better. From my position on the east, I will first bid farewell to Robby, then sail upwind – miles out to sea – on a long "zig", and then – after a tack – will clear the port entrance in one long "zag". If anyone does notice a sail crossing the port entrance it is unlikely they will want to intervene, or have the time to do so before the entrance is behind me.

The maritime authorities are usually quite pragmatic. Their priority is safe maritime operation. If that logic is applied then all should be well.

There was probably no need for the decoy tactic, but it does no harm. I am already mostly past the entrance, when two sails – who *have* attracted the attention of a police launch – come into view from behind a kink in the mole. Some minutes later we are together as a group of three sails, bathed in sunshine, tracking diagonally shoreward, and the police launch – adjacent to the mole – appears the size of a pea.

Sand scuds across the beach at Knokke-Heist

8. English Channel

The historical names of the sea area between modern day France and England are various. To the Anglo-Saxons it was their South Sea. Early Latin sources aggrandised it as the British Ocean, or sometimes the Gaulish Ocean. The terms British Sea, and sometimes English Sea came later. For a time, the Royal Navy called it the Narrow Sea.

As maritime travel made the world smaller, its status as a strategically important channel – rather than simply a divide – resulted in the term The Channel. Convention has it that the modern-day French name *Canal de la Manche* comes from reference to its sleeve like form.

IHO *Limits* (1953) determine that the English Channel borders the North Sea on a line between Leathercoat Point – just north of St. Margaret's on Britain's Kent coast, and the Phare de Walde, a steel-frame lighthouse on a drying beach to the northwest of Calais. The western limit is drawn between Land's End in Britain, and Île Vierge – an island that lies off the *Finistère* (also "Land's End") coast of France.

***

The Channel is narrowest at the Dover Strait. During epochs of low sea level, when Doggerland connects Britain with Scandinavia, The Channel is an inlet. Prior to the creation of the Dover Strait, glacial "ice dams" had sometimes led to the pooling of the waters of the Rhine, Thames and other rivers. The water level would build behind a chalk ridge. On two separate occasions, the lake broke-through as a catastrophic flood that drained to the sea-level inlet. These breaches carved the Dover Strait. Plunge pool depressions in the seabed "a hundred metres deep" and "kilometres in diameter" have been identified, that are indicative of the scale and power of the mega-floods.

Neanderthals would – perhaps – have witnessed and been awed by these processes. Humans came later, and were occupying Doggerland as the sea level rose again to swallow it and reunite North Sea with English Channel, about 6500 before the current era.

English Channel

extent and track

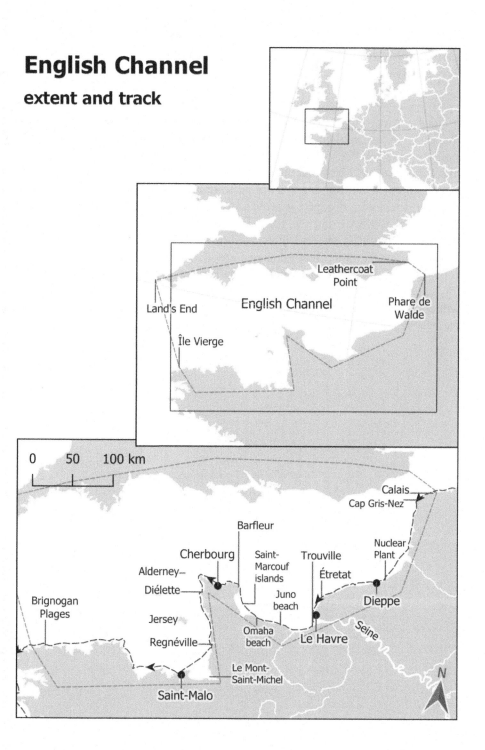

Leathercoat Point

Land's End

English Channel

Phare de Walde

Île Vierge

0 50 100 km

Calais

Cap Gris-Nez

Barfleur

Nuclear Plant

Cherbourg

Saint-Marcouf islands

Trouville

Alderney–

Étretat

Diélette

Juno beach

Dieppe

Brignogan Plages

Jersey

Omaha beach

Le Havre

Regnéville

Seine

Le Mont-Saint-Michel

Saint-Malo

N

The Dover Strait today is 18 nm (≈33 km) wide and is the world's busiest international seaway. Maritime traffic has transit rights under UN law; ferries criss-cross the Strait day and night; and a tunnel runs beneath it, through the chalk.

***

Tides and currents in the Channel are strong: amplified by its sleeve-like shape. It is an ecologically rich and important fishing ground. Where sunlight reaches, beds of maerl – a type of red algae with a hard structure like coral – grow. These habitats act as nurseries for target fish species such as cod and pollack, but are vulnerable to damage from trawling. Maerl was also, until recently, dredged at scale on both sides of The Channel for use as agricultural fertilizer, but the practice is unsustainable due to low regrowth rate. Near to fertile shores, there are coves of the western Channel with beaches of maerl, rather than of sand.

Throughout the ages, the English Channel has been both a natural route for, and an impediment to, forces of invasion. The sea battles it has witnessed are numerous, and on 6th June 1944 it carried a flotilla of boats to the beaches of Normandy for the D-Day landings.

Blighty

17 September 2017

The sun's great arc reaches the horizon. Low-hanging cumulus is backlit with a fiery halo, and an orange track is laid-out on the water. The board arrows westward in game pursuit. It rides high and free, slices the waves, hurls aside golden spray. But the orb's clockwork precision is unmoved by such enthusiasm. The sun descends, marking the passage of time.

Approach to Calais

I give up the chase before Calais port. At the Phare de Walde the beach is miles wide. That is no place to alight. It is narrower in front of the mole where I land. Discernible as a silhouette on the maritime horizon, to the right of channel-crossing ferries, that are stacked in line like dominos, is land. Home is near: a corner of my British Isles.

Impending darkness demands that teary eyes are postponed. It is a long walk over the flat beach. The first journey to the dunes is with sail and barrel. When I go back for the board I find that it has been swallowed by the night, and am fearful the rising tide will carry it away, until finding my own footprints to lead me back to it.

On a calm night, the dunes are a good place to camp. Amplifying my melancholy mood has been news that a good friend from Menorca has been struck by a brain haemorrhage from which he will not recover. And the knowledge that behind me are the leftovers of the recently cleared "Jungle" migrant camp.

Perhaps these are the reasons why I do not seriously consider crossing the water, to complete and celebrate a voyage from the Arctic to Clacton, and calling it quits there. Because life will end soon enough; the opportunity to continue will be gone.

Dieppe

20 September 2017

The artificial headland of Calais port kicks up a spirited sea. The equivalent obstacle across the water – the Port of Dover – had tested aptitude and mental resolve over three difficult days on my windsurf round Britain. These waters on another day would be equally problematic, but today's lumps are just posturing. Cap Gris-Nes – a natural headland of low cliff, and the closest part of France to mainland Britain – is the next landmark. I stop for a photograph and dangle feet in the water that has changed from brown to green.

I had been enjoying the view of cliffs – of somewhat higher land – but further on the terrain sinks again. Now there is more sand: a narrow band tapering into the distance. And the occasional estuary with sandbank accompaniment. The mussel farms provide some novelty. Row after row of wooden *bouchots* – stakes – are driven into the sand, upon which the mussels grow. It is safest to give the semi-exposed *bouchots* a wide berth. The tractors, and farm workers who tend to the bivalves, would make a good Lego set. It is low tide at the end of the day. Sea and land are estranged by at least 500 metres. One trip for the board, another trip for the sail, and a final trip for my luggage make it a 2.5 kilometre haul to bring the gear above the tide line.

60 nm further on, the chalk cliffs return. The undulating coastline is every bit as notable as its English, symmetrically-opposed cousin across the water. The scale matches Beachy Head. The formations as are striking as The Needles. In a few days' time I will be wowed by the arches at Étretat.

The cliffs change in character and appearance. Recently eroded or rain-washed parts are more brilliantly white. Green thatches of vegetation inhabit the cliff where there has been slippage. Rust-orange streaks add a third principal colour. Where the cliffs dip in a vee shape, hamlets nestle; and where they briefly fall away, towns reside.

***

Creels – lobster pots – marked by floats with flag-topped canes, are numerous. Since they are tethered, they give a useful indicator of the strength and direction of the current that streams past them. Navigational marker buoys are helpful in the same way.

After a dent in the coastline I come inshore, and absentmindedly duck inside a yellow marker, attentive only to the small bow-wave on its eastern front. The board slides past the buoy in a current that is becoming lazy as low water approaches. I am also out of energy. In a daydream I sail across and enjoy the slidey swirliness of an upwelling of cooling water from a nuclear power station. Beyond the facility there is an attractive beach with majestic cliffs behind. It looks nice for a stop.

The sand is firm and flat. Two men walk towards me: military, heavily armed. They arrive. It takes a while for me to realise my error. With very rusty French, I try to apologise for sailing the wrong side of the yellow buoy. The infraction had been a genuine mistake. I had only been a few metres in the wrong. Three armed police also show up, bringing their total to five.

One of the new arrivals understands a few words of English. I delay being carted off by explaining that the board will float off if left on the sand, so it at least needs to be moved to the shingle at the top of the beach. That buys time during which my passport details are radioed in, contents of barrel inspected, and my photos for the day deleted from my camera. It seems that the terrorist threat has been downgraded, until a radio crackles to life, and an apologetic *gendarme* gestures towards the police car, making an offer that cannot be refused.

Blue lights and sirens blaze as the French countryside whizzes past in excess of 100 miles per hour. Presumably, clocking-off time is due – because once at the station there is absolutely no rush. A female *gendarme* is the resident linguist, though even her English makes me proud of my French. The infringement is filed somewhere; I am let off with a verbal wrist slap, and dumped back at the beach shortly before midnight.

***

The following morning comes a short hop to Dieppe, where my dad, brother, and niece will arrive for a visit. They stay overnight, and also deliver some technical supplies. The few hours we have together are over all too quickly. The town is pleasant and interesting. The castle offers good views, and has a perfect lawn for handstands with little Alba. At the time of writing – when all contact is virtual to slow the spread of Covid-19 – such moments are remembered with particular gratitude.

A good-luck hug from Alba the following day. Photo: Gregg Dunnett

Contacts

Autumn 2017 – France: North Coast and West Coast

Favourable tides are harnessed like a ratchet, and the weather holds fine, such that westward progress is reliable. Also, my website is receiving more daily sign ups than I can attend to. The final tally of contacts in France reaches 154 offers of places to stop! A thoughtful follower has been publicising my journey.

Some contacts are at particularly strategic locations, where it is probable that I will stop. But in most cases link-ups are uncertain. My internal rule is to "sail first" and work out a stop later. It is mentally difficult to cut short a good day to make a link-up happen. Preferable are more-distant contacts, who require extra effort to reach, but add more miles to the tally. Frequently, it does not work out to stop, and when this happens there is a sense of letting people down. Where there are clusters of contacts my policy is to accept the first offer of support, rather than choose between them. Sometimes, contacts know exactly where I am, and are tracking my progress in real time, and perhaps find me in person before I reach out to them. For other contacts, it is obvious that my message to them arrives unexpectedly. In all cases, having offered to help, people go to tremendous lengths to actually do so.

I tend not to give much prior notice of arrival. To do so would often put people out needlessly, or suggest that a stop is confirmed when it is not. It is simpler to "wait and see" before sending a message. Perhaps it works out one way, or perhaps another.

Many link-ups remain of the spontaneous kind, and there is still plenty of sleeping on the beach. Under Normandy's cliffs, sleeping on the shingle is a joy. The mast snuggles into the stones, my mattress is safe from punctures, and everything stays clean. The fine weather currently being enjoyed is like a free pass, because to launch from the shingle beach when the sea is rough would be impossible.

Baie de la Seine

28 September 2017

There is a battle against the tide to reach Le Havre, but a very warm reception from jolly locals once there. Laurent and Corrine provide a comfortable place to sleep, which softens the impact of sunstroke-induced migraine and a night spent throwing up. By the afternoon I am recovered enough to cross the Seine estuary, scraping beyond the shipping lanes before the air goes calm, and then paddling to land. It is satisfying to sweat out the last beads of illness.

Light winds gift me a few days at Trouville. First, with Stive at the surf school; and then with Caroline and family. Once again, departure is tinged with a happy sadness.

The beaches of *la Baie de la Seine* – The Bay of the Seine – witnessed the D-Day landings. I sail until Juno beach, where a lone piper sends *Amazing Grace* out over the water. The rendition is hauntingly beautiful.

Later that day the board glides between the remains of the Mulberry harbour at Arromanches. The Mulberries were like grand scale pop-up ports that were used to land men, vehicles and supplies. Dolphins keep me company. The following day ends at Omaha beach. The tide is low; the expanse of sand is wide; and the gear is heavy. I shoulder the load – tired at the end of another hard day, but aware that the day has not really been hard.

Rising from the sands of the beach are the curved wings of the memorial *Les Braves*. These days of sailing bring reflection: About fraternity; about the European project (with fondness); about Brexit (with sadness); and about our complacency that the future will work out OK, despite our insistence on putting it in jeopardy.

Raz Blanchard (the Alderney Race)

29-30 September 2017

The Raz Blanchard is a tidal race between the Channel Island of Alderney and the northwest corner of the Cherbourg Peninsula. The current can run at more than 8 knots. It is one of the few passages of this journey that I have sailed previously – or attempted to. I was a child, and we were on a family holiday:

Our yacht had rarely been pushed to sail so fast, but despite streaking through the water her progress relative to land was ever slower. At an area of overfalls – where the sea was like a treadmill of standing waves – the boat slammed violently, but she could not break through where the current flowed strongest, and eventually the attempt was aborted. We had arrived too late. Tidal races are all about timing.

My second attempt would begin from Cherbourg, where I had arrived the previous evening at the end of a long but fulfilling day. En route I had detoured via the curious Saint-Marcouf islands; and then – near Barfleur – been waved into a small bay by surf photographer Jérôme Houyvet, who had planned an interception by following the tracker updates. Coffee was brewed on my camp stove, and Jérôme explained some local history. Apparently – in the year 1120 – the White Ship foundered on rocks outlying Barfleur. Almost all of those on board were a) extremely drunk, and b) drowned – including the heir to the English throne – whose premature death led to a succession crisis and civil war in England and Normandy: a period referred to as The Anarchy.

I avoided the rocks, and 13 nm of upwind zigzags later reached Cherbourg, where contact Olivier and family welcomed me ashore and into their home. Multiple delicious *crêpe complete* (ham, egg and cheese) and *crêpes beurre-sucre* (butter and sugar) filled an empty stomach. For a few hours the threat of the sea was far off, and I was melted like the butter on the crêpes – by two-year old Juliet's adorable smile.

***

Early next morning the port police are briefly attentive as I trespass through Cherbourg harbour. On the sail to the corner of the peninsula occasional downpours arrive and these kill the wind. The stream direction – however – is favourable, so I drift, making progress of about one knot, even when becalmed. The current will go slack as the tide changes, and the Raz Blanchard will briefly slumber. This would be the best time to pass. But if I arrive late, and the flood tide has set in, the current may be too fast to overcome, and standing waves may enrage the sea. Every puff of wind is precious. All energies are directed toward eating away at the 15 nm approach.

The corner is strewn with low-lying rocks, and marked by Goury lighthouse that stands upon a more prominent skerry. The previously misty skies clear as the beacon is approached. Sunlight dazzles off the now white-capped sea, agitated by a wind that has a free run from the south. Seaward of the lighthouse – towards mid-channel – there is rough water: an indication that slack tide may already have passed. But the pull from the sail inspires confidence to pick a way through inshore, amongst the rocks where the tidal flow is reduced. Between the lighthouse islet and the foaming white water of its adjacent skerry the gap is about fifty metres narrow. The water is choppy, and the sea beneath the board breathes to the sighs of the North Atlantic. I zigzag through – between the rocks – executing tacks that are nervous and unsteady.

I punch south a few kilometres, until almost-but-not-quite beyond the clutches of the current. Here the land rises, and cliffs reflect a jostling sea. Before they can be passed, a fresh raincloud arrives that kills wind and progress. I can no longer advance and will soon be swept back. For a half-hour the zigzags do nothing more than lessen the haemorrhaging of distance. History seems liable to repeat itself. But a gentle breeze returns, and soon build to a no-nonsense force 5. Some more zigzags get me past the obstructing cliffs, and then… Bam! I am through, punching into a now heavy sea, maintaining distance from land to give sea-room over breakers that pound the shoreline, spearing through swells that leave my face awash.

The wind direction allows a straight run towards the only bolt-hole available: the port of Diélette, 8 nm to the south. The board sails free and rampant. Conditions would be problematic on another point of sail, but that is a secret we do not tell the sea. Instead, we tell it that we have a right to be here, that we can live with its moods. We adopt some Gallic defiance. Show me wind and I will show you speed to break your race!

The 70-metre-wide gap at Diélette is a chaos of waves, but this is not a day for measuring up. We attack it straight, and we are in! And the Raz Blanchard – for this voyage – is history.

The Bay of Le Mont-Saint-Michel

1-2 October 2017

I have more nerves the following day. Will it be another section of red-route coast – designated no stopping by a duel between wave and rock? How far will need to be sailed to find safe port? The wind forecast indicates potential for another rough ride. The grey sky hangs low: threatening rain, and poor visibility. To the south of Diélette there is a nuclear power station that requires a seaward detour. Many factors prod at my anxiety.

Some nerves are good. They help guard against complacency. They mean that I tie the barrel to its cradle with extra care. After knotting, the barrel is double-secured by a tensioned strap.

Beyond the power station, rock gives way to beach. Rather than receiving the brunt of Atlantic swell, the low shore is protected by Guernsey, Jersey, and other islands and shallows. Despite continual rain, my concerns for the day evaporate.

Kind people had spontaneously offered a bed last night, and ahead there is a contact signed up. It is motivating to have a target, and a miserable evening for sleeping under the sail. I text-message a *Bonjour!* to Patrick and receive back a welcoming reply.

35 nm south of Diélette is a small estuary. I hook-in round a sand spit, then follow a line of moored yachts that indicate the position of a narrow channel. Either side of the channel the water is ankle deep. Patrick's marker is at Regnéville-sur-Mer, so that is where I head for. Although it seems that the tide cannot drop any lower its trick is only half complete. Soon the creek will be fully dry, and the boats stranded far from the sea.

The board glides silently through misty drizzle. Respite from chop and wind-buffeting is welcome. Tiptoeing through the gloom is magical and spooky. It is the kind of weather when souls come back from the dead. Out of the mist appear faceless figures. Hooded. But unlike those in the cult-classic film *The Fog* – which I hid from as a child, alone, behind the sofa – these hoods are fluorescent, and belong to yachting jackets. The arms in the jackets move up and down in a welcoming way. Up close, there is also a drenched border collie.

Patrick and Anne are wonderful hosts, and Regnéville is delightful. Its substantial houses are built with rocks borrowed from a castle that became redundant after the middle ages. My guides insist that the Yout' Club is a required stop. I accept the offer of a visit, though wonder what relevance the Youth Club has, and am curious that we must go to Bar L'Escale to find out. Once inside, I realise that the bar doubles as the Yacht Club. Indeed, the

Yacht Club is an essential port of call before and after heading out to sea. I wrap my hands round a warming *chocolat chaud* on both occasions.

Adjacent, there is a *Le Tabac* that carries *La Presse de la Manche*. Thanks to Olivier's efforts in Cherbourg "Le Tour d'Europe a planche a voile!" has made the front page.

***

The following morning the tide is low. The sea is 4 kilometres away and there is no possibility of reaching open water from Regnéville. We load the board on to Patrick's trailer, and drive along the coast to where the expanse of sand is only 2 km wide. Patrick borrows a tractor, and the pain of hauling gear such a distance is saved. This is the first and only day of the entire journey where launch and previous landing locations do not coincide. Once afloat, I first sail back to north of the estuary to ensure continuity of route.

***

There follows a 30 nm crossing to Dinard, just beyond the port-city of Saint-Malo. This is to avoid the interminable shallows of the bay of Le Mont-Saint-Michel, where there is a tidal rise and fall of around 15 metres. To begin with, the breeze is stiff and progress good. A problem I am unaware of is that the barrel is "upside-down", meaning that it is rotated so that things that should be at the top are in fact at the bottom. This means that the tracker – normally a "top" item – has a harder time than normal receiving GPS fixes and sending them to the website. When overcast weather arrives mid-crossing the tracker loses communication with the satellites altogether, which apparently leaves me stranded 15 nm off the coast. Some hours later, when I am back close to land, a volley of SMS-texts arrive. I learn that concerned tracker watchers have been petitioning my brother to mount a rescue. To his credit, he has resisted. His reading of the situation was correct. He judged that the failure to log positional updates probably had a technical explanation. A continual slow drift would have been more indicative of a genuine problem. Nonetheless, he seems quite relieved to receive my call that all is OK.

The landing today is complicated by a high-tide arrival. I head for where a contact had placed a marker on the beach. But instead of beach there are waves that slop up against a concrete wall. I somehow haul myself and gear up, until upon it, before strolling to the opposite side of the mini peninsula to find a gentle slipway caressed by perfectly flat water!

Numerous contacts have registered in Dinard, and chance links me up first with Philippe and his daughter Clementine, and then more of their family and friends. They are relaxed, fun, kind, and welcoming. The support in France has snowballed. Lately, the nights being camped are few and far between.

North Brittany

7 October 2017, from log entry

The westernmost stretch of Channel Coast is wilder and more remote. The sailing most days is challenging, and exposure is keenly felt. This log post was written reflecting upon the days to and beyond Île Vierge. The island is the base for the World's tallest lighthouse, and also where the English Channel transitions to the Celtic Sea.

***

North Brittany offers a beautiful coastline with many well protected bays. At low tide, rocks are everywhere. They form barriers that block or hide the route to the beaches. It is confusing from a navigational perspective. The marked channels that indicate a route in are welcome finds.

The currents beyond the rocky, labyrinthine shoreline tear east for six hours, dither for half an hour, then tear west for six hours. It is futile attempting to sail against the current if the wind is light.

Wind is mostly out of the west: Headwinds, in the face. My hat helps to mute the howl. The board is being pushed hard. The daggerboard creaks. Attention to the slot flusher keeps it hanging on.[14] Industrial strength superglue reattaches the troublesome gasket.

The rest of the gear? That is doing as well as can be expected. The sail materials are weak from too much sun.

Help? That comes from everywhere. Kind people are all around.

450 nm of La Manche coast have now been sailed. The signs of autumn – conkers, the days pulling in – lend urgency to the westward push. Glances back to the North Sea, which is often painted red with wind on the forecasts – are a reminder to not take sailable conditions for granted, but to push on. I am not there yet – there are some big headlands coming up – but progress towards a milder winter seems to be within reach.

---

[14] The slot flusher was first mentioned in the North Sea (part 2), where it was referred to as a rubber seal. Here, a more correct term is used. The slot flusher partially seals the underside of the daggerboard slot whilst still allowing the daggerboard to be deployed or retracted. When correctly installed it leaves a smooth, flat surface on the underside of the board that massively reduces drag from the slot. They are difficult to stick and prone to tearing away.

The best slot flusher glue is rubber-toughened cyanoacrylate.

Île Vierge, which has two lighthouses,
one of which is the World's tallest (82 metres)

9. Celtic Sea

The Celtic Sea might alternatively be described as the Western Approaches to the English Channel, Bristol Channel, and Irish Sea.

Its name was first recommended in 1921, by Ernest Holt – a British army officer who later based himself in Ireland and dedicated his life to the study of fish. Holt provided a suggestion for a Celtic Sea area that was – broadly speaking – homogenous in terms of ecology, geology, and hydrology. Later, marine biologists, oceanographers, and the oil industry began to use the name. Popular usage has become more widespread in France than in the UK.

The IHO now provide a precise definition of the Celtic Sea's limits.[15] It meets with the Bristol Channel at a line between Hartland Point and Saint Govan's Head. It meets the Irish Sea at a line between Saint David's Head and Carnsore Point. And – of relevance to my calculations – it meets the English Channel at an imaginary line between Île Vierge and Land's End. The westward extension roughly corresponds to the continental shelf boundary; and in the south it shares a limit with the Bay of Biscay sea area.

The Sea has rich and diverse fishing grounds. Water depth over the Celtic Shelf is mostly between 100 and 150 metres. There has been some oil and gas extraction, but with limited commercial success. Large scale projects for floating wind turbines are underway to harness the eolic resource.

The Celtic Sea coastlines of France, England, Wales and Ireland are rocky and indented. Moderately high cliffs and sandy beaches are typical. Tidal effect and currents are significant.

---

[15] The main text of IHO *Limits* (1953) is inaccurate with regard to the Celtic Sea and Bay of Biscay extents. The corrections to be found on page 39 confirm these as inaccuracies and clarify the actual limits.

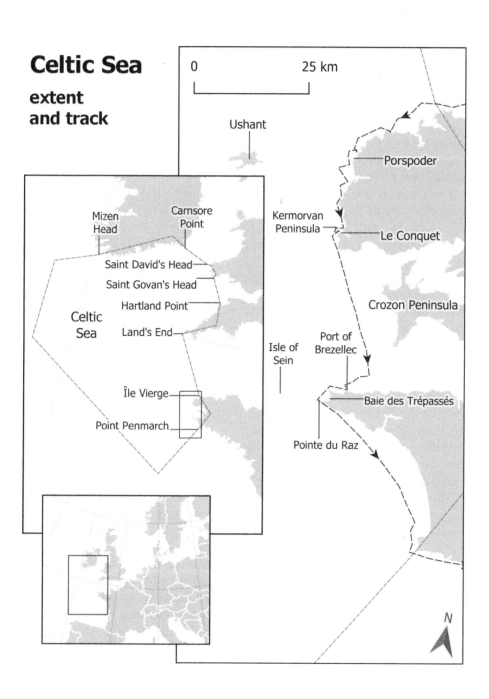

Celtic Sea

extent and track

0   25 km

Ushant

Porspoder

Mizen Head

Carnsore Point

Kermorvan Peninsula

Le Conquet

Saint David's Head

Saint Govan's Head

Crozon Peninsula

Hartland Point

Celtic Sea

Land's End

Isle of Sein

Port of Brezellec

Île Vierge

Baie des Trépassés

Point Penmarch

Pointe du Raz

N

Finding a way

9 October 2017

The coastline bends to the south, and the wind direction follows, remaining doggedly on the nose. France's most westerly mainland location – Pointe de Corsen – is a relatively minor promontory, and is somewhat protected from Atlantic swell by the islands of Ushant and the Molène archipelago. A more engaging puzzle arrives shortly after, when attempting to reach the small fishing port of Le Conquet.

The previous day's sail had been aborted due to fog. I threaded into the protected, drying anchorage of Porspoder – grateful to find a route through the rocks to land. Scant distance had been made. It became a day for inspection and maintenance. The daggerboard is cracked from the continual and bruising upwind sailing of previous weeks. There is little I can do to strengthen it, but the casing gets repacked to reduce the play and hopefully limit further damage. Water floods through my drysuit's leaky socks now. I have tried repairs, and experimented with plastic bags, but the only real solution is to accept wet and wrinkled feet. The fog remained into the evening. A message from Patrick (Regnéville) persuaded me to call on his brother, who lives nearby and had offered food and a bed. As Patrick had claimed, his brother is an excellent cook.

Today starts foggy. Cool, moisture laden air. Autumnal. There is a bar for café crème and croissant – being patient is no hardship. A beautiful day is breaking through as I set sail upwind.

With visibility restored, this is no longer a threatening coast. Later, the tide sets hard against. The current is negligible in the scallop-shaped bays, but it is stronger and cannot be escaped at the outcrops.

There is a small fort and picturesque lighthouse at the extremity of the Kermorvan Peninsula. I approach in the back-eddy of its lee, close enough to exchange *bonjours* with an amused fisherman on the end rock, then punch out into the stream, fully expecting to overcome it.

But the current is too strong. Soon, the board is simply being swept downstream. And the power in the sail – previously a healthy pull – is gone. By the time I have sailed 100 metres seaward of the headland, I am already 200 metres downwind and downstream. I persevere. If I sail far beyond, perhaps the stream will weaken, and it will be possible to claw my way past. Neither does that work – the deficit grows to become over a kilometre. Total failure!

I return inshore to escape the current, and over the next half hour re-sail the same bit of coast, until positioned once again in the back-eddy, level with the outcrop. Another *bonjour* is exchanged with the now laughing fisherman, who – I guess – accurately predicted the outcome of round one.

The strategy of round two is based on current being deflected out to sea off the headland; and employs a small rock, that is strategically located 25 metres to windward of the tip of the peninsula. The current races over and around the rock, creating a back eddy and turbulence downstream.

The board creeps forward to the end of the peninsula. Beyond here is where the current zings past. At the moment of inevitable slide into the current, all efforts go into clawing 25 metres to windward, such that the rock's back eddy can be reached before the current sweeps the board beyond it. The deflected current adds to the board's speed, increasing the apparent wind, and power in the sail. 50 metres downstream of the rock, the board enters its back eddy. The slower water movement is sensed as an island of calm – albeit a narrow one. A neat tack now turns the board so that it faces back towards the rock. Sheltered downstream of the rock, it is easy to sail back towards it.

The net result is 25 metres gained, and the impasse solved. A second short zigzag is sufficient to clear the fast flowing water altogether, and – having avoided being spat to seaward a second time – I can continue on my way.

Current off the Kermorvan Peninsula

Raz de Sein

10-11 October 2017

The most notorious navigational hazard of the French coastline is the Raz de Sein – a tidal race between the Pointe du Raz headland and the Isle of Sein. The isolated location of the point brings comparisons with Britain's Land's End. When I solo windsurfed Britain in 2015, Land's End was memorably traumatic, in the true clinical sense of the word. Large waves, a heaving swell, confused currents, desperately little wind, and a huge dose of fear all combined – unrelentingly – over many hours. The experience was eventually processed, and no doubt added to mental resilience that has served me well since. The most notorious of the other headlands and passages of that journey – including Cape Wrath and the Pentland Firth – were, when I experienced them, more benign. Such places have much myth and legend. The Britain journey also taught me that there are many skippers who are vendors of second-hand stories; and others who have helpful advice.

It is a great comfort to have friends living on the Pointe de Raz. Franck and Karine lived for a number of years in Menorca, before the pull of remoteness and reliable surf relocated them to a finger of land pushing out into the Atlantic. My plan for the Raz de Sein is to ask Franck.

A direct crossing from Le Conquet to the north side of the Pointe du Raz means that a large chunk of Brittany's coastline is observed only from far offshore. The crossing is in effect a traverse of the Iroise Sea – a name given to the body of water bound to the north and south by the isles Ushant and Sein respectively; but which is not a sea in the official IHO sense. The easy hop is a gift. A number of Portuguese man o' war jellyfish drift past. Their inflated air sacks – translucent mauve-pink and in the form of a Cornish pasty – act as sails. Today's wind will land them on the Crozon Peninsula.

Franck has suggested the Port of Brezellec for my landing place, or the beach on the west side of the outcrop that shields it. With more swell forecast tomorrow, the east facing "port" seems a safer bet, though is not a particularly easy landing, being in a windless corner at the base of a steep cliff. Barnacle encrusted steps carved from the rock lead out of the sea to a path that winds up to the clifftop. I wonder if I am being overly cautious, choosing to exit the sea from here, when there is a perfectly nice beach just round the corner. But once on a firmer platform the decision seems wise: It is a good place to leave the board; and to have a secure launch point tomorrow is one concern fewer.

As I reach a false summit on the cliff path a man arrives. "Hello Jono", he says – which throws me, because this is not the Franck I remember. In fact it is Eric – from windsurf magazine *PlancheMag*. Eric has tracked me here to say hello and offer help if needed. Shortly after, Franck shows up too, his voice and features are reassuringly familiar. A wealth of windsurfing experience unites our small group: we speak the same language without having to speak much at all: no complicated plans are needed, and that is immediately calming. Eric takes a few pictures, then ghosts away.

Franck's vehicle is a Volkswagen camper of the original generation. On the way to his homestead, we stop for a peek at the *Baie des Trépassés*, which translates to Bay of the Dead. The origin of the name is unknown. Beyond the tip of the bay's long left arm are broken rocks, a pair of lighthouses, and the Isle of Sein. The panorama is stunning. This is immediately my favourite part of France, and I have clear intent to shortcut through those rocks.

When they lived in Menorca I hadn't known Franck and Karine that well. It seemed to me that they were nice and decent people. That seems to be the case for all my friends. I have so many friendships now that it leads me to question if the term is correct. But what is the alternative? Acquaintance? The only difference between acquaintance and friend, is that acquaintance does not specify whether the "known other" is liked. To leave that ambiguity won't do. No, I am happy to consider that – without doubt – all I meet are friends. And if all I meet are friends, then a stranger is simply a friend who I have not yet met.

What others make of me, that is for them to decide. I may be a friend, an acquaintance, or an oddball. Or perhaps I may not have registered at all.

And why are people so motivated to get behind my little journey? The project is such a silly endeavour: just sailing my windsurfer day after day. I have a growing awareness that it means something for more people. Others – including those who follow the journey online – may see someone who is valiant, lucky, privileged, odd, or to be admired or to be pitied. Regardless of what they think of me, those who are following also must notice how other strangers offer their support – how they nurture me on this journey. These people see a glimmer of the base element of humanity – which is simply love – with no agenda beyond wishing another human being well. If we operate with this attitude as our default, it will become our default, and our lives will be better. There really are no negatives.

The journey may also provide encouragement to take an alternative path. Franck and Karine have long been carving their alternative path. Their home is in a gently-folded valley on the south of the peninsula, where the hurricane force winds of winter storms would rip the roofs from most houses. But their larch-panelled home, with thick walls of straw and earthen plaster, topped by living grasses, allows the wind to bend around and over. Through belief and trying they are making their eco surf-camp work. I am inspired by what Franck and Karine have achieved. When we see each other

Looking back after an easy passage through the Raz de Sein

putting our heart and energy into our respective projects we spur each other on. If a project does not merit our best, is it really worth doing?

It is late when we turn in, after some excellent gourmet *crêpes*, and my eco-outbuilding guest accommodation is deliciously comfortable, clean, and cosy.

***

To reach the Raz before the current is at full strength we make an early start. I paddle out from the calm under the cliffs as dawn breaks. Upwind to the Raz is easy – uneventful; and the passage through the fearsome race is too. Further out, a yacht transits the main channel between the lighthouses, but I keep close to the rocks off the point, and there is a sufficiently-wide gap, with a smooth carpet of water, that the board navigates like a well-mannered pooh stick.

The turbulence downstream lasts perhaps a mile. Then comes some reef, and a long expanse of sand. There is some swell running today, and the coastline has no good shelter, so it is best – and shortest – to stay offshore all the way to Point Penmarch. On the north side of the rock-strewn corner the Atlantic breathes to its resting pulse, tumbling white over the skerries. To the south, it is like a lunar rock field, and the sea is as flat as at my native Clacton.

Calmer waters south of Point Penmarch. Photo: Eric Doux

Today's sail crossed a sea boundary to the Bay of Biscay. A weight has been released. Perhaps, after my experience at Land's End, I had feared this coast – and specifically the much talked of Raz de Sein – more than had been appreciated. After all, who does not listen to legend?

10. Bay of Biscay

The Bay of Biscay is a gulf bound by an imaginary line between Point Penmarch in Brittany, France; and Cabo (Cape) Ortegal in Galicia, Spain. To its west, separated by 2500 nm of open ocean, is North America.

The North Atlantic jet stream is a high altitude "river" of air from which cyclonic depressions are born. During winter, the jet stream typically wanders to lower latitudes and brings high winds and seas to Biscay. Even in the absence of strong local winds – more typical in summer – clean, powerful swells travel uninterrupted to the Biscay coast. These are born of winds on the other side of the ocean, and eventually become the waves that make Biscay a surfing mecca.

The oceanic side of Biscay is deep; and its rise to continental shelf particularly abrupt, striated, and square-on to much of the incoming weather and ocean currents. Where the transition occurs, sea conditions can be particularly hazardous. In the age of sail – when craft had limited ability to make headway against strong winds – Biscay was a particularly dangerous trap. The corner between France and Spain is a graveyard for many ships and sailors.

For modern mariners – including alert passengers on the ferry services to northern Spain – Biscay's deep waters are a likely place to observe cetaceans. Regular sightings include the fin whale, which is the second largest animal on the planet after the blue whale; and the Cuvier's beaked whale, which makes the longest and deepest dives of any mammal.

Commercially important deep-water fish species include hake and anglerfish. In shallower waters target species include sole and bass, and pelagic species such as mackerel and anchovy.

The northern French Biscay coast is shallow and indented, with some outlying islands behind which shellfish production is commercially important. Further south are many miles of continuous beach. Biscay's Spanish coast is backed by high mountains.

The south of the sea area conforms roughly to the limits of the Cantabrian Sea. Though it receives no mention in the IHO catalogue, the accepted coastal limits of the Cantabrian Sea are from the river Adour in the French Basque country, to Estaca de Bares – Spain's most northerly cape.

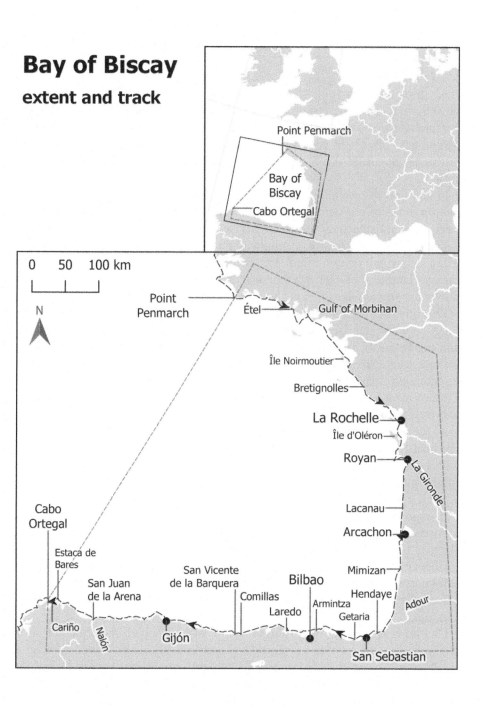

Bay of Biscay
extent and track

Point Penmarch

Bay of
Biscay

Cabo Ortegal

0   50   100 km

N

Point
Penmarch

Étel

Gulf of Morbihan

Île Noirmoutier

Bretignolles

La Rochelle

Île d'Oléron

Royan

La Gironde

Cabo
Ortegal

Lacanau

Arcachon

Estaca de
Bares

San Vicente
de la Barquera

Mimizan

San Juan
de la Arena

Bilbao

Comillas

Hendaye

Cariño

Laredo

Armintza

Getaria

Adour

Nalón

Gijón

San Sebastian

Charlie

South Brittany starts gently. For a few days it seems as if the change of the seasons may be compensated for by decreasing latitude. Support remains comprehensive, such that nights camped are the exception. Many of the people who offer help have young children, and busy lives. It seems that the last thing they need is a hanger-on, but the determination to be supportive is strong.

In addition to providing a psychological boost, regular support is a major help in terms of physical preparedness. The kindness of strangers means that I eat and rest better than would otherwise happen.

Typically, stops are for a single night. Although on occasion a stay is extended by one or two more. The first longer stop arrives at Étel – after an estuary landing between surfing waves – where I link up with Charlie, a university friend who I had not seen in decades.

That day, like so many, had been like a whole life lived. Earlier it had been foggy: a white out. Like a ghost ship, a yacht had appeared. It was at anchor, and the flags off its stern helped me to identify it as a committee boat for a sailing event. Shadows in the cockpit had held out their arms – signalling a direction to sail in, presumably a safe route to shore. That was very odd! First of all it was a coincidence to almost bump into them, and secondly it was as if my arrival had been expected.

At the beach, a crowd of children descended upon me. Each took a part of the board until it became as light as a feather. There were dozens of junior and youth windsurfers. Patrick – the event organizer – then hosted an impromptu Q&A that lasted just long enough for the fog to clear – and then I was off again, with that uplifting hour as a favourite memory.

It is great to see Charlie. We became friends in my last year at Swansea University. We surfed and biked and played Mario Kart and somewhat to my surprise one of the "cool crowd" became a buddy.

I never tried to be cool, but did try to fit in socially at university. Heavy drinking was the norm. Alcohol always had a bad taste for me, but it was an effective tool for masking social incompetence and anxieties, and at the time was fun.

Charlie and I were on different rungs of the social skills ladder. For example, he seemed able to effortlessly converse with a multitude of people inside a noisy and crowded pub. As a student I would have scored a big fat zero on this ability. My tactic then was to drink more, and come out of my shell once slurring. Some decades later I realise that some talking therapies might have been more helpful.

Issues of self-worth became more keenly felt in the years that followed university. The sense that I had not achieved career success, whilst my peers were reaching skyward, came to have a strong negative impact upon my wellbeing.

Then I windsurfed round Britain, and realised that there is no good that comes of comparing. And that we all have struggles, and at last I saw us all as equals.

So not only is it great to see Charlie, but it is greater still to meet him as an equal, for what may be the first time.

Reunion with Charlie after landing at Étel

Storm Ophelia

16-17 October 2017

Charlie and partner Annou put me up for over a week, during which time Storm Ophelia – formerly known as Hurricane Ophelia – hammers the European Atlantic coast. During the cyclone's approach the sky is observed Martian red. The cause is dirty air, that is laden with both dust from the Sahara, and pollution from wildfires on the Iberian peninsula. There is a sense of the apocalyptic. It is a relief to be spared the thought of going sailing.

Ophelia tracks along the west coast of Ireland, and at the time of writing is considered the most significant storm of the last 50 years. The windspeed at Fastnet Rock reached 103 knots (191 kmh), the highest ever recorded in Ireland. Early warning meant that Ireland was well prepared, resulting in just three deaths. The flames that Ophelia fanned on the Iberian peninsula were more deadly, with around 50 lives lost.

In the wake of the storm, I sail from Étel, round the Quiberon peninsula, and through the entrance of the Gulf of Morbihan. The launch is critical. A sandbar across the river mouth is breaking at about 2 metres, and is a playground for surfers who are getting fully barrelled by the powerful waves. After being dropped off by Charlie on his way to work, I study the setup for 45 minutes. The outflowing river water turns sharp left, then runs parallel to the coast inside the sandbar, before punching to open ocean as a powerful rip current. There appears to be a path out.

If there is not, I will likely break everything, and will struggle to make it back to shore. The stakes are high.

Having made the decision, speed is of the essence, because the situation may change as the tide drops further. Thirty heart pounding minutes later, I can say that the call was good: the turns had been correctly identified. There is time to admire the surfers' skills as the current delivers me seaward between breaking waves.

Once out I stay out, far from shore. Towards the end of Quiberon peninsula there is a stiff breeze and a rock field to negotiate. Though potentially hazardous, the many reefs also form a barrier to the swell. On my small craft the actual rounding of the peninsula – by the most inshore of all available routes – is stress free. Once on the east-facing side of the outcrop, the sea is calm like a reservoir. A simple landing recommends itself for a picnic of hot coffee, bread and cheese.

The entrance to the Gulf of Morbihan is an easy reach, and inside it is safe like a salty lake. I sail to within a few miles of the village of Le Bono, where Charlie and Annou live.

The remaining days for me are time relaxing, attending to repairs, being a responsible adult for my hosts' youngest child – Oliver – and being an irresponsible adult tour guide for a night-time paddle trip in the Gulf. We go surfing, though to be honest I am not that keen. The fear of what is to come is too present. I prefer collecting Oliver for the cycle home after school. It is nice having not much to do, and distancing myself from fear.

A tranquil islet in the Gulf of Morbihan

Six Hops to La Rochelle

23-28 October 2017

It is not long before another scheduled stop with friends. Six days of sailing are sufficient to reach long term friends Ian, Solenne and Lily-Rose at their home in La Rochelle:

Noirmoutier

An ideal wind angle allows for a straight-line broad reach from Morbihan to the uninhabited Île Dumet; followed by a close reach round the next stub of land; after which it is possible to free off and blast across 20 nm of open sea direct to Île Noirmoutier. About 5 nm from the island, the passing water begins to pull at the board, and it is immediately clear that the occasionally problematic slot flusher has resumed its quest for an independent life. That settles a dilemma about which side of Noirmoutier to pass. Inside there will be flat water: it will be easy to stop in order to make repairs.

With the glue dry, the afternoon sail behind the island is pleasantly novel. Many small boats are aground upon mudbanks, waiting for the now incoming tide to raise them. Once freed, they speed away with their haul of shellfish. If my navigation is not astute, I too will run aground. As the funnel between mainland and island narrows, it becomes increasingly difficult to locate water sufficiently deep to sail in. Satellite imagery helps to identify the channels, and at an increased zoom level an unexpected causeway suddenly appears. The fin scrapes through the mud, until a narrow road is eventually reached at the midpoint of its 2 nm traverse.

Now it is my turn to wait, until the road floods and it becomes possible to continue south. A helicopter takes a detour – presumably to check that I am equipped to float, rather than in distress. It seems likely that someone is watching from a distance. For motorists whose vehicles break down, or become stuck after a panic-stricken reversing attempt, there are periodic crow's nests which may be ascended. Later, I hear of a friend (once removed) who experienced exactly this emergency, and can attest to the lifesaving importance of the crow's nests.

The evening camp is upon a soft bed of pine needles. Eric and friend call by with a flask of tea to share. There is absolute peace in the forest, beneath the sail, sipping hot tea. And when the cups that warm our hands are empty, my companions slip away into the night, with barely the crunch of a twig.

Saint-Jean-de-Monts

Eric and his son Mathieu beckon me ashore midway through the following day. The beach is unexpectedly wave free: unseen sandbanks provide shelter. A picnic is laid out that includes oysters with a twist of lemon. Although I prised oysters from the rocks in Brittany, and sampled those, these are the first that I eat not half-suspecting food poisoning to follow.

We meet up again further down the coast. Eric and his family – and the local Fédération Francaise de Voile (FFV) – are helpful and hospitable. This evening's treat are chestnuts grilled over a fire.

Eric wishes me luck, and difficulties too. I understand his reasoning: that difficulty and hard times are necessary for growth and insight. I agree with that sentiment. A frequent self-doubt is whether I struggle – or suffer – sufficiently. Any claim to suffering seems exaggerated. Effort is not suffering. Physical toil is not actual hardship. If I do suffer on this journey, it comes from worries of the mind – fears, rather than any discomfort in the present. I am not convinced that it is even possible to suffer during the adrenaline high of physical fight or flight. With the tempest upon us we simply act, and are more in the present – more gloriously alive, perhaps – than at any other time. It is our minds' anticipation of the storm – and the projection of its consequences – that brings suffering. That mental anguish can sometimes be a struggle.

Saints Gilles-Croix de Ville

A windless day, and with waves enough to make a beach launch out of the question. Fortunately, Saint-Jean-de-Monts has a long pier, the end of which reaches beyond the breaking waves like a horizontal ladder to open water. Quite a crowd has gathered by the time I am ready to leap from pier to board. A platform at the end of the structure makes the jump more like a hop, which disappoints the spectators.

The sea beyond the breakers is glassy and its surface never still. The swells are the energy of the sun: Its radiation heats our planet – and stirs our atmosphere – to create winds that scrape over the sea, to whip up waves that now manifest as lines of swell. It is the energy of the sun that will break all my gear if I stray too close to the beach. So I stay offshore, and paddle for 8 nm until the nook of protection offered by Saint Gilles Croix de Ville.

Bretignolles-sur-Mer

Similar conditions – and another paddle – propel me to Bretignolles. Again the FFV are hospitable, but since I have a contact here I reach out – because it would seem rude to not let Nicolas know that I have arrived where his marker is placed.

From the moment we meet, I suspect that my host has not warmed to me at all. That evening, a time-out is called during our fondue evening meal. Nicolas and wife Anne-Sophie go the kitchen and engage in hushed conversation. It seems that my intuition is right, and the end of my visit is imminent. When they return to the table an announcement is made: the couple have decided to gift me a new wetsuit.

Nicholas and Anne-Sophie are much younger than me, and their means are clearly limited. The next day, I accept instead a fresh pair of wetsuit boots. However, the enduring gift of my hosts is a reminder that – when the evidence is uncertain – it is always best to interpret intention through a positive lens.

La Tranche-sur-Mer

Olivier and Marianne first hosted me in North Brittany, and this weekend they are catamaran racing near La Tranche-sur-Mer. A rule of thumb of mine is to renew and strengthen existing connections, so I am pleased to coordinate a reunion. We meet up in a near-empty bar and are relaxed enough to have a good giggle, before going our separate ways. By this time I just want the nearest bed – and that is the one under my sail.

Before shuteye comes, a message from Eric arrives. It is a picture of a Lego expedition windsurfer complete with barrel, and next to it the smiling face of the architect – Mathieu. Brilliant!

La Rochelle

The final hop is an easy one: up the inside of Île de Ré, paddling alongside the endless rows of buoys from which mussels are suspended, and beneath the towering Ré bridge. On the approach to La Rochelle a gentle breeze for sailing fills in. There are hundreds of sails to be seen. The area between Île de Ré and Île d'Oléron is the French equivalent of England's Solent.

Ian and I say hello like I've just arrived back after popping out to the shops. My friend "appreciates cleanliness", so our first priority is to keep the rig off the sand so that none of it sticks and ends up in the car. We do pick up a few grains though, because the derig is interrupted by the arrival of a chap named Jeff – who has a van with a big number 17 on its side. I recognise Jeff as a shore-based spectator from a few miles before landfall was made. The usual questions follow. I am practiced at responding to them by now. It is always a pleasure to be generous with time at the end of a day's sail. Jeff is a warm character, and adamant that I must look him up when I head south from here. He points to the van: "Jeff 17 – Jeff dix-sept. Remember!" – and I tell him I will.

Repairs

29 October – 7 November 2017

Ian and Solenne are the perfect hosts – and La Rochelle the perfect place – for a mid-voyage refit. The gear is less than six months old, but has already endured a lifetime of hard labour.

The construction of the board is like an egg: in that it is structurally strong, but the outer shell is prone to damage. Some knocks are inevitable because the loaded board is heavy and awkward to lift, and landing locations are frequently unforgiving.

Boisterous seas and many hours of use have also accelerated age-related wear. The upwind push along the English Channel was particularly tough on the daggerboard and its casing. When ploughing through waves the board complains with cracks and creaks. This is a concern.

The sail has suffered too. Though I care for it above all else its laminate plastic films have been weakened by sunlight. Minor scrapes – that six months ago would have been inconsequential – now result in holes that need patching. The disposability of sporting gear troubles me. In a world where environmental cost is taken seriously there would surely be more focus on developing materials that have a longer useful life.

Severne Sails kindly agree to build a replacement sail. The drysuit seals are replaced at home in a fog of contact adhesive. The mast is reinforced with Kevlar and epoxy. Every component of gear receives attention.

All shared moments are a gift. On a day between jobs we enjoy a surf on Île de Ré. I notice that it brings pleasure to be remembered by Lily Rose from previous meet-ups. The bilingual 5 year old is a bundle of fun with an afro of blond hair and no off switch.

I am without dependants. There was a time when I wanted children – or thought I did. I assumed that I would have a family, though was scared and pessimistic for the future of any children that I might bring into this world. Later, it seemed more urgent, and it seemed almost necessary for my own happiness to have kids. Self-interest overrode my fears for the wellbeing of future lives. I knew of many people of my age who were starting families – so there was a biosocial urge to conform, to do the normal thing. But at the times when kids seemed a good idea, they would have been inadvisable attempts to shore up relationships that had endured too long, though I was fearful of losing.

Children are adorable, but I have no desire to be a parent. And the planet and its inhabitants will do better if there are fewer of us. As for family, that surely is everywhere, if we are open-minded as to what it means.

Anyway, back to the sailing.

La Gironde

8-9 November 2017

The comfort of La Rochelle evaporated soon after departure, and became a struggle to go downwind in 25 knot "wind over tide" conditions. Instead of flat water in the shelter of Île d'Oléron there was a corrugated sea. It was not the gentle re-start I had hoped for, but at least it was simple to stop for a time-out. Some easier miles were added late in the day to reach a pleasant camp location on the south of the island.

Jeff-dix-sept shows up again in the morning and we discuss strategy for today's leg. I'll sail out of the channel to open sea, along the coast, then up into the Gironde estuary to be sure of missing any swell. Easy. Jeff reckons I should be able to cut straight into the Gironde by following the beach, and the stretch of coast I am heading for is always flat.

Navigational preparation for what I now know to be the largest estuary in Western Europe is woefully inadequate, but I do at least have the sense to programme into my GPS the location of the outer marker of the Gironde channel. The wind today is forecast to be helpful – a gentle northerly – and there is a slight hurry to get going, to not squander this breeze. The days are short now, and it is preferable to reach safety with a margin of daylight in reserve.

The scenic run out of the channel is on flat water. The day could not seem more benign. There is a fairy-tale world all around to visually explore: golden beaches, gentle waters, lush forest. Enchanting. And then, without intentionally leaving one world, another is entered. I am carried – as if through the fur coats of C.S. Lewis's Wardrobe – to a world where I feel as alone as the last living being. This world is the antithesis of nurturing: it is mother nature with a maternal instinct bypass. Waves climb like caged animals. They stand tall and vomit onto the snake pit sea. It is a world that would drown me without a thought, and I am scared.

Line of sight is foreshortened by the steep lumps. A red channel marker occasionally comes into view and marks a route out, in theory. Around the buoy and to its north are crumbling waves of muddied water, around 2 to 3 metres. I must avoid those. To its south are steep lumps – smeared with skid-marks of dirty foam – that teeter indecisively on their way towards a more substantial collapse closer to shore. That way is the least bad option. Current and breeze continue their outward push. There is no reason to look back, or consider a retreat – because with the ebbing tide that option is gone.

The channel – for on another day it might be called that – bends to the right, though is poorly defined in practice. A given wave or set may break

Searching for a route to deeper water after launch from Île d'Oléron

within the channel, or outside. Choices are a shimmy left or a shimmy right. I dodge the peaks, with my heart in my mouth.

The sandbanks either side eventually recede into deeper water. At 1 nm from land, the channel becomes open water. But the waves still lift, and it feels too close to where they pound. At 2 nm from land, the swells roam peacefully. That is the distance from the shore at which I sail.

These distances from shore are not predetermined. Water depth, swell size, wind direction, wind strength, and the coastline type determine what distance from shore feels safe. Today's track shows that comfortable safety was felt at 2 nm, which is indicative of a fairly solid swell, and fairly shallow water.

Progression along the coast is made without difficulty, and almost too soon the La Coubre lighthouse – beyond the foot of which I had hoped to turn into the Gironde – is prominent. The sea looks *wrong* – in that there is a fringe of white where I had expected open water. Beneath the white must be a sandbar that extends seaward from the lighthouse. I edge closer, though am still too distant to identify any potential route through, if there is one, which I doubt. The waves build into towering walls. Their approach to the corner is square-on, and the ones around me are in their final moments of existence. When they unload onto the sandbar they will do so with ferocity, projecting forward a curtain of blue water. At this distance from the bar, already there is no safety. I have been lulled inside. A set of waves approaches. I swing the board round and scramble for deeper water: sailing straight at the would be assailants to summit before they lurch. Five times I go from dungeon to rooftop as the set passes through. It is clear that there is only one safe route in, and that is around the sandbar to the shipping channel entrance.

The barrier forces me seaward until 8 nm from land. For most of this distance the white wall appears interminable. And with each passing mile the waves crunch harder. The offshore swells – that become waves – have less distance to travel over shallow water, so retain more of their power before breaking on the barely submerged bar. The power of these beautiful assassins is felt within. I sail parallel to the bar, and even in water depth that seems prudent am frequently sent scuttling for more depth as each set arrives bigger than the last.

Finally, there is a sighting of the buoy that marks the end of the sandbank: the entrance to the Gironde channel. The bank then simply ends. It slides into deep water and is gone. Ships presumably use the opening year round, so my reasoning is that it should be safe and clear on an unexceptional day like today. It is nonetheless a huge relief to have this assumption validated. Once inside the bank, it is in effect a different sea: a protected sea – more akin to a lumpy Thames Estuary than Biscay. It will take a while to re-establish contact with land, and I have some nerves about a dying breeze, and my ability to fight against the current of the outflowing Gironde.

The complications do not arrive. 8 nm later I am sailing on calm coastal waters. There is no impediment to looking back now, to survey the sea just sailed. From here to the horizon is tranquil, blue-green, and empty. It is as Jeff-dix-sept had promised. There are no waves, or sandbanks, or wardrobe gateways to alternative worlds.

***

I write in a subsequent log entry that:

There is not usually fear at the time – just glimpses of awareness. Mostly, once you're in it you get on with it. And then, upon landing or entry to safe waters, a kind of euphoria kicks in, and it is tempting to think "that's that – done and dusted." But it's not done yet. A deeper processing still needs to happen. The fear needs to be felt. Perhaps written.

Aquitaine Coast

13-20 November 2017

The long and straight Aquitaine Coast of southwest France is fully exposed to Atlantic waves. For 135 nm (≈250 km) there are no easy landings. Patience, and a dose of luck, will be needed to safely reach the border with Spain, and guardian angels like Jeff-dix-sept will play their part too.

After the shared nerves of that tricky sail into the Gironde, Jeff is host and guide for the next four days of unsettled weather. His rural dwelling – near to a tidal inlet managed for the cultivation of oysters – is a calming retreat. The wine that washes the oysters down is exquisite. One day, we visit the city of Royan where Jeff has a windsurf and I am interviewed over lunch by delightful Nathalie Lamoureux – an Everest-ascending journalist for *Le Point* magazine. Later, history again comes to life. Jeff tells of the allied destruction of the city in 1945, and of its subsequent reconstruction. We visit the city's reinforced-concrete cathedral: a towering, light-flooded space in which to feel peace, or perhaps awe, or maybe to simply find refuge. Disregarding any religious function, it is a building that seems worthwhile.

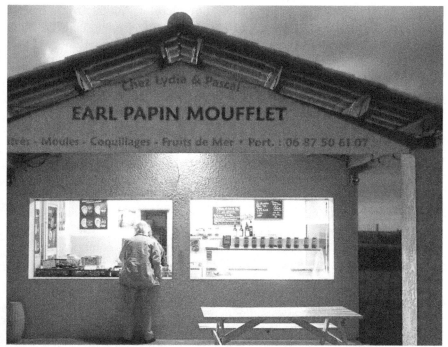

Jeff at the local oyster take-away

Experiences with people like Jeff underline to me what support really is. True support is patient: it allows people to get their shit back together and prepare for going solo once again. Thanks Jeff.

A suitable weather window arrives, allowing for departure. A dear friend waves me off from the end of a precarious breakwater.

***

The Aquitaine Coast begins south of the Gironde Estuary. Sailing conditions are good: the waves expire upon mile upon mile of empty sand – so there is no bounce-back to contend with; and there are no hills – so the wind is clean. A touch more breeze would be helpful, and would facilitate the launchings and landings, which are the most notable events of each day's sail.

The exit from the Gironde Estuary is incident free: no huge detour required. The only delicate moment, at the end of a 16 nm sail, is the landing at Montalivet beach. And a gust of wind arrives to help with that.

The following day's landing is at Lacanau. The surf is bigger, and although the outer bar is successfully negotiated, on the inside there is almost no wind. A surging reform [like a wave reborn] picks up the board until the nose points irrecoverably downward. Once in the water, my main concern is the mast. Tons of water swirl and surge. Swimming is ineffectual – hindered by the submerged sail. Legs kick and my spare arm flaps in the frothy soup. Finally, a brush of sand is felt underfoot. Another surge pushes me closer in, and then traction can be gained. A gasping, semi-drowned, backpack-wearing rat emerges from the sucking waves, hauling behind him a precious rig and lifeless board.

A humbling experience, but vindication too: that these landings are too hazardous. They are a form of Russian Roulette. This time the mast survived; damage was limited to a broken batten, and some splits on the sail. There was really nothing I could do to get in unscathed. Perhaps it would have been better to delay the final approach; to be more patient in that zone between the outside waves and the reform? But that was risky too, because a bigger set could have marched through and mown me down. Anyway, what's done is done. To get in with only light damage counts as a success. The night is cold, but made warmer by Lacanau Surf Club who lend me their minibus as a bedroom.

Launch the next day – after sail repairs – is predictably complicated. For a long ten minutes I struggle to control the board. The ocean surges: one moment around my ankles, the next up around my chest, then disappears again to leave the board marooned upon the draining sand. It is exhausting, and seemingly futile, but eventually an opportunity arises: the waves go flat, and I snare a messy getaway. The path ahead is briefly clear: time enough to climb the swells to deep water and safety.

Once out, there is no easy way back, so I stay offshore, and scrape to the entrance of the Arcachon basin. A last-moment change of plan results in a very risky landing on Cap Ferret: a spit of sand that encloses the basin. Before this I had been resigned to a horrible night-time attempt to find the marked channel into the basin – and had gone so far as to forewarn my brother to hold back on sounding any alarm. The crashing-in gamble pays, but these are all gambles, and the smart money is on not rolling the dice.

Adjacent to where I land – for advancing further is impossible – the current runs out so quickly that it forms a quicksand beach. The quicksand is considered dangerous. A warning sign reads *Plage Interdit* – Forbidden Beach. There are cameras, though I doubt they are monitored.

The next day is windless. I am late for the brief opportunity of slack current to paddle into the basin, so spend a second night at this beautifully wild spot.

My timing is better the next day, which is also windless. The tide is low and the shortest route to the water is over the Forbidden Beach. Quicksand or otherwise, it is the least unpalatable of the launching options. At the water's edge the sand swallows me thigh deep. Strange indeed – were it not for my board I might really get stuck. A military-style Jeep-like vehicle tears along the upper shore. Moments later it spins to a halt at the *Plage Interdit*. Doors are flung open and uniformed figures pour out as I leap on the board and begin to paddle. We all know that the men are too late to intervene.

10 minutes earlier the sea had been covered with a dancing, serrated chop, and 10 minutes later it will return to that state, but now it is flat. A black RIB – also military-styled – emerges from somewhere inside of the basin. It speeds across the water in a long drawn-out arc. They are looking in the wrong place, but eventually find me, and then just sit and watch, like a distant shadow, as I complete the paddle to less complicated water.

Inside the basin is like a lake, and there is a faint breeze to sail by. I stow the paddle, haul the rig upright, gently flip the battens and – in a microsecond – the sail's main panel splits from top to bottom. It is a major failure, but a convenient place for one to happen, where repairs should be possible. I cross the basin, land, and knock on a random door, hoping to leave my gear in the occupants' garden, whilst I go in search of a sailmaker. The generosity of the elderly couple who reside here goes far beyond that: they run me into town to buy a few acres of strong Insignia adhesive cloth, and repairs are completed in the garden. It is dark and cold by the time I am finished, so I camp there too, and am grateful for a hot soup delivery from Madame Bouchon.[16]

---

[16] This kind lady's surname (the name she gave) somehow escaped my notetaking, so the one used here – although it fits – is probably an invention.

Going south, an added complication is the "DGA (Direction générale de l'Armement) Essais de missiles" – the launch site from where France tests its missiles by firing them out to sea. Requesting permission to windsurf past the range is somewhat complicated: the operative at the end of the telephone line – after thinking about it for a few moments – is decided that he does not speak English. It is more satisfying to establish permission in French anyway – and luck is on my side: no missiles for the next 48 hours.

Departure from the basin is on the last of the ebb, out the main channel, between sandbanks that are temporarily high and dry. At a lonely place several miles from land there is a shockingly narrow and wave threatened gap to the sea proper. I climb over the swells, then turn south, until once again sailing parallel to endless beach. The missile testing installations are passed during the day, and eventual landing is at Mimizan, where the feature of a small river is helpful for getting in.

The next day is windless, and there is no way to get out through the surf. Cold air above the warm sea forms a mist that lingers until evening. Psychologically, it is uncomfortable to be waiting – running down the clock of this weather window. By the end of the day I feel tired, withdrawn, detached, isolated. At dusk, a couple with a young child trudge across the sand and offer a bed for the night. It is not easy to accept their help: in my eyes I have become an unworthy alien, intent only on progress, and lacking in basic humanity. But this is a familiar trap, and I know to be gentle with myself, and accept their offer of connection. Aurelie, Loys and little Hélia coax me back to being fully human.

Early the next day we drop dear Hélia off at her *Ecole de la Plage* elementary school, and then it is my turn to be cast free. I launch with the fog that is being blown out across a nearly-calm sea. The morning is spent lost in whiteness. I look forward, but think back: with big smiles and a flood of gratitude. The sun breaks through, and stays with me until the end of the endless beach.

Bienvenido a España

21-22 November 2017

A zoomed-out view of this journey puts Spain somewhere about half distance, which had been helpful to make the total seem less intimidating. Having lived for many years in Menorca, the country seems like home. Though that concept is an expanding one.

This is now the Cantabrian Sea, which – the reader may recall – is not a sea listed by the IHO, but it does nonetheless possess a distinctive character from the Biscay area sailed thus far. Its coastline is – mostly – difficult-to-access slabs of rock, but there are also indents that provide opportunities for seafarers to find shelter, and many fine beaches that add curves to the jaggedness. Higher ground introduces significant local effects upon the wind. Steadier winds are offshore; and it is frequently necessary to head a long way out to find any wind at all. Inland it is mountainous for the first time since Norway, but this coast has no outlying islands to block the waves.

I had been piloted into Spanish waters by Josema, a windsurfer and fisherman from Hondarribia. In no wind, most of the distance had been paddled. Having a boat to follow took the guesswork out of finding a way through the reefs – which was necessary – as every 5 to 10 minutes areas of ocean would fold into deep peaks and troughs as passing swell trains snagged on submerged rock.

Landfall was made up the river: at Hendaye, in France, which faces Hondarribia, in Spain. I moored on the dock at the Decathlon watersports R&D facility, and linked up with new friends who had put me up the previous evening, and enjoyed a tour of their workplace.

A mini-flotilla of Decathlon employees accompany me back to the open sea the following morning. Then I sail solo round a mighty headland that completely blocks the wind, so requires a huge detour; and then thump against a strong headwind to Playa de la Concha, San Sebastian. Friends who live there had said 20 years ago that I must visit, and finally I have made it. Itziar and her father Jose-Mari are there on the beach, and local Basque TV are there too for the milestone of this first landfall in Spain.

San Sebastián

22-27 November 2017

The family live in the hills behind San Sebastian. Itzi is now a doctor. Partner Iñaki – who I have subconsciously dialled in to be another medic, is a bus driver, which is refreshingly down to earth. Needless to say, Iñaki is a lovely guy and we have a great game of Basque Pelota – whacking a ball with wooden bats on an open-sided covered court, until my shoulder goes numb. The couple have a happy two year old.

Another day – with Itziar, and little Iker riding upon shoulders – we hike to the peaks and look down at the late autumn colours from high up. That builds a good appetite for San Sebastian and *pintxos* from local bars.

Many houses and businesses are displaying Catalan flags, as symbols of solidarity with Catalan nationalists who are protesting that their recent independence vote has been declared illegal. My opinion on independence-matters generally is that there are more important problems to be tackled, and that humanity will have a rosier future when divisions between groups of humans cease to become our focus. In contrast, Itziar is firmly of the opinion that the Spanish state oppresses the autonomous regions: particularly Catalonia and The Basque Country.

It seems cowardly not to engage with the reasons for this sentiment. In a historical context there is no argument – Franco brutally oppressed the regions, but I ask Itzi to tell me how this oppression is expressed today, and suggest that the current day indicators all point towards a resurgence of Basque identity and autonomy, the same as is happening in Catalonia. Where is the repression then? It seems that Itzi is softening slightly – in the absence of concrete examples of actual oppression. But then she figures their game: "They still *want* to oppress us!" There is no counter to that.

I am distrustful too. Relating to the leaders of Catalan independence it is their character that bothers me. Jordi Pujol – the driving force of the movement – is a financial criminal. For me, he has with more in common with Putin than with Braveheart.[17]

Pleasingly, our conversation avoids all the mud-slinging pitfalls of online debate. But this is a highly polarized topic, and it is difficult to imagine how either of us could change our views.

---

[17] "Former Catalan president amassed huge fortune through crime, judge says" https://www.theguardian.com/world/2020/jul/17/former-catalan-president-amassed-huge-fortune-through-judge-says

***

After a few nights it is time to move on – or at least show a willingness to. In reality, the lumpy sea conditions and absence of wind will not permit that today, but I go along with the charade – suit up, go afloat, fail to make meaningful progress – and then return once the futility of the attempt is clear to all.

Conditions the next day are marginally better. A dozen bottlenose dolphins, slowly tracking westward, are unperturbed that I join their pod for a few miles. They help to suspend the normal concerns of lone sailing far offshore. The final miles must be paddled, but there is an easy landing at the fishing port of Getaria.

A statue in the town commemorates Juan Sebastián Elcano – the first man to have circumnavigated the globe. My subsequent research finds that a flotilla of five ships – commanded by Ferdinand Magellan – set sail in 1519 in search of a new trade route to the Spice Islands. They crossed the Atlantic, and followed the coastline of South America southward to where Magellan found a passage – the Strait of Magellan – that leads to a large body of water that he called *el Pacífico* – "the peaceful" sea, our Pacific Ocean. Late in the voyage, after the death of Magellan at a battle in the Philippines, Elcano became captain of the one remaining ship that was to complete the circumnavigation.

There were 18 of the original 240 mariners still alive and aboard at the end of the voyage. Elcano is most celebrated, but a lesser known detail is that in an early part of the voyage he participated in a mutiny. He is a villain who became a hero. Or a villain and a hero. The world is less black and white than we tend to assume.

I am intrigued by the character of these men who sailed to the unknown. What motivated them? Was it the prospect of fame and riches? Or something deeper, a restless urge to roam? Some innate predisposition, or acquired tendency, to cast off in search of novelty? This interests me, of course, because I wonder if I am like them.

Bilbao

Support in Spain tends to arrive unannounced, then snowballs.

Some miles short of Bilbao the wind builds to require a fully tensioned sail, and backs to become more on the nose. With 32 nm already sailed fatigue is setting in. The flat set of the sail is a sign that the wind must be strong, though I am spared its howling by the snug fit of a fleece-lined hat. Collisions with white horses are another indicator that the going is tough.

Ahead is a minor but potentially tricky headland, beyond which an unseen lee shore faces square-on to the wind and waves. I am uncertain of finding a landing there. Inshore of my current position, shielded by a steep outcrop, is a narrow gulley that leads to a walled harbour. Though awkward, it is a viable option for getting in.

At the approach to the gully the outcrop blocks the wind. The water surface is a chaos of random chop. There is urgency to be away from where waves may break. Cursing Spanish expletives I hurriedly set up the foam blocks to balance the sail. Then on protesting knees paddle the remaining distance in.

Armintza has a rugged and honest feel to it, a freshwater tap, and a bar. I assume it is where I will see out the next few days of forecast bad weather. I sort the gear out. Then a man shows up with the smile of a life-long friend and enquires "Jono?" That is how I meet Alejandro, who has been tracker-guided to this unlikely landing spot.

The bad weather days end up as a crash course in having a good time. I have Alejandro's flat to use as base. A confusion of new names and faces arrive: *pintxos* with Lander one day, lunch with the Juanma the next. Particularly memorable is a tour of Bilbao with Alejandro and umbrella-wielding Iban. We follow the scything brolly, and a literal high spot is the upper gallery of the Puente de Vizcaya "Hanging Bridge".

Fernando, Helena and family adopt me for a day. When the rain stops we visit the islet of Gaztelugatxe – aka Dragonstone to Game of Thrones fans. 241 steps and a twisting walkway connect the island to the mainland. At the summit of the islet there is a hermitage from where I survey the recently sailed coastline. We observe the custom of making a wish and ringing a bell. Then the rain starts again. We go back to the house – tired after all those steps – eat cake and sink into the comfortable furniture. Soon we are all asleep, as if napping with strangers is the most natural thing in the world.

Bilbao could be a longer chapter, but let's say it ended there, in that perfect moment.

Alfonso

3-19 December 2017

It is now December. And this is Spain – a country to where tourists escape for winter sun. The Arctic seems far off. I am complacent about the cold of winter. For more than six months the goal has been to get south. I have sailed most days, and those days not sailed have been sat out only after a negotiation with myself. Exceptional experiences have come thick and fast. Each month – even some weeks – have seemed like a whole life lived. I have barely had time to think back: to encode, catalogue and organise the memories. There is a processing deficit, and I wonder if I am squandering these gifts of experience. Perhaps, when I look back, there will be nothing there. The physical and mental intensity may also have depleted my immune defences.

Laredo is an east-facing bay that promises flat water for the approach and landing. It is an untroubling sail from Armintza, but the meagre headwind makes for slow progress, and continuous light rain robs warmth from my body. Pumping the sail helps generate some heat. But the effort is difficult to maintain, and soon – again – my body shivers uncontrollably and my teeth chatter. Darkness descends long before shore is reached. Lights flash in the distance: headlights from the vehicles of local windsurfers who have been tracking progress. Patiently they guide me in.

Landfall is adjacent to the "Real Club Náutico de Laredo". The reception committee usher me into the club. I wrap myself in woollen thermals and down jacket, take hot tea, and then some more hot tea, but cannot rid myself of the cold. The path of least resistance to shutting my eyes is home with the parents of a contact. A hot shower at last stops the shivering, though a now banging headache prevents sleep.

I hallucinate my way through the next morning. An eccentric chap called Iñaki whisks me away for a tour of the historic port town of Castro Urdiales. The local warmth somehow keeps at bay whatever illness I am suffering from. There is not a breath of wind, but a weak sun brings colour to the day. The coastline on the next hop – paddling round the headland – is stunning.

Conditions the following day are too favourable to lose. Illness can wait. Cantabria is at her beautiful best. Golden-sand beaches punctuate the dark cliff-line. Beyond are the greens of pasture and copse. And in the far distance – etched beneath an intense blue sky – are snow covered mountains: the Picos de Europa. The splashes of turquoise sea are deliciously refreshing. An easterly wind animates playful white horses. They seem not just alive, but joyful to be alive! We stretch our legs together. Tell me a white horse has a soul and I would not disagree. The herd moves west. There is no fear between us today. But the day is short. A descending sun glints off the ice fields of the Picos, and then is lost behind the peaks.

I land at Comillas, tired and cold after having fallen a few times late on. There is a patch of grass to sleep upon but first I go for a coffee, and inside the bar a man in a suit digs for my story. The suit is big enough for two at least but Josema fills it and could be a stand in for the capo in a Godfather movie. "*Ven conmigo*," he says. Come with me. And I do. And we go by car the 500 metres to the small fishing port, which is walled like a squash court and has a narrow opening to the sea that now fills it. At the port are Enrique and Alfonso, working on an engine in a small boat that they eventually bring to life. And I don't remember so well the details, because my fever is rising, but there is a big heavy wooden trailer that brings my gear to a hut that stores fishing nets.

And then I remember in the hut, but before that there was another bar and Alfonso had insisted I come, and then we left and outside were Alfonso's wife and children. And they gave me a big *bocata* that was foil wrapped and hot from its fresh tortilla filling, and they told me to go and sleep. And in the hut that dripping *bocata* and the paracetamol and the caffeine settled inside me and they made the delirium nice. And cocooned by the nets and the safety of the hut I closed leaden eyelids and surrendered to sleep.

Comillas port with (left to right) Josema, Alfonso, me, Enrique

***

The sea does not yet give permission to stop. Next day is mirror calm –
truly without a ripple. After breakfast at the pharmacy I paddle away from
Comillas beach. Leaving from the harbour are Alfonso and crew in a black-
and-white steel boat with a high, curved bow. It will be a fine day on the sea,
and I am happy for the opportunity to wave a fond adios to Alfonso.

The carbon shaft of the paddle had been last repaired in France, and the
adjustable section is now an aluminium tube. A problem with aluminium is
that it eventually fatigues and breaks. Today, the aluminium section breaks.
It is a good day for it to break, and only a short distance to the town of San
Vicente de la Barquera. On a bank of the town's protected estuary there is a
rowing club where the helpful coach sorts out clearance for me to stay.

Illness... Broken paddle... Convenient place to leave the gear... Is the
universe trying to tell me something? I decide that it is. Menorca is a simple
bus ride and hassle-free flight away. I hadn't wanted to break the journey at
all. But the simplest way to restore gear and body to full working order is to
pitstop in Menorca. At the Minorca Sailing workshop I can resolve the
paddle problem; and my good friends John and Sarah will feed me back to
health. I return to Menorca for 10 days of rest and recuperation.

Upon resumption of sailing I briefly feel strong. It is rare to see craft at sea
in winter, but on this occasion there is a boat and it looks familiar. I sail until
close, and indeed it is Alfonso hauling nets, about 2 nm off the coast. The
sea is rolling and nauseating but the catchup brings jolliness.

Heading seaward from San Vicente de la Barquera. Photo: Santiago Pérez

Winter

20 December 2017 - 21 March 2018

At Gijón I meet with Montse and her partner Ignacio who have taken delivery of a replacement custom-build Severne Turbo GT sail. The sail is perfect. All the panels are made of laminate films that will resist tears even if punctured. The creation is beautiful, strong and light. The original sail is now so heavily patched that the rig literally sinks if not attached to the board. On one muddled landing I lost the rig and was lucky to hook it with a leg before it slipped beyond reach.

For the onward sail the swell has returned, making landings hazardous. Failing light advises for an attempt at San Juan de la Arena. The town is at the estuary of the river Nalón and the course of the river has been extended seaward by a double line of rock moles. The entrance is clear of breaking waves, but the outpouring of fresh water and cool air rolling down from the mountains make my zigzag attempt to sail upriver ineffectual. A rapid transition to the paddle – now repaired with a stout section of carbon tube – is called for. I paddle alongside unscalable boulders for a kilometre, until the chute they form becomes a concrete wall that bends into a basin and there is a ramp to exit from the water.

The town has a number of bars where cider is served from a great height as is the Asturian way. Dinner is a plateful of succulent Biscay prawns. I sleep on a finger of land in the middle of the Nalón, on a patch of grass next to the concrete wall I had sailed past earlier. It had been deserted then, but now fisherman work from the wall and stay throughout the night. They dip their nets for glass eels – the larval stage of elvers, which are themselves juveniles of the adult form of these finless fish. The wormlike glass eels fetch a good price in Spain and the fishing is highly regulated. Positions on the concrete wall are assigned by lottery. These European glass eels will have spent the first few years of their lives drifting with the Gulf Stream. Some that make it to a life in freshwater will reach maturity, and hopefully a few will make it back to the Sargasso Sea to spawn.

The Sargasso Sea – a glaring omission from the IHO's list – is the only sea without a land boundary. It lies in the western North Atlantic and is bound by a gyre of rotating currents. In 1492 Columbus first documented the *Sargassum* seaweed after which the sea is named, and which acts as a nursery for many species. A sobering reality is that an explorer today would find that the Sea is home to the North Atlantic Garbage Patch.

It is a cold night. And the next night – after a day too windless to sail and too lumpy to paddle – will be colder still. Now accustomed to the presence of the nearby eel fishers I pull the sleeping bag up around my face and wait for sleep. But a visitor – Marino – arrives beforehand.

Marino takes the award for random act of kindness of my journey. He wishes to help me through the chilly night, and has prepared a battered holdall and trekked through the darkness to deliver it. Inside the holdall is a sleeping bag of the bulky rectangular style, a bottle with freshly warmed hot milk and *Cola Cao*, and a packet of cardboard-like biscuits – a traditional companion to the Spanish chocolate drink.

Some details of my story enable Marino to reminisce on his own. He too is a wanderer. He has wandered from his native Peru, worked a time in Norway from where he reflects that he should "never have left", and is now in San Juan de la Arena: from "somewhere over there" – signalled by a vague arm movement towards the town. There is a bitter sadness in how he talks: disdain for the electricity company who have cut off his supply, and racist words about Moroccan immigrants. When Marino is gone I wonder what to make of his visit. Marino's current framing of his personal history does him no favours. But we can tell ourselves different stories. It is not the events in our lives that make us but how we interpret them.

In a few days it will be Christmas. My brother and family are in Madrid at María's parents' flat. I am also invited, but do consider sailing through the festivities instead. Perhaps it is Marino's visit that prompts me to put family

The golden beach at San Juan de la Arena

first. Fate also provides some nudges: there is an airport that is so close by that I can walk to it, and Pepe the friendly harbourmaster has keys to a fisherman's lockup where the gear can "sleep safe." I walk the golden beach, then bush-whack my way to the airport perimeter fence and follow it round to the terminal building. Some hours later my aeroplane begins its descent to Madrid Barajas. Air travel is remarkably simple.

Christmas

The days of Christmas are fun, disorientating and dislocating: Subway rides with excited niece and nephew, nice food, busy streets, rampant consumerism. So many lives so disconnected from the natural world. If cities were zoos they would be banned on animal welfare grounds. My mind takes me to a more restful place: to the golden beach with its white, rolling surf. Then a relapse into illness takes hold.

Illness and Convalescence

Family jets away, and – lost in Madrid – I need a plan sharpish. A lifeline arrives in the form of an offer from friends Marcos and Olga to stay with them a few days at El Espinar, a rural village outside Madrid, and a local train ride away. The plan is to shake off this cold and then get back sailing, but this time the illness is far more severe. For a few days I am totally incapacitated. The family demonstrate remarkable kindness and patience at having the worst house guest ever. They care for me until I have the strength to move on.

I call Pepe and he provides reassurance that the windsurf gear still sleeps well – *"duerme bien,"* and has a small appetite – *"no come nada."*

Without this care I would have been in much greater trouble, very possibly a hospital case. Instead, dosed up to my eyeballs, I make it back to Menorca.

Restart

After two months of convalescence I feel sufficiently restored to be paying close attention to the Biscay weather forecast. For the entirety of January and February the north coast of Spain has been receiving a battering of wind and swell. The waves have not dropped below three metres and have regularly been double that size, and the wind has continually been out of the west. Even had I been on location and in rude health, it is possible there would not have been a single opportunity to sail.

With March already well advanced the forecast at last promises a break in the weather. I head back to Asturias, and walk through lush Spring vegetation to San Juan de la Arena. Pepe has been good to his word – board and gear are in good order. I rig the sail. It is a rough night. Sometimes the wind blows up the valley. Sometimes it blows down. Regardless of how I arrange the sail shelter, a few minutes later the wind switches to flick away the roof.

It is too wild to sail the next day. I leave sail and board attached together on open grassland so that the wind blowing up the valley leaves them unruffled. I go for a coffee to kill some hours.

When I return the gear is upwind of where it had been left, at the foot of a wire topped fence, and the beautiful sail has had shreds torn into the upper panels. Films that were as new as a child's skin have the puncture wounds of a rabid dog's mauling. The leech of the sail is severed and limp. The scene leaves me dazed. *How has this happened? Is this even real?*

I know from my uncomfortable night that it is real. The wind must have switched 180 degrees and sent an almighty gust that picked up the gear and slammed it into the fence. There is no other explanation. It is an inauspicious restart and perhaps a negligent mistake. It could be argued that I should have derigged the sail. But a derigged sail is more vulnerable to pilfering fingers. No, mostly it is just a result of the numbers game: multiple rolls of the dice. With all the misfortunes that can happen, one of the many possibilities will happen – eventually.

There is good fortune too. The new and high quality films resisted more catastrophic damage; and my sail repair supplies are at one-hundred percent. In what remains of the day I butterfly-stitch the leech back together with Insignia cloth to patch the worst-mauled parts. The emergency repairs will add some weight to the sail, but for a while at least they should hold.

At last – after four days of waiting – the swells recede such that they roll into the Nalón rather than tumble. I launch into the current and am swept toward open sea.

Cabo de Estaca de Bares

28 March 2018

I punch into a stiff headwind towards Spain's most northerly point, expecting this to be a landmark sail. A fishing boat gives an encouraging blast of their foghorn in the lee of the cape. Then the rain comes and obscures all company and sight of land. I sail further than necessary on port tack for additional sea room. The shadow of an eastbound ship comes into view and prompts a tack back onto starboard. Cabo de Estaca de Bares is cleared with ease. The board ploughs through the rough sea towards the shelter of the next headland. Visibility fades back in. Revealed is an immense and jagged outcrop. Despite the grimy weather, the sailing is exhilarating. Directly ahead is the port of Cariño. The name is welcoming, a translation might be "gentle fondness". It is easy to sail to gentle fondness. And once there – on a foul day like today – it is difficult to sail back offshore to where I know there are real dangers. The headland from where I have come is dwarfed by the one that lies ahead. Out there will be squalls twice as fierce. The offer of Cariño is persuasive. I sail into the port. Really, that was the only offer. And already I am uncomfortable, because there is a storm coming, and Cabo Ortegal still lies ahead.

Friends of a friend arrive and see to it that there is no physical discomfort during the next three days of howling wind and torrential rain. Sam and Mel are native Cornish and now nearly as native Galician as their daughter Lorena. They lead a Good Life existence in a lush green valley. For 12 years they lived in a horsebox whilst they built their house. The horsebox is now a nicely decorated guest room and is where I stay.

Sam and Mel cook proper food like lasagne, game pie, and roast dinner. They drink proper tea and proper coffee. Sam also surfs and has a spare board and wetsuit of the correct size. We surf an excellent wave at Villarube. As a group we also visit the lighthouse at Cabo Ortegal, and take a trip to the breathtaking cliffs that run from Cariño to Cediera. In terms of sea cliffs that face the ocean, these are highest of mainland Europe.[18] The wholesome nourishment and cliff tourism are excellent preparation for the upcoming sail. Occasionally it stops raining, though not for long.

The friends who have linked me up with Sam and Mel are Carolina and Rufus. Carolina has a fine old boat in Ribadeo that was built in Falmouth by

---

[18] The Cariño to Cediera cliffs are 621 metres high. Hornelen cliff in Norway is significantly higher (860 metres) but looks down to an enclosed fjord rather than open ocean.

her father and sailed engineless across Biscay. Caroline and Rufus put me up after the "Camino de Santiago" Hostel Association decided that I wasn't a proper pilgrim, and therefore declined to open their inn! God works in mysterious ways, and it has to be said that he nailed that one, because Carolina does a roast that even Sam could learn from.

I sheltered from Storm Hugo during a prolonged stay with Carolina and Rufus. We saw immense waves pounding the harbour at Viavélez, and headed high into the mountains to leave the sea behind for a day of retreat. Carolina also has a fantastic bookshelf of nautical adventures. When this book is complete, it will be submitted to the curator for her consideration.

In every section of my book, the stories told and people mentioned are just a subset of all those who truly contributed. For those who do not feature in person, please know that you are represented by the Sams and the Carolinas.

Cabo Ortegal is the westernmost limit of Biscay. Beyond the Cape – undiluted by further subdivision – is North Atlantic Ocean.

Punching out northward of Estaca de Bares

11. North Atlantic Ocean

The Atlantic Ocean is the second largest division of World Ocean. It is comprised of both North Atlantic and South Atlantic parts and these meet at the equator. To its west are the Americas, and to its east are Europe and Africa.

According to IHO *Limits* (1953) the Atlantic's southern extent reaches Antarctica. But if IHO *Limits* (2002 draft) is adopted then the Southern Ocean will be recognised, and the oceanic boundary will be at a latitude of 60 degrees south.

The Atlantic's northern boundary is where it meets the Arctic Ocean. The Atlantic-Arctic shared limit is therefore also coincidental with the southern limits of the Norwegian Sea, Icelandic Sea and Davis Strait.[19]

The modern name Atlantic Ocean comes from Greek literature and mythology. Accounts such as the Iliad and the Odyssey describe Oceanus as the gigantic river that encircles the world. While Atlas (a Titan) lends his name to the "Sea of Atlantis" which lay beyond the "Pillars of Hercules" (mountains on either side of the Strait of Gibraltar).

Both North and South Atlantic have gyres. They rotate in opposite directions and set up westward flowing equatorial currents. In the case of the North Atlantic, its gyre rotates clockwise, and carries warm water westward as the Gulf Stream, which is responsible for the mild climate of Western Europe. Without the warmth of the Gulf Stream the coastline of Norway and perhaps much of the UK would be locked in sea ice for much of the year, as is the case for equivalent latitudes in Canada.

The Mid-Atlantic Ridge is a mountain range that follows the boundary between the continental plates beneath the Atlantic. It divides the Ocean longitudinally and links up with similar ridges in the other oceans. The network of ridges is the longest and most extensive mountain range on the planet. Some of the peaks of the Mid-Atlantic Ridge break the surface. In the North Atlantic, the islands they form are Jan Mayen, Iceland, the Azores archipelago, and the Saint Peter and Saint Paul archipelago.

The seas at the coastal margins of the Atlantic are shallow where underpinned by continental shelf. Beyond, they are much deeper: 4000 to 5000 metres is typical. On the west-facing Iberian peninsula the shelf drops away quickly. At some locations – notably Nazaré in Portugal – subsea canyons allow ocean sized-swells to reach shore.

---

[19] The Icelandic Sea lies to the west of the Norwegian Sea. The Davis Strait lies between south Greenland and Baffin Island, Canada.

N

Bay of Biscay

Cedeira

Cabo Ortegal

Malpica

Muxia

Cabo Finisterre

Carnota

La Coruña

Muros

Islas Cies

Viana

Porto

Aveiro

Nazaré

Tagus

Cabo de Roca

Lisbon

Cascais

Sesimbra

Milfontes

Azenha do Mar

Arrifana

Cabo San Vicente

Sagres

Ilha do Farol

Fuzeta

Cabo Trafalgar

Strait of Gibraltar

0   50   100 km

North Atlantic Ocean

extent and track

Arctic Ocean

Arctic Ocean

North Atlantic Ocean

0°0′

South Atlantic

It used to be assumed that the deep ocean was devoid of life, or depended upon "sea snow", composed of organic material falling from above. That changed with the discovery of ecosystems located around hydrothermal vents and seeps. It is speculated that the moons of Jupiter have similar conditions to those found in the deep sea. They may be a good bet for the nearest extra-terrestrial life.

The Exclusive Economic Zone of coastal nations extends up to a maximum of 200 nm from land. Beyond this distance is the high sea: International Waters where there is a principle of freedom of access. Fishing in the high seas is in theory regulated by Regional Fisheries Management Organizations (RFMOs) and their member countries. In practice the RFMO guidelines are often not enacted upon by the member countries, and compliance is difficult to enforce. Technological advantage – rather than bountiful oceans – enables record catches. Life from the oceans is harvested with greed rather than fished in a sustainable manner.

Mineral scraping from the ocean floor is an additional threat to deep sea ecosystems. Nations and corporations are already jostling for a share of the spoils. Exploitation has the potential to lift vast blooms of smothering sediment.

For most of us, the deep sea and the high sea are out of sight and out of mind. The remoteness that once made them safe now makes them vulnerable.

In the Balance – Cariño to Cedeiro

29-31 March 2018

Sam and Mel are upbeat about the conditions. In Galicia these brief windows between low pressure systems are the good weather days. The last drops of rain have fallen. Puddles in the street now accurately reflect back the grey sky. Glimpses of water beyond the harbour show a gently rippled sea, settling the matter that today is a good day to sail.

My hosts have put up with their visitor for three nights already. Today's better weather brings with it a natural assumption that I will be sailing. We head to Cariño's *vivero* to collect the board from where it has been residing next to the seawater-filled lobster pens. Sam and daughter Lorena have a skip in their step that brings forward the inevitable launch despite the dragging of my heels.

Were it just me here I would take a time out: head for a coffee, phone a friend. It would be helpful to explain my apprehensions. But in this situation that isn't an option. After all, I have sailed all this way to get here and will definitely be continuing. And outside the port it looks like a decent enough day. My hosts have done their bit – so now it's my turn. Time to move out and move on. Back to the routine for us all. I set about rigging the sail, performing each stage of the process with particular care. That settles the mind and helps to keep fear in check.

When I got up this morning I knew what was coming. There is an inevitability to it. As there was an inevitability that the WW1 soldiers who went "over the top" of the trenches would do so when their fateful day came. Though my experiences bear no comparison, I am sometimes grateful for having what is perhaps some insight into their states of mind. I wonder what I would have done in their place. Though my fear may be misplaced or trivial, perhaps to them it would be recognisable.

My sense of foreboding today is caused by the knowledge that a four metre swell has been pounding the coast through the night. How quickly will the sea have subsided? What will be found beyond the jagged pillars of Cabo Ortegal? I can turn back if necessary – I tell myself – though a tactical retreat is more easily imagined than performed. To reach safety there are 15 nm to zigzag against the wind – that's 30 nm of sailing – alongside cliffs that in places reach to more than 600 metres in height.

There are reassuring aspects about the day too. The various wind forecasts are all in agreement and predict a rock steady 15 knots. Swell and sea conditions will be moderating. Turning back early-on is an option. At the end of the leg the natural harbour of Cedeira guarantees a way in through deep and therefore safe water. 15 miles upwind is a respectable but unexceptional hop. Today's gamble is the wind and the sea.

The loaded board is heavy and cumbersome on land. Launching is inelegant. But once afloat the first puffs of an offshore wind catch the sail and a beautiful transition occurs. The board glides. My body arches sideways to counteract the weight of a leaning rig and this steers the board in smooth curves over a shallow bed of white sand. It feels good to be afloat, alone and free. This world is a simple one. Gone are the calculations of the minds of others.

Outside the port is protected: the lee of the Cape. I sail parallel to rising cliffs. From this angle they appear to terminate as isolated jutting peaks that rise from the ocean. When I had been depleted after sailing round Bares this view had filled me with trepidation. Today I am fresh and there is wonder and excitement too.

The high terrain of the Cape bends a current of air in its lee. A following breeze carries me to where stray gusts rough and tumble with the main west-southwest flow.

The flat sea becomes undulating. It bends round the pointed islets, squashed up like the folds of an ill-fitting carpet. The time between the folds – the swell period – tells of their provenance. Swells that have travelled from afar have a slow heartbeat: perhaps 20 seconds between each pulse for a swell that has travelled the width of an ocean. Swells from closer-by are more tightly packed. Off Cabo Ortegal, the swell lines come frequently – their origin would have been the same swirl of low pressure that brought all that rain. The waves do not carry the ominous power of a long-period swell, but closer neighbours make for steeper peaks.

Waves grow in height and slow down when they feel the ocean floor. The effect is known as shoaling. A powerful 20 second period swell will feel the ocean floor at a depth of about 300 metres. Even a modest 10 second swell reaches down to 80 metres. When a swell moves from deep ocean to shallow coastal water, shoaling occurs: the "sea" becomes shorter and steeper. It is differential shoaling that causes the swells to bend round the islets. 40 or more metres beneath me the swells are feeling the ocean floor.

I proceed with caution, using the shelter of the headland to tack up close – or where feels close – to the islets. The lighthouse is perched on a precarious ledge at the outcrop's craggy end. It is dwarfed by the cliff backdrop and appears miniaturised from here. Possibly there are visitors looking. The thought of spectators makes me bolder. Perhaps they have a camera. Maybe a long lens too. If anyone were to notice this tiny craft – this out-of-place beach toy – they would most likely call the coastguard.

Clear of the islets the wind blows steadier and from the west. The board noses upwind into the oncoming swells. A transition happens: from feeling relatively safe to feeling utterly exposed. Swells roll under the board and I

Cabo Ortegal lighthouse dwarfed by its backdrop of cliff

am sent climbing up steep faces. Superimposed on the undulating terrain is the veneer of a recent gale. I read the oncoming sea, and the sense of being alive is heightened!

An invisible boundary has been crossed. This is now Atlantic Ocean proper.

The board powers forward. The sea surface resembles a giant waterbed being jumped upon by an invisible behemoth. Pits form out of nowhere to swallow the board and then there is the lurch of a quick rise of a passing swell, and a brief gasp of visibility. The wind – thank God, goodness and Windguru[20] – is as predicted: in the goldilocks zone of being neither too light nor too strong.

The boom – the carbon tube from which I hang – gives stability, and the board carries enough momentum to punch through smaller, crumbling waves. It is the larger ones that threaten to topple that cause an intake of breath. They approach unannounced; arrive suddenly as abrupt walls. Even a partial collapse would sweep me away. It is down to luck where the board ascends. I can slow up – and sometimes do – for a route over the top that reduces stress on the daggerboard, but at such short notice there is little choice in which section of oncoming wall to steer for. The board takes aim and goes straight.

I am far from land – north not just of Cabo Ortegal but also of Bares. But still it feels too close to the coast – as if I am tempting fate by playing in the

---

[20] Weather forecasting website.

surf. So I sail further, searching in vain for *mar noble* – a predictable and trustworthy sea; finding instead only greater isolation.

And then – somewhere out there – comes a place and a moment when I am three quarters buried. The board slides into the deepest pit yet and I feel sick inside as the wall in front inhales. It grows tall and steep. The tip of the mast looks upward towards the ramparts. My imagined friend, a seagull who sometimes sits atop the mast-tip, would have alighted by now; would be being lifted on an updraft to safety. Every man or seagull for himself. The mass of water takes a form that gravity does not allow. I cannot steer around the wall because the board knows only straight. I am not a seagull, and there is no route out.

It will not be the first time I have been buried by a wall of sea. I know what to expect. I know this moment and what comes next – or at least I think I do. To find its level the water will tumble as an avalanche down that precipitous slope. The carbon tubes of mast and boom will snap. The board may be lost and carried away, leaving me in deep water and deep shit.

I am in the wrong place, at the wrong time, and on the wrong vessel. That wave does not belong in this sea – but then neither do I.

The underlying swell marches forward, deferring the impending avalanche, matching the pace of the hanging wall to maintain upright its spineless, wobbling flab. It is too late for a race to the roof of the wave – that would be futile – so I ease the sail – an instinctive act of preservation – sensing that by treading softly the avalanche might not be triggered. The wall teeters on the brink of collapse. I am as defenceless as a puppy and whimper like one as I gingerly ascend its long face. The falling water would bury me. That prospect seems very real and I am deeply fearful.

For a count of three the outcome is uncertain. But the wave passes beneath me and I tiptoe over its peak.

***

That wave was an outlier. Its constituent parts had ganged together for just a few moments and the threat it posed had been real. It was bad luck to find it; and good luck that it did not break.

There are more big waves to climb over, but no others that suggest they will wipe me away. The sea becomes less rough as the hours tick by. I zigzag at 2 nm from the coast and there is wind all the way to Cedeira. Arrival is celebrated with Sam, friend Tino, and an incredulous kayaker. I am in an altered state: dazed, but also deeply satisfied and serene.

The sail is one of the most epic of my journey. Though I doubt my memory for some details, the emotion of the account, I know, is accurate. The emotional memories are locked in. It seemed probable that I would not make it over that wave. It seems plausible that the outcome was in the balance.

La Coruña

1-7 April 2018

It comes as a surprise that I sail. I had not wanted to face another heavy day – not yet – and the tapas bars of Cedeira had been my plan. But a check on the ocean had found it benign: a free pass to move on. The psychological repair work can wait, or happen at sea.

The coastline is crenelated, picturesque rather than awe inspiring, and bathed in sunshine. A small swell washes over various rocks and reefs, indicating their location. Lunch on board, with feet dangling in the cool water, improves the day and my mood further. It is another leg of upwind sailing, but even the wind angle is partially cooperative: allowing for a long tack on starboard.

Maritime towns and cities are best arrived at by sea. Those who come by boat are delivered to the heart of the place. They benefit from a front door arrival and are spared the urban sprawl of the outskirts. When I have the courage, I opt for front door arrivals, though I do not always have the courage, and quite often end up at little-used side entrances. The front door of La Coruña is guarded over by the dominating Torre de Hercules. The tower is the oldest lighthouse still in use and dates from the second century. It gained a protective second layer in 1791 with the result being a particularly robust appearance.

As the tower is being approached the day has transformed into another where concern for reaching land is foremost in my mind. 5 nm ago I headed offshore to cross the wide mouths of the Ría[21] de Ferrol and the Ría de Betanzos. Now the wind is funnelling out of the Ría de Coruña at 25 knots. The final zigags to reach the Torre are a real fight. Wind tears at the sail, and the daggerboard creaks in protest.

Inside the Ría – before safety can be truly claimed – there is the manmade obstacle of a kilometre-long rock mole. Beyond the mole I notice a windsurf sail. It is the sail of a Raceboard and – undoubtedly – it is being expertly handled. Most recreational windsurfers stay close to their bit of beach, but this sailor is a solitary open water wanderer. Our courses dovetail in a natural way, and shortly after we are sailing upwind in formation: me following, Jorge as guide and shepherd.

---

[21] The Galician rías are large coastal inlets similar to Norwegian fjords or Scottish sea lochs. The divide between the Upper Rias – Rías Altas – and Lower Rias – Rías Biaxes – is at Cape Finisterre.

We land at the Playa de Oza, at a windsurf and sailing club. As is often the case at the end of a sail I am dazed from the effort and disorientated because everything is new, but the conviction that I am with family is absolute. The other sailor is Jorge Maciel, who represented Spain at two Olympic Games and is the heart of the club. I am introduced to a bunch of people who are so warm and open and obviously good that it fills me with love for humanity. A key to the club is handed over and I am told to stay for as long as the weather requires.

To my immense good fortune, a week passes before a comfortable day to move on arrives. During that time, the sail that had been damaged by the rogue gusts of Asturias receives a proper repair courtesy of Velas Finishterra; and David from BoardsbyNeira patches the cracks of the daggerboard. David and I go surfing too, though the water is cold and soon I am shivering in the ill-fitting borrowed wetsuit.

Marcos takes me for a viewing of the coastline ahead, which is always a great settler of nerves. Pancho lends me a bike. I visit the Torre, the end of the mole, and shortcut to the Atlantic facing beach of Orzán. I like the city, though it is the antithesis of bike-friendly. Huge drop-off curbs, uncrossable roads and narrow lanes that leave no space for cyclists. There is little option but to ride on the pavements and this seems to be accepted practice.

I cycle west of Orzán, overlooking the sea, along a nice coastal path that is the exception to the bike unfriendly rule. Coastguard vessels and helicopters scour the sea. The weather is fine but windless, and waves as high as houses break hard and hollow. It is beautiful but dangerous. The search is for the body of a young woman who was swept from Orzán beach. The ocean can for a long while go calm, but then will surge. A fisherman on dry rock, or walker on dry sand, can be knocked over and dragged away. It can happen and does, and even people who are experienced sea folk – if they do not know of the tsunami-like nature of long-period swells – may be unaware of their danger.

There is a sculpture of an octopus sliding its way through the handrail at the edge of the path; the Estrella Damn beer factory bar to visit; and another night out with Mori, Carlos, Carmen, María and Ana. The three mermaids are a welcome distraction and take my mind away from the sea. I fall in love another three times, and am attentive to their lesson of how to eat "tequeños", which are a Venezuelan-inspired snack with proportions that resemble a – ahem – cucumber.

Mori mentions something about having me roped to a mast, and later I become aware of the aptness of the cultural reference. For those as unversed as I was, Homer's *Odyssey* tells of Ulysses' epic voyage back to Ithaka after the Trojan War. On one part of the journey Ulysses and his crew must sail past sirens, whose voices are so beautiful that sailors who hear them would throw themselves overboard and drown in an attempt to be with them.

Ulysses orders that his crew stuff their ears with beeswax, and that he himself be tied to the ship's mast, and that his demands to be released go unmet. Ulysses – alone – hears the sirens but is unable to drown himself, which allows his odyssey to continue.

Note that Ulysses is the Roman name for who the Greeks call Odysseus. He crops up elsewhere and the name used reflects that used locally.

The La Coruña group were all fantastic company. Pictured here with (clockwise from me) Carmen, Mori, María, Carlos and Anna.

Malpica, and Basecamp Muxía

9 and 13 April 2018, from log entries

A solid upwind sail from La Coruña ends with an uncomplicated landing at Malpica. The small harbour is the first stopping opportunity on Galicia's *Costa do Morte* or Coast of Death.

My first bed is the unforgiving concrete dock, but Team La Coruña have been mobilising contacts and in the early hours I am woken bleary eyed by intrepid night owl Neli. Minutes later we are driving to a surely-haunted house in the pitch black of deepest Galicia. Neli gifts me a lucky garlic, which only adds to the sense of supernatural presence.

Today, in favour of sailing is a light easterly breeze. A contraindication is a four-metre swell. I endure self-inflicted torment for a few hours before deciding to try for progress. Near the shelter of land there is absolutely no wind, I make it a short distance beyond the harbour wall but am unable to sail in the confused sea, and fall repeatedly. Back to port. Zero miles.

The resulting puddle of self-pity soon evaporates. It can be difficult to wait, or turn back, but they are useful skills. A bonus is that having made an attempt I can now be gentle with myself for the rest of the day.

I meet Tono from Buceo (Diving) Malpica. He is a wealth of information about the many nearby wrecks. Fragments of dinnerware are produced with emblems that identify the craft from which they have been recovered. The treasure hunter also dives for sea urchins that will be exported to France for the dinner table.

Although a young man, Tono remembers well the Prestige oil tanker disaster of 2002. The vessel was holed in a winter storm and then denied access to ports in France, Spain and Portugal. Ecological disaster would have been averted had the Prestige not been forced to remain at sea, but instead she sank and her cargo of Heavy Fuel Oil reached the coastline of all three countries.

Tono says I can stay at the dive centre until conditions improve.

I consider the sea from above piled-up concrete blocks that protect the port. A short way out, dolphins work as a team on a shoal of unseen fish. With Neli's garlic that makes it a double-lucky day. Superstition is not my thing but on this coast all help is welcome. Today's good fortune was failing to sail myself into a complicated position: Had I made it round the outcrop to truly exposed coast, the limp breeze and express-train sized groundswell would have been traumatically difficult.

***

Another day of monstrous sea is sat out at Muxía, while plotting an attempt on Cape Finisterre. It is 18 nm to Spain's "Land's End" and there are no options to cut the leg short. Mountaineering terminology comes to mind: This is "Basecamp Muxía" and a suitable weather window is needed for an "attempt on the Cape".

Muxía, a natural harbour, has a wide and deep entrance. I run to the headland that guards it to watch the departure of the 50-foot ketch *Le Labo*. The crew of the yacht conduct research into plastic pollution and had welcomed me aboard last night. They are headed for the Mediterranean and trying to make up for lost time. At my vantage point by the stone church above the surf, salt hangs on the still air. As *Le Labo* heads for open water, each swell sinks her entire hull so that just the sails are visible.

I know how it is out there. The troughs would swallow me whole, as they did when I sailed Britain's Land's End on that formative journey. In the dungeon-like troughs there would be no wind. Some puffs might reach above. But not down below – where I would be – robbed even of awareness for what is near, or for where I am headed. Strange currents would pull the board first this way, then that way, then the other. The surface of the ocean would be alive like the skin of a great beast that is dreaming of fight or flight. To stay upright would require the straining of every sinew – and the effort would bring exhaustion. And there would be no engine to escape from this world. No option for stepping off the hell ride. To attempt a premature exit would be to invite death, by drowning or by gashing on rock.

I snap out of my imaginings, but will leave Finisterre for another day.

Le Labo departs from Muxía

Finisterre to the Isles Cies

16-20 April 2018

Carnota

This account will skip Finisterre, Spain's westernmost mainland point, because it is more of the same: More fear. More zigzagging upwind. More "required distance" with too much wind, and waves that batter a lee shore. And I'll skip the relief of getting round. And the dazed arrival at "I don't care where" because all that matters is that it is land. Though I do want you to hear of the kind locals, who noticed the drowned rat on the dock of their little village and provided refuge during two more "damned rough" days. Thankyou Javier and Sandra.

And I'll keep brief the account of heading south from there, in far too much wind, that – predictably – was a headwind. And the surprise – unwelcome – of shallow water even far out to sea, and an inner maze of reefs that duelled with the swell and barred the route to shore. The wind howled. The objective – the safety of the entrance into the Ría de Muros – though not far – was too far. I have no sense of authorship for the U-turn that ensued. It just happened, and a moment later I was sailing at full tilt with the wind, to where there appeared to be a dip between reefs. And heading in like this the strong wind was a help because the board could match the pace of the breaking surf and the backs of the waves lifted us high over the dangerous shallows. It was quite a ride in, and the beach that was found – Carnota – is one of my favourites of this journey. It was a few days before I moved on. There was a bar with knowing fishermen; and mermaids on the rocks who were marine biologists, and for a few happy hours they provided company as we counted limpets.

Sixteen years ago, oil from the Prestige came ashore here and lined the beach a metre thick. Thousands of volunteers descended upon the community to help with the clean-up. The remaining thick, sticky Heavy Fuel Oil eventually biodegraded. It is rare to find oil on a beach nowadays, but plastic is – sadly – ubiquitous. On nearby Praia de Louro a winter storm has left a collection of plastic flotsam. Plastic pollution decomposes into microplastics; microplastics absorb toxins; and these ascend the food chain, with increasing concentration in higher organisms. When we pollute at the continental shelf, we poison ourselves at the supermarket shelf.

Cape Corrubedo

If the sail to Carnota was wild, the one that followed became wilder still. It began in a sprightly sea and a stiff breeze. The board raced downwind; bounced off the lumps; slung water at my stinging eyes. Either side there were skerries and some matched with my memory of a previously consulted chart.

That was the warm-up. Later came brief respite in deeper water off the Ría de Muros, and then ratcheting intensity over 10 nm as Cabo Corrubedo drew closer. The wind built and the waves stood tall as if hoping to catch a glimpse of the lee shore beneath them. The board raced through deep furrows and snagged the angular walls like an out of control bobsleigh. The sea was predictably empty. Desolate.

Off Cape Corrubedo the pulse of the Atlantic was stronger. Mature swells swept past; and the wind – unobstructed by a lee shore – blew harder. It rattled the wilted leech of the tensioned sail. It was too windy for normal sailing. So I sailed like a Viking would: like Tord had done in the Skagerrak Sea. The deep troughs of this sea – this ocean – did at least provide some shelter from that wind. Though where was my good sense and caution to be found? *I would cherry pick the calm days*, I had told myself, when this journey was conceived...

It was necessary to go far beyond the Cape – halfway to America it seemed – before the angle seemed right to gybe. Then – after that cautious turn – the board rode freely with the marching swells. I positioned it high on the faces to observe where the waves broke and the skerries lurked. The charts had suggested a route through – though my memory was uncertain. I stayed at altitude: on lookout – edging closer, for another cautious zig and zag, until a smooth passage of rounded swells was glimpsed. The geometry was perfect. The sail pulled the board onto a deep and fast reach and it sliced a clean diagonal between islet and headland.

Land arrived soon after. It had been another physically and mentally draining sail. Later that day I launched again, nervous as hell of the next unknown miles.

Islas Cies

The more southerly Rías Baixas receive partial shelter from outlying islands. The east-facing shores of the islands offer safe landings. It was a relief to be inside the islands. But even as I enjoyed Ons and the Islas Cies on a summery day it was relief tinged with fear for what would come after. The unprotected coast of Portugal offers almost no natural shelter, and is renowned for huge waves. If Galicia – with its rias and abundance of natural harbours – had been this tough, how would I fare on the Portuguese expanse? I had no answer to that.

And even as I sailed between the Ons and Cies archipelagos – on a supposed day off from stress – the wind dropped, the Atlantic did what the Atlantic does, and I could barely stay upright. Only the thought of guaranteed shelter ahead made it tolerable.

The archipelagos are gifts of the natural world. The fortress-like west coasts shield forests that descend to meet gentler east coast shores. Sweeps of fine white sand, and skerries that team with life, gradually fall away into the clear and tranquil depths. The islands are important grounds for resident and migratory birds, and also attract tourists who arrive by yacht or tripper boat.

At Montefaro, and island of the Cies archipelago, the crew of an anchored yacht invite me aboard for a late lunch. It is nice to be around people, and it is better still to finally reach shore, and have hours to kill on what will soon be a deserted island. I had hoped to find solitude. At sea I am alone, but the sailing demands focus and there has been no space for idle time. I need that now: some time without demands; a pause from the fear; a putting aside – for a while – of the unremitting stress.

The island empties out: A ferryboat rounds up its catch of day-trippers; and the yachts depart. I wander on a path through the woods, onward to a blinking lighthouse, and – from the craggy summit of the island, nestled in soft grass next to the seagulls – watch the sun set over the Atlantic.

I cry on the descent. The island is a safe space that allows the dam of emotion that has been building to be breached. I plead for a day of sailing – just one fucking day – that is easy.

Twilight has almost become night when I arrive back at the board. I am composed now, but mentally drained and physically tired. Before bed I message Helene – just a "hello how you doing?" She tells me that I had "good progress last week despite big swells and much wind." I like it that she knows there has been "much wind." I remember to ask her how preparation is going for a ski across Greenland she will begin in a few weeks' time. She reports an eagerness to start, and is pleased to have "three dried reindeer hearts and some moose meat for daytime snacks." And that makes me smile too.

The Trades

22-24 April 2018

I depart Cies the following day when the tourists come, and paddle over a windless sea to Baiona. A nothing move; a positional tweak whilst the weather turns a page.

Just round the corner lies the Portuguese coast, and there is still no solution to that riddle. The mariners who fed me at Cies had warned of northerly winds that blow 25 knots from dawn to dusk. That would be a lot of wind for a small craft on open water. Large waves would build, with whitecaps heavy enough to fell me. But it is not windy now, and the forecast for tomorrow does not speak of a sizeable Atlantic swell. So perhaps there will be a tame introduction, and shipwreck on day one of this next leg will be avoided.

Viana do Castelo

The tame introduction becomes more spirited where Spain – a backdrop of hills draped with low cloud – becomes Portugal – and the terrain descends and the sky clears blue. The wind settles steady from the north and the board rides free in zigzags: out to sea – gybe, in towards shore – gybe, repeat, repeat, repeat. I sail with feet wedged firmly in the rear straps, apart from at the gybes, which the barrel robs of elegance, since my possessions occupy deck space that would normally be used to turn the board by foot pressure. It becomes properly windy later on, but by that time I have escaped into the shelter provided by the mole at Viana do Costelo. 30 nm have been covered: a good run, completed without incident.

Viana – it turns out – is the first of several large ports in the north of Portugal. The distances between them are not trivial, but with a favourable wind are within range. These ports all feature a river, with an opening to the sea that has been twisted south and held open by the construction of rock moles. The north bank mole is always larger, and extends a kilometre or so out to sea, and is usually curled like the oversized pincer of a right-clawed crab. To the currents, and to the mariner, the curled claws are headlands like any other: overfalls spill beyond them, and in their lee is found calmer water.

At Viana, there are visiting and local windsurfers. The friendly community do me proud, organising a place to stay and store gear, and educating me on Portuguese essentials such as *pastéis de nata* – a mini custard tart, and *francesinha* – a meat sandwich covered with cheese.

Porto

Another day of useful north wind delivers 30 nm of progress to Portugal's second city. Not knowing where to stop, I sail upriver and try my luck at the marina, hoping that the board and I might be allowed to overnight. Space is at a premium, but the marina employees are friendly and helpful, and link me up with Sasha who offers a berth on his boat. Sasha is en route to the Azores, and a new beginning mid-Atlantic. His yacht has been in Porto all winter, and he is making final preparations for the crossing now that better weather has arrived. His best friend is the marina dog – "Marina" – and Sasha now regards himself as Marina's rightful owner. But the marina workers disagree: Marina is their dog! Sasha confides to me his kidnap plan: an early start and an extra crew member. I keep that confidential, until now.

***

Sasha lends a bike and I cycle alongside the Douro to the port's centre. Though my visit is short, it delivers a glimpse of the depth of history here: Vessels from Porto's shipyards helped make Portugal a colonial power. Its notable residents voyaged to West Africa, and the Americas. It is thought that Magellan was born here.

Multiple threads begin to mesh together: The Azores, 800 nm to the west; the Azores High – a weather system associated with stable summer weather and the winds that I am now enjoying; Porto's location and significance during the age of exploration; why the voyages of discovery each took multiple years; my own struggle for progress whilst the Azores High was being battered out of existence by Atlantic low pressure systems; and the sudden change in weather that came after. It all points to one thing: that I am benefitting from the push of the Portuguese Trade Winds.

I am heading south when Elcano, Magellan, Vasco de Gama, and other historic seafarers would have set off on their great voyages, in vessels that needed the wind on their sterns. Our seeming coincidental timing is suddenly understood as something more inevitable. It brings me closer to their experience, I notice, with a lump in my throat.

Aveiro

I leave early, already familiar with the pattern of breeze and waves that build through the day, and it blows hard on the way to Aveiro. The 30 nm leg is completed in downwind zigzags, such that the distance sailed would be perhaps 50 nm ($\approx$ 93 km).

The gybes are difficult and tiring, so I do fewer of them. But going out to sea the wind blows stronger still, so eventually I do gybe, and for a while my rear thigh does not burn. Somewhere during the passage – about halfway – it became prudent to harden up the zigzags, to win back a little control at the expense of directness of route. There had been little option as the winds and the waves built. I sail inshore as far as I dare – the shipwrecking potential of the waves is self-evident – then gybe again.

From about 10 nm the mole is visible. It looks to be close, but I am being deceived by its scale. I sail high, but if I sail high then the objective is not closed in upon. So I sail low for as long as there is a path. And a salt-stinging eye blink before that path closes; before the board, and I, and whatever lump of water lie ahead all combine; before the explosion of spray actually happens – I again come high, and recover a semblance of control.

When it comes, the crash is a heavy one. Another brutal deceleration. A sinew-straining effort to maintain compact form. But that form is prised open – and my weakness exploited and magnified. I am hurled forward, slung round by a harness that won't let go, and buried underwater in a tangle of cumbersome gear.

It is a humbling fall. I had been playing a foolish game of pedal-to-the-metal Russian roulette. The mole had seemed near though it is still 7 nm downwind. The rolling, breaking sea is significant in size but not inherently dangerous provided the gear holds up, and – most importantly – provided that I do not lose contact with the gear. A leash is used to connect me to the board in heavy conditions.[22] Foolishly, I had been reluctant to expend energy with an earlier stop, meaning that I had been untethered until now. I clip on – belatedly, chastised. Then reach for a Mars bar.

There is a wild sea going past the mole, but I am a more centred and prudent sailor than before. I pick my way through the overfalls; and these bring, not fear, but a welcome order to the sea. And then there is a rolling smoothness of outflowing river water; and the wind is good and strong, meaning that a sandy beach within the harbour can be reached.

The final kilometre back to shore is sailed slowly in mindful appreciation. It is deeply satisfying to complete a difficult stretch. But pride should be tempered. Today, good luck was notably evident. That crash with the unclipped board had invited another outcome. I had left the barn door wide open. In another world the Universal Joint would have broken, and the board would have galloped away.

---

[22] It slightly embarrasses me to reveal that a safety leash was not added to my inventory until at La Coruña. I should have had one from day 1.

Nazaré

27 April 2018

The location where the largest waves on earth are surfed is almost calm the day it is reached. I stop in the turquoise water beneath the nose of the outcrop. Above me there is a fort that is now a visitors' centre dedicated to the spectacle of big wave surfing. I look up to where thousands of onlookers crowd to witness and be awed by miniature surfers riding 100 foot faces. Sometimes the waves form a tube – or barrel – that completely enclose the rider. Today there are no other surfers. Nazaré is all mine. The sail is massaged by the gently sloshing water and my legs dangle freely in its refreshing chill. This is a moment to be enjoyed. It is the subsea topography that makes this place special: a deep-water canyon allows Atlantic swells to roll in and be focussed exactly *here*.

The old hand surfers would say I am too far inside. A pang of fear prompts a seaward scan for early warning of a rogue set. The horizon is flat. Then a swirl of current spins the board. This is the moment of near perfect alignment. I paddle hard and the board reacts so that the famous headland is now framed in the background. Neither would the old hands approve that I am lined up for a fin first take off: too showy by far. But it is necessarily this way. How else would the battered container be in shot? I release the shutter. It is the picture I had been planning for, and to which I already know the caption: "Jono Dunnett and his perfect barrel at Nazaré".

My Dolphin Teachers

3 May 2018

The trades are briefly interrupted by winds that blow from the south, and upon their return are less vigorous. Either the stronger winds lie farther offshore; or the Azores High is weak, or has been displaced. It is early in the season after all.

Towns and harbours hide behind natural steps in the coastline, and there are easy landings at Peniche, Cascais and Sesimbra. On the day of the rounding of Cabo de Roca – the most westerly point of mainland Europe – there is a rare total absence of swell. That provides an opportunity to land and overnight at Guincho: a beach that has some renown in the windsurf world for its gnarly onshore wind and wave conditions. I tiptoe in and tiptoe out whilst the Atlantic giant sleeps.

Lisbon is leapfrogged with an offshore crossing of the Tagus estuary. At 4 nm from land I am invisible, so a potential permissions problem that I had been alerted to remains theoretical. I enjoy the sail, and the arrival of dolphins brings the reassuring sense that all will be OK. Dolphins usually tolerate my clumsiness, but these are shy individuals, and my turn towards them is too quick, and that scares them away. I accept their lesson, and from that day leave it to the dolphins to make an approach.

Some days later, perhaps it was that earlier misstep that allowed me to simply *hear* the call from behind. I dismissed it as maybe the caw of a tern, and returned focus to pumping the sail for both balance and a little more speed. A few minutes later the call comes again – this time much closer – and moments after a trio of extra-long open kayaks skewer themselves level. The friendly "surfski" paddlers are on a 14 nm downwinder; obviously faster than me – which is briefly humiliating. They also know exactly where they are headed – so I am keen to follow. We end up at Milfontes harbour: a finger-like gulley with an entrance so narrow that it could almost be leaped. The Portuguese have demonstrated much kindness wherever I have landed, and here is no exception: a shower, a beer and a slap-up feed rounds off another excellent day.

Natural Park of the Southwest

4-7 May 2018

The southernmost 100 km of Portugal's west coast are rocky, and cove studded. The area corresponds to the Southwest Alentejo and Vicentine Coast Natural Park. There are no major towns or mole protected ports. Any yachts that sail this coast would bypass it entirely. Even in good weather there would be nowhere for them to stop.

Milfontes

Vila Nova de Milfontes is enchantingly beautiful. The countryside abounds with spring flowers. I walk a sandy track between the village and its port a half-dozen times. The terrain is gentle. A soft meadow treats the senses to reds, yellows, and gently swaying silver-greens. A modest cliff is topped by succulents and other plants that prefer a drier climate. Burnet moths reflect iridescent under the sun's warming rays. Low tide exposes a reef and its tapestry of life. The faintest of sea breezes arrives late in the day, and falls away soon after.

My lodgings here are the shell of a quayside building that is occupied by a man who is presumably otherwise homeless. The abode has no doors or windows, and is missing a front wall: features that contribute to an airy feel. It is like a grander and more substantial version of my own sail shelter home. Perhaps the regular occupant is destitute. Though in a sense he is a rich man. Perhaps it is his clear-headed choice to live here, rather than somewhere more homely but less inspiring.

Azenha do Mar

I am ready for the breeze when it comes the next day, and manage about 10 nm before it once again dies away to nothing. A slight chop fades within the hour and the paddling thereafter is agreeable. Two-hundred metres from the coast a pair of fins briefly break the surface alongside me. The lazy swim action and long body of the animal unmistakably identify it as a blue shark. Likely there are sometimes scraps to be had from the local fishing boats.

Now, when children ask – as they inevitably do – if I have seen any sharks, I can give them the answer they crave. I can also explain that blue sharks kill humans at a rate of less than one fatality per century. Whilst humans kill blue sharks at an estimated rate of 10-20 million per year. Most sharks are caught as bycatch, de-finned and left to die.

Milfontes harbour

I land at Azenha do Mar. The fishing here is at an artisanal scale. All craft are winched from the water up a steep log-lined concrete ramp. Sections of concrete wall link adjacent rocks and afford some limited protection to the ramp. The boats are all near identical: high-sided, twin-engine, and open, and it can be deduced that the fisherman of this coast exploit often short-lived fair weather windows. Our strategies are similar.

The surrounding cliffs form an echoing crucible, and spikes of rock emerge from the sea as stacks. These are favoured nesting sites for white stork. The elegant birds stand tall and tranquil at the summits. Occasionally they alight and glide on their two-metre wingspan. They seem like pterodactyls, and this seems like a Jurassic world.

**

At the cliff top there is a fish restaurant that is doing a roaring trade. Inside is full, but a table comes available outside and a wait for food is of no concern. There is another solo diner, and perhaps a conversation would be nice, but she – like me – is too timid to initiate one. Fate lends a helping hand. Big drops of rain begin to fall and I will clearly soon be drenched if I do not move, and her table is beneath a covered terrace...

We exchange stories. She tells fragments of a life that has included psychotic episodes. I tell her an unlikely tale about windsurfing here from the Arctic, and it is clear that she wants to believe me but cannot quite bring herself to do so. I want her to believe because – although to be cautious is wise – to be cautiously trusting is enriching too. After dinner, when the rain has stopped, I suggest we walk down to the fishing boats so that she can see the board and sail. The path down to the water is dark, and there are no other people. My suggestion had been unfair – but she follows nonetheless – and thanks to her courage is able to confirm my story. This may be a forgettable tale for the reader – and perhaps it was for her – but for me it has significance: It seemed that I had passed on a message that others had passed to me, and that I believe to be true for all humans: that our healthy, uncorrupted nature – our core – can be assumed to be good.

Arrifana and La Tormenta

The Atlantic moves to the rhythm of a new groundswell today. I launch into a fickle breeze which soon fades until there is nothing for the sail to pull against. There is a cost – lost minutes and expended effort – in preparing the board for "paddle mode". And the head-down work of stabilising the sail over the tail of the board is predictably nausea inducing.

As I paddle, the sky behind me fills with cumulonimbus cloud. A storm is brewing. It explodes high into the troposphere, and then spreads, until its ominous shadow has swallowed the entire day. Drumrolls of thunder emanate from within the smothering blanket. On open sea I am a lightning rod, but there is no quick route to land.

With the arrival of a wind chop it becomes too unstable to paddle from a standing position. The board slaps at the agitated sea as I dig at its surface. My knees protest. Occasional rogue gusts of cold air grab at the sail, and since it is tied to the board, a half-capsize results. I switch mode – try to harness those rogue gusts – but now they are nowhere to be found. Each switch is a physical effort, and the awkward focus on knots brings a fresh wave of nausea. The storm – *tormenta* – brings torment. I curse this wretched day.

The wind chop is being generated by surface winds – fed by downdrafts of cold, high altitude air that spread from the centre of the storm. The winds do not carry as far as the associated choppy water propagates. A near simultaneous flash and thunderclap land. The jolt startles me but stiffens resolve. The physical demands of today – 12 nm, the lumpy sea… I confront those with disdain.

By the final headland I have emerged once again into sunshine. A trickle of breeze runs around the promontory. I self-appraise the passage and am happy with my choices. Not all risks can be avoided. Determination to keep moving had reduced the exposure time.

At the harbour the coastguards are waiting for me. "You've caused us a lot of trouble," the English speaker of the pair informs me, with an accusatory tone that seems unnecessary. Though it is probable that I am their man who has been "swept out to sea on a surfboard." The pair become less chastising after I direct them to the website tracking map – which is an increasingly useful tool to demonstrate competence. Nonetheless, the Maritime Police are called, and an hour later are on the scene. A report is filed to the "Sesimbra to Lagos" coastguard. There is also a stern warning that "beach craft" are not allowed to cross the Tagus river at Lisbon. This is interesting to know, though it is unlikely I will be sailing back that way.

The police truck makes its departure up the cliff-side track. I overhear the conversation of onlookers who are curious about the quayside events of the last ninety minutes. A family have returned from a fishing trip, and with their fisherman guide are gutting the catch. The fisherman points in my direction and explains that a kayaker got into difficulties and had to be rescued.

That strikes a nerve. Dead centre. In fairly clear terms I set the record straight. And as quickly as it had arisen, the pulse of indignation subsides.

The fishing family donate some mackerel which I enjoy later – cooked in abundant olive oil, with mash potato from powder – and complemented by a Sagres beer, pastel de nata, and an orange. Delicious.

From here – tomorrow morning – I will make the final dash round Cape Saint Vincent – beyond which lies the south facing Algarve coast.

A stop to take in the moment with Cape Saint Vincent as backdrop

168

Algarve Coast – Portugal Final Days

8-11 May 2018, from log entry

Muito Obrigado Portugal. What a beautiful country: unassuming and quiet people with open and kind hearts; colour, light, wildflowers, clear waters; headlands that resist the pulse of the ocean, beaches that absorb its impact; hidden coves and harbours; and wind!

***

An early morning dash saw me to and round Cape Saint Vincent. The wind doubled in intensity at the following headland – Sagres Point – and there was a strong offshore wind to overcome to reach the town's beach.

From Sagres, another early getaway helped escape the strong winds on the corner and set up a 50 nm total with eventual finish – paddled – on Ilha do Farol. The island is minimally inhabited aside from abundant bird and sea life. It is a perfect spot to spend a last evening enjoying Portugal's gentler, Algarve coastline. The ocean-toughened west coast inhabitants calls this part the Portuguese Mediterranean.

From Ilha do Farol I sailed to Fuzeta – where I had been aiming for the previous evening but had come up short. There, collecting shells for my niece, contacts from Club Naval Fuzeta sailed across, laden with gifts and beers. It was a most touching moment to conclude my Portugal adventure. There have been so many positive experiences from north to south of this country.

Had I not been pushing on to meet brother and family I would have been keen to stay and rest for the afternoon. As it was, I sailed on and crossed the border to Spain.

Today is a day to while-away with family. The type of day that is more fully appreciated when life is recognised as an eyeblink.

Cabo Trafalgar

12 May 2018

Wind is moving air. To understand the wind: study a stream. Watch it bend and flow round obstacles. Observe where it flows fast and where it is more tranquil. Look closely and you will see that at some places it becomes turbulent, or bends back to run seemingly the wrong way.

Within a certain range of incidence, when a wind meets a shoreline – particularly a higher one – it will tend to bend so that it blows roughly parallel to the shore. The sailor who is sailing a coastline will notice this: because most days will be sailed either into a headwind, or with a wind that is coming from behind. As a consequence, rarely will the route sailed be the most direct.

For upwind sailing, think of a switchback path that zigzags up to an otherwise unscalable peak.

For downwind sailing – with the air from behind – whilst in theory a straight down descent is an option, in practice it is still easier and more efficient to add an element of zigzag.

Eventually, I get lucky and am gifted a day with an angled tailwind that is neither too strong nor too light. With relative ease nearly 100 nm are claimed whilst sailing mostly parallel to a low-lying coast. There had been wind and light for more miles, but the pull of a three-digit tally – though tempting – seemed greedy. The board is beached at Cape Trafalgar: a historic site – a boundary of seas – and a wild space for an atmospheric camp.

***

The crow-flies distance achieved that day was a record that would not be bettered. Which is not to say that it was a maximum in terms of distance sailed, or particularly notable in terms of difficulty or effort.

12. Mediterranean Seas and Straits

There is a branch-like bay of the North Atlantic that physically separates Europe from Africa and Asia. The branch is knotted: at times as wide as a sea, and elsewhere narrow enough to be bridged. The branch extends eastward for over 2000 nm, and all but its easternmost tendril coincides with the extent of the Mediterranean Sea.

The Mediterranean Sea itself – as defined by IHO *Limits* (1953) – is subdivided into a Western Basin and an Eastern Basin. The Western Basin "reaches from" and includes the Strait of Gibraltar. The Eastern Basin "reaches to" though does not include the Dardanelles. The two Basins meet between Sicily and Tunisia, where The Mediterranean narrows to a width of about 80 nm.

Both the Western and Eastern Basins are – in places – further subdivided into subsidiary seas and straits.

The Mediterranean Region – a term used within IHO *Limits* (2002 draft) – includes the Mediterranean Sea, its basins and their subdivisions, and also those connected seas and straits that lie further east.

Currents in the Mediterranean Seas are in most places driven by salinity and temperature differences rather than by astronomical tides. There is an overall anticlockwise circulation in both the Eastern and Western Basins. Inshore, currents are typically gentle and more variable in direction.

Approaching Cape Trafalgar lighthouse (far right of shot) and the Mediterranean Sea

Mediterranean Sea
and Mediterranean Region

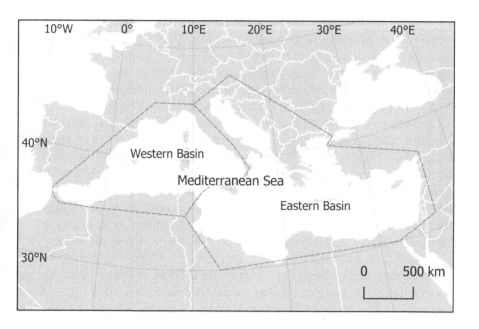

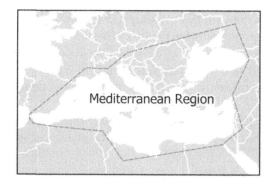

13. Strait of Gibraltar

The Strait of Gibraltar is both a unifying link and a dividing barrier. It is where Sea and Ocean meet; and it is where Europe and Africa are close enough to each know the outline of the other.

Spain and Morocco occupy the Atlantic side of the Strait. On the Mediterranean side – where the Strait is only about 8 nm wide – the British Territory of Gibraltar faces the Spanish autonomous city of Ceuta. The imaginary lines that officially delimit the Strait intersect land at Cape Trafalgar, Cape Espartel, Cape Europa, and the Almina Peninsula.

Long-running disputes relating to the territorial waters and ownership of Gibraltar and Ceuta are unresolved. Britain claims only 3 nm of territorial water for Gibraltar, and argues that this leaves part of the Strait as international waters. This is significant, because under the UN Law of the Sea if any part of a strait is in international waters then vessels may transit the entire strait unimpeded. Many vessels exercise this right, including submarines – which may do so submerged. Additional to a high level of "through traffic", there are continual ship movements *across* the Strait.

Around 6 million years ago the continents of Africa and Europe drifted together and closed the Strait. It then took about 500,000 years for the Mediterranean to evaporate. Rising sea levels eventually caused a great flood that carved the Strait to its present depth of up to 900 metres, and the Mediterranean was restored.

Surface water of the Strait flows inward to the Mediterranean, whilst a deep current goes outward to the Atlantic. Far more water flows in than out, which partially compensates for the loss of water from the Mediterranean by evaporation.

Temperature and salinity differences mean that water in the Strait is highly stratified. The interaction of these deep layers can generate internal waves. The curious banding that can sometimes be observed on a calm sea – alternating glassy and rippled patches – is sometimes a surface expression of internal waves. Satellite pictures frequently and more clearly detect the phenomenon.

Strait of Gibraltar
extent and track

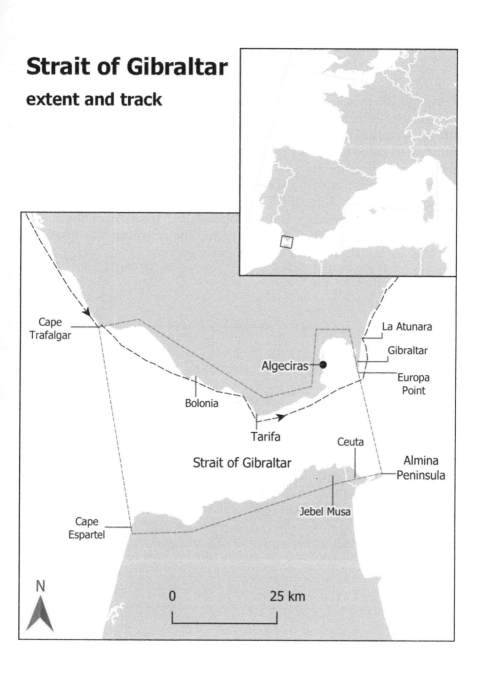

The Strait is of fundamental importance to many migratory bird species and is rich in marine life generally. There are – however – concerns for the resident killer whale population since shipping-activity and pollution impact their ability to hunt and successfully reproduce.

***

In antiquity, the Strait was considered a gateway to an all-encompassing *Oceanus*. The mountains that bound it had either been smashed through or pulled shut. In both versions it is Hercules who is credited with the heavy lifting. In recognition of his efforts, the dominating peaks on each side of the Strait were called the Pillars of Hercules. The European Pillar we now call the Rock of Gibraltar.

Today, criminal activity across the Strait is rife. Drug running is particularly brazen. An established method is to traffic with high-powered RIBs. The gangs patiently wait in international waters until there is an opportunity to deliver their cargo to shore. The deliveries take just a few minutes and law enforcement craft can rarely get close.

A ferry – seen beneath Jebel Musa – crosses the Gibraltar Strait

Conscious Pilots

13 May 2018

From Cabo Trafalgar I head offshore to shortcut a concave indent of coastline, and hopefully find more breeze. A few miles out there is what initially appears to be an old boot, and then – at less distance – a flailing and injured turtle, and then – once alongside – it appears that the animal is healthy. The handsome loggerhead hinges its flippers in a determined, mechanical way: an enthusiastic rather than an elegant swimmer.

I think back to yesterday's sail. There had been a drift net marked by a seemingly endless line of pink buoys: a wall hanging from the surface until who knows what depth. I eventually gave up on an attempt to go round the net and instead forced the net underwater to hurdle it – an option that will not be available to my turtle friend. Increasingly, I am of the opinion that humans dominate the natural world like colonialist rulers. We assume full and exclusive rights over all life and resources, and impossible conditions are imposed upon other species. If we are to become good custodians of our planet there will need to be more equality for nature.

Sea turtles pre-date humans by about 100 million years, but we are in danger of wiping them out. Good luck mate. Good luck avoiding the nets, the boat strikes, and the plastic bags that look like food.

The next encounter of the day is when I am spotted by the spearfishermen occupants of a small and tippy fibreglass boat. They change course and head seaward, and after a few minutes are within hailing distance. The outboard goes quiet and two wetsuited figure stands up and cheer *"¡Ánimos! ¡Tu puedes! ¡Ya te queda poco!"* – Go on! You can do it! There's not far to go now!

"Gracias amigos!" I bellow back across the water. The fisherman must think that they have spotted a migrant attempting to cross from Africa to Europe. We are too far apart for the confusion to be easily resolved, so instead I pump at the sail with renewed enthusiasm to signal that all is well.

I pass the familiar and rather beautiful beach of Bolonia. Lush green hills provide a backdrop and above those is a blue sky crisscrossed by aeroplane vapour trails. Around the next headland is the beach that precedes the town of Tarifa.

For windsurfers, Tarifa needs no introduction. It is famed for strong winds that are accelerated as they funnel through the Strait of Gibraltar. The strongest wind is the Levante – the east wind. The Strait would be impassable with the Levante in full whistle, so I am keen to slip through whilst it draws breath. I make a just quick stop, time enough to say hello to a friend who will soon be a mum.

There is more breeze and the sky is busy with kites when I resume sailing. Entanglement is avoided and the rocky outcrop of Punta Tarifa soon lies to port. This is the most southerly point of mainland Europe. There is also a sense of having truly reached the gateway to the Mediterranean, and of a transition to a new chapter of this journey.

A leant-over cardinal mark indicates a healthy inward-flowing current. Near to shore there are back eddies, but about a kilometre out the conveyor belt becomes settled. Africa appears to be close: colour and detail can easily be discerned. The distance between continents is less than half that which separates England from France. The mountain Jebel Musa stands tall and is the obvious candidate for being Africa's Pillar of Hercules.

The Rock of Gibraltar – the European Pillar, no doubt about that – is 15 nm from here. The industrial port of Algeciras is the gaping inlet that precedes it. There are ships all around. It is unclear where some of them are going. A steadily-expanding oxide-red bow bears down up me. Where is that one going? Will it swing north towards Algeciras? Or maintain its line towards the Atlantic? To the ocean is my guess – and with that expectation I adjust course to port.

A moment later a dorsal fin breaks the water. A dolphin! And the next instant there are more – a dozen more at least – too many to count, and all in close quarters. These are common dolphins: a smaller species than the bottlenoses I usually see. They swim alongside – breaking the surface for air, or power forward to make zigzag dashes across the bow, or swim rotated – for a view straight up as I look straight down through the clear water that lends a turquoise tint to their white flanks.

Mesmerized by the animals, I lose track of time. For 10 or 20 minutes my eyes and attention are not on the ship. Whilst the dolphins surround me it feels safe to trust in them.

As I sail with focus beneath the water my course drifts off to starboard. I have questioned since who was leading. The new heading is easier for me to sail, and marginally faster, and the dolphins might prefer a livelier pace. So perhaps it was me who decided that we should cross the bow of the ship, and head out more towards mid-Strait.

But the ship did not go out to the Atlantic as I had thought it would. It went into the Bay of Algeciras. My original course change would have maintained a collision course rather than avoided one. Did the dolphins know this? Did they choose to engage in order to guide me safely past that ship? Did I follow them, or did they follow me?

I can easily believe that I was guided – cajoled, encouraged and distracted – into following the dolphins. The animals were deliberate with their intervention. And their sonar and local knowledge would perhaps have given them awareness of where the ship was headed. Ultimately, I cannot know who guided who. But I am sure that a goodbye marked the end of our encounter.

Once past the port of Algeciras, and level with the Rock of Gibraltar, when all sense of stress and danger is passed, it is time for me to peel away. A few seconds after doing this all the dolphins are suddenly gone. I am alone again. It is as if they were never there. I feel sad for a moment. And then – from out of nowhere – a single individual leaps from the water with a jump far more extravagant than any seen thus far. Briefly the animal is suspended mid-air, at eye height. It is clearly communication. The splash subsides and the water goes calm again, and I no longer feel alone.

I make land that evening at La Atunara, in the Alboran Sea.

Common dolphins, the same species as those that guided me through the Strait.
This picture borrowed from an encounter in the Black Sea.

14. Alboran Sea

The Alboran Sea lies between the mountain ranges of the "Gibraltar Arc": the Rif mountains of northern Morocco, and the Baetic Cordillera mountains of southern Spain. The Sea has an east-west extension of about 350 km. Average depth is over 1000 metres.

The western limit of the Sea is where it meets the Strait of Gibraltar. In the east, its limit is at an imaginary line between Cabo de Gata in Spain and Cap Fegalo in Algeria, with these capes being separated by about 150 km of open water.

The Sea takes its name from the centrally located small island of Alboran, which itself was named after the Tunisian pirate Al Borani, who used the island as a base. The Isle of Alboran has been in Spanish control since their victory over the Ottoman fleet at the 1540 Battle of Alboran.

Biodiversity in the waters is high, which is partly the result of the Alboran Sea being in a transition zone between Mediterranean and Atlantic. Circulation within the sea is similar to that observed in the Strait of Gibraltar, with incoming surface water and an outpouring at greater depth. An abundance of plankton favours pelagic fish species and of particular commercial importance are sardines, anchovies, swordfish and tuna.

The East Atlantic subpopulation of bluefin tuna migrate into the Mediterranean to spawn. Since the Phoenician era they have been fished by the "Almadraba" method that corrals them into a tight space where they are slaughtered. This was sustainable for centuries, until the value of bluefin soared as a result of demand for sushi in Japan. The fishing fleets boomed and prosperity came to the towns that could benefit from the bluefin migration.

Advances in technology helped to sustain catches for a while, but by 2006 the bluefin tuna population was "close to collapse." Campaign groups such as WWF became vocal on the issue, helping to raise public awareness, and at last the catch limits – that had been in place for years – began to be enforced and adhered to. Assessment a decade later found the East Atlantic bluefin population to be making a slow recovery.

Alboran Sea
extent and track

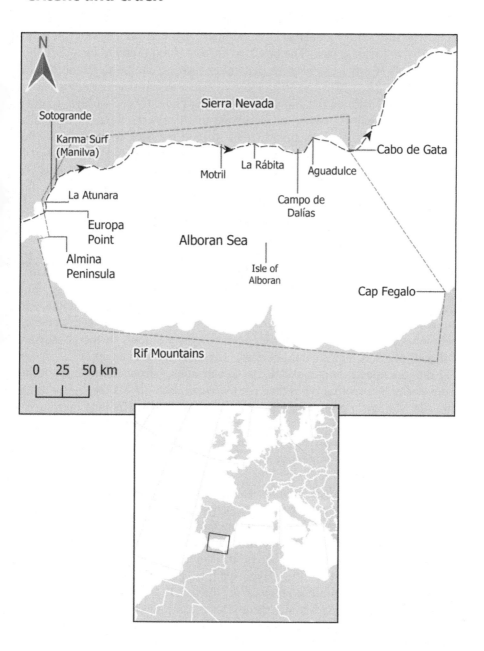

La Atunara

13-21 May 2018

Alongside the Rock of Gibraltar the evening breeze dies away to nothing. A patrol ship with "Aduanas" – Customs – painted on the side observes patiently as I paddle past. The beach to my left is too urban to be a desirable camp location – there is no secluded cover – so I continue to the port at La Atunara.

Landfall is made on the slipway of a fishing club. There is a high security fence and behind it a ribbon of wasteland that keeps the adjacent town at a distance. Paco the security guard wants to send me back to sea because the club is private. I can't stay, he explains. Though apparently I could stay if it were Paco's decision, but it isn't his call to make. I find contact details for the club president and call him – which makes Paco nervous – until the president understands and becomes a little bit proud that I landed at their slipway and wish to sleep next to their fence. And then Paco becomes proud too: because he managed my arrival so expertly.

This is a landmark day to celebrate, so with the gear being monitored by Paco on CCTV screen I take a walk towards the centre of town in search of a meal. There is a sense of this being a place that outsiders do not visit. The centre – if there is one – evades me, and there are very few people about, and no restaurants. Bars, on the other hand, are plentiful: metal rods cover each window of every shoe box house. Some of the windows in the houses are "shops" of a sort, but it would be easier to buy drugs than an apple.

I dine as upmarket as possible: a "kebab house" front-room (only room) conversion. No seating other than a windowsill, but – if it's OK? – I will eat in. The Moroccan proprietor has no problem with that. His next customer – the only other customer – demands alcohol and there is none on the premises. He spits a stream of racist abuse at the kebab shop owner who weathers the tirade impassive like a punchbag, though the blows must crumple him inside.

For different reasons, I could be a target here too: The fair skin, the crocs, the salt-stained drybag rucksack. A privileged tourist. But not a regular tourist. Also the unkempt, unshaven, un-showered, physical appearance of a homeless person. An appearance of minimal value. Perhaps there is also a message that I would be unwise to prod. That is my hope.

I also speculate that the dayglo-yellow Personal Locator Beacon – prominent on the shoulder strap of my rucksack – provides a measure of protection. That theory comes from the natural world: brightly coloured insect and frog species that are not themselves poisonous but that mimic those which are. The PLB indicates that I might not be a tasty meal.

La Atunara port, with the Rock of Gibraltar behind

And if these strategies are not sufficiently compelling there is the ultimate deterrent: my Windows Phone. Truly, no-one wants one of those.

Back at the club, Paco's replacement and some club members have fished some horse mackerel from the pontoon and are gently cooking them over a barbecue. They invite me to join the group. We eat fish, and drink beer through the calm and peaceful early hours.

***

In the morning sunshine I check-over the board and find serious damage. The rubber gasket that helps seal the daggerboard casing has partially detached. That is a recurring issue but this time, rather than an adhesive failure, it is the outer shell of the board that has ripped off. The low-density inner core is fully exposed, spongy, and waterlogged. A professional repair is needed.

A sailboat captain – Pablo – Captain Pablo – who has been keeping in touch sending nautical charts and various other messages of encouragement – reaches out to ask how the passage through the Strait went. After our conversation – and the damage report – he sends a link to the website of a local custom-surfboard business: Karma Surf. I check the website. It explains karma seemingly not as a cynical marketing tool but as a guiding philosophy. I dial the number for Antonio, already sensing that in him I have found a kindred spirit.

Antonio listens and then exclaims "*¡Vete de allí¡*" – Get out of there! – upon hearing that I am stranded at La Atunara. That it is said only half in jest needs no explanation. We agree that I will sail the 7 nm to Sotogrande, and that Antonio will pick up the board from there once I have arrived.

A whisper of onshore breeze makes it an easy sail. I observe the coast in something of a daydream. Inshore of me is a long sweep of sand. Suddenly there is movement. A kilometre or so back, a brace of shiny and black jeep-type vehicles move at great speed along the shoreline. They cover another kilometre of beach and then turn inland and are gone. If that was not a drug pickup, then it was a good decoy act.

La Atunara's sizeable port is behind me now. Fishing would have been a major employer at the town before the collapse of the bluefin tuna population during the 1990s. Since then it has been dragged deeper into an underworld of hashish and tobacco smuggling.

I land at Sotogrande. This is a gated compound urbanization of overly ornate villas. The building style is classy in the way that Donald Trump would approve of. It is a reasonable assumption that much of the wealth here is ill-gotten black money that has been whitened by conversion into material assets. The fortunes of La Atunara and Sotogrande are two sides of the same coin.

Antonio arrives. Between us the gear is loaded ready to be whisked away. The camp gear I keep hold of, ready for a sleeping plan that will come later. Then Antonio swings open the door and says to get in.

***

Karma Surf occupies a plot that is also home to Antonio and partner Maria. Fragrant lemon and loquat ("*nispero*") trees make it a welcome retreat from the busyness of the coastal strip just up the road. Partially hidden by the trees are Karma Houses that provide accommodation for holidaying guests, and in one of them a tired sailor rests up.

A week elapses before Windsurfer *Phantom* is declared fit to continue its voyage. Each day for a few hours Antonio fires up Aussie Gold internet radio and performs his artistry to some classic tunes of the previous decades. The torn underside of the battered hull is rebuilt. Its dented surface is reviewed, repaired and re-faired in its entirely. And finally – when it is perfectly smooth – three fine layers of light-grey epoxy paint are spayed on to leave a hard and water-slippery finish.

I offer payment to Antonio for his labour and costs but it is waved away – though not entirely, because it is left that there is an obligation to make a return visit when the journey is done. If I know Antonio, then it is an obligation without time limit. And if I know myself, then it is a visit that will be made.

Antonio and María have an open door policy

The Sea of Polythene

22-28 May 2018

The flood of experiences continues. A week of scenery passes: Runs of 15, 18, 25, 39, 20, 35 and 57 nautical miles.

In the shadow of the Sierra Nevada mountain range the winds had been elusive and ephemeral. Beyond – approaching and rounding Cabo de Gata – the board had streaked in zigzags across a deep blue strewn with whitecaps. Its master had squinted from the glare; been invigorated by the drenchings of spray; revelled in the freedom and recklessness of the charge.

The sea here is a different animal to the Atlantic proper. The thumping pulse of ocean crossing swells is absent. Tides are so small as to go unnoticed. The riches of an intertidal zone are missing, and from my perspective are missed.

A shocking addition is the plastic pollution. I notice it on the calmer days. A translucent shape in the water is more likely plastic than living or natural. And there are slicks of pollution, observed nearer to settlements – which occupy where rivers large or small meet the sea. Their waterways outpour as streams of plastic, that once in the sea broaden over tens of kilometres until they become indistinguishable from the sea itself. Having sailed through a slick, and afterwards back into a blue that is once again pristine, I ask myself if it had been a one-off: an outlier not representative of the general state of Spanish Mediterranean waters? And I begin to believe that. And then I find another slick and am once again appalled.

A major local contributor of plastic are the polythene greenhouses of the Almeria region. Their abundance on the terraced lower slopes of the Sierra can be observed from the sea, but a satellite image is more helpful to appreciate their near total coverage of the Campo de Dalías coastal plain. The Sea of Polythene allows for the year round cultivation that provides much of Europe's fresh produce, and the reflective properties of the white plastic is a possible explanation for the average temperature in the region to have bucked trends and actually dropped in recent decades.

On land I meet kind people. The towns within the greenhouse belt are not prosperous but have tight and caring communities. The people I meet wish to shield me from petty thieves or other threats they perceive I may be vulnerable to.

An example is at La Rábita, where the reincarnation of Bob Marley helped move the board to a safer location, and then a caring family offered shelter and soothing drops for bloodshot eyes. And next morning grandad accompanied us back to the steeply shelved beach, and the youngest generation swam the board out beyond the dumping shorebreak, whilst I did the same with the sail, so that with their help a complicated getaway was made easy.

Another example is at Motril, where I ended up sharing a security caravan with José – I think that was the name. He was another Antonio really – another guru.

And there are more of you who once again I cannot adequately mention or thank.

A side-on view of polythene greenhouses in the Almeria region

15. Mediterranean Sea Proper – Part One

The Mediterranean Sea was reached when Cabo Trafalgar was passed. But this part of the Western Basin – between Cabo de Gata and Cape Sant Antoni – is the first to be sailed that is not also within the bounds of a more specific IHO subdivision.

Cabo Tiñoso, near to Cartagena

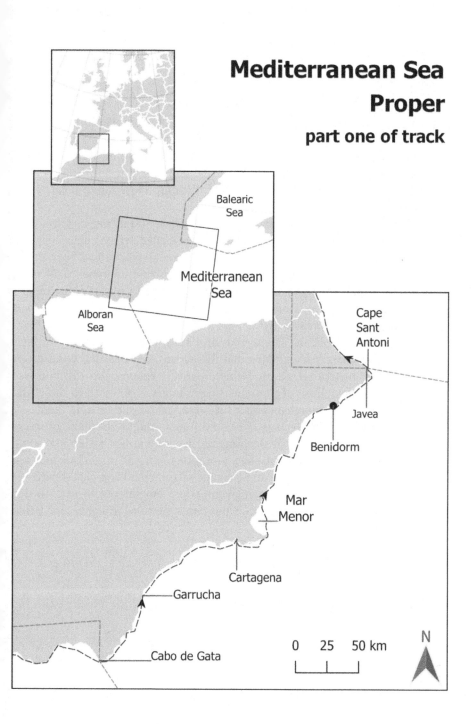

Mediterranean Sea
Proper
part one of track

Balearic
Sea

Mediterranean
Sea

Alboran
Sea

Cape
Sant
Antoni

Javea

Benidorm

Mar
Menor

Cartagena

Garrucha

Cabo de Gata

0   25   50 km

N

Cartagena

29 May 2018

Some mornings the sea begins calm as a lake. I sail or paddle barefoot, perhaps with drysuit peeled down to the waist. The warming rays are heavenly.

Normally a breeze builds – and the sailing may become wet and lively later on. Fatigue is a companion towards the end of every sail. The decision about the last chunk of miles is the most difficult. How far to push? How long until sunset? How accessible is land?

Conditions become difficult towards the end of a 50 nm run to Cartagena. There is a good planing wind, and sizeable waves that are so closely-packed that there is barely room between them to squeeze a gybe. I had been dimly aware of a lone yacht attempting the same downwind approach, and upon reaching the natural harbour entrance sit for a while to observe the ketch's awkward labour. She rolls and yaws so violently that the imagined chaos below decks sounds as real as the wind.

The yacht club folk at Cartagena are kind and welcoming to their unannounced visitor. José explains that the ocean floor near the coast drops away to 4000 metres of depth, which partly explains the difficult sea conditions. The upwelling of nutrients brings marine life close to the cliffs. Whales are visitors – though a calmer sea would be helpful to sight them.

The following day the wind is light, and it is a struggle to make progress against the diminished but still sloshing sea. Board and water slap like sumo wrestlers, quashing momentum. The vibrations carry to my skull and are unpleasant – almost painful – like the scrape of fingernails on chalkboard.

But progress is being made, and eventually I am far out to sea. In this world the shearwaters glide between the peaks and the troughs, and I find that I am happy after all.

Mar Menor

30 May – 1 June 2018

The Mar Menor – translation: the Little Sea – is a saltwater lagoon that is annexed from the Mediterranean by La Manga "The Strip" – a 20 km long sandbar-type divide. I sail on its Mediterranean flank, past towering hotels that look down upon the lighthouse at Cabo de Palos, and come ashore next to Puerto San Pedro at the northern end of the strip – where development has been more restrained. I ascend a hump of sand – hoping for a glimpse of the Little Sea – but the ridge is a false one. Instead, there is a view of saltmarsh, and flamingos whose shocking-pink flashes are reflected double on the mirror-calm water.

My arrival is expected, and has been planned for. Chemi and friends from the local Mar Menor windsurfing community are soon on location. I am treated as guest of honour. David from Jaws Windsurf Shop readies me for summer with a long sleeved lycra, new boardshorts and replacement sunglasses. And we eat. Boy, do we eat!

Chemi's group of local enthusiasts are buoyant – quite literally! – happy and upbeat. They are rightly proud of their beloved Mar Menor. Most of them learned to windsurf on the protected water and most would still rather windsurf there than on the waves of the open sea.

So I sense their pain – almost their shame – when they acknowledge that the Mar Menor habitat is out of balance. I hear how in 2016 agricultural pollution contributed to the usually clear waters becoming a "green soup". Toxic algae blooms are bad for tourism, so there was an outcry and a regulatory response of sorts. My hosts talk with optimism about the future, though I sense their lack of conviction that the problem will not repeat.

Nearby, Frank and family put me up for two days. That gives swollen, tendinitis-riddled fingers a break from the constant pull-pull-pull of downwind sailing; and rests eyes that are reddened from salt and glare. Mountain bike rides on the dry and dusty tracks make for valued shared experiences. The sun shines incessantly. Frank is easy-going: everything is "Fine! Fine!" On the second day we sail together and add a few gentle miles to the tally, and that is "Fine! Fine!" too.

***

In 2019 and 2021 the Mar Menor again suffered from devastating eutrophication, with mass suffocation of marine life on both occasions.

The Other Nick

5 June 2018

I first met Nick when he was a teenager. The Jones family used to holiday at Minorca Sailing where I worked as a windsurf instructor. Anne – Nick's mother – was a Clinical Psychologist, and she considered that I had the potential to be one too. That seemed to be where my degree should take me. For a while it was a path I followed, though I was too unresolved myself for it to be a sensible one at that time.

The family and I fell out of touch, though about 10 years ago I did hear that Anne had died of cancer. To mark her passing I waited for a day when Fornells Bay was as calm as the one when we had sat on our boards – silent and motionless – to watch an Osprey fish. Special times together often do not require words. On this occasion there was no Osprey fishing, just a posey of wildflowers floating on the water's surface as I paddled away.

***

The message from Nick Jones is a welcome surprise. It arrives via the expedition website after he registers as a Local Contact. He says that he is based in Javea – just south of Valencia – and that I am welcome to stop and stay at his flat. Nick also mentions that he sometimes works with the windsurf coach Jem Hall. That makes Jem a mutual friend. "Small world!" I observe in my reply that confirms it would be great to link up.

***

I sail past Benidorm – staying well offshore of that mass of high-rise development – and am then pleasantly surprised by a section of wild cliff. Nature was wise to fortify parts of the coast. A natural spring exits from the cliff face as a waterfall: a rare and precious wonder in these parts. Where it cascades there is an oasis of green on the otherwise barren rock.

There is no easy stopping without a major detour, so it becomes a full day afloat. My needs are basic: food and warmth. It is difficult to put on the drysuit at sea, but after doing so I am warm, snug and content. A break to eat a generously filled *bocata* restores some energy. It tastes so good that my mouth drools at its memory. Then comes more developed coastline. Then more cliff. Until a corner is turned: Cap de la Nau. The headland's name is in Valencian Catalan rather than Spanish. That is evidence of my progress and perhaps of Spain's too. Javea – Xàbia – is just a few miles away now.

I am a little nervous waiting for Nick. Not about how we will get on, that will surely be fine. But about whether I will recognise him – because it has been a long time.

It is a normal worry, and – as it turns out – not misplaced, because it is difficult to match this Nick to the younger and gawkier one I had known previously. He projects solidity now. This other Nick's voice is calm and assured, and his accent more northern than home counties. What a change. "How long has it been?" I ask, though no reply is forthcoming.

The windsurf gear can stay at the Club Náutico, so with the efficient teamwork of people who have done this before we manoeuvre board and sail to the indicated hangar. We are in sync moving the gear, but conversation is trickier. "How's Simon" I venture, but it is as if the question travels right through him. We gently lay the sail on some parked up Optimist dinghies. "I heard from Nick, about Anne." Silence. There is a tension building between us.

We shut the doors to the hangar and head over to where the barrel waits next to the water. I search Nick's face and fake a smile of recognition. He takes a step back. I recognise him even less than before. This other Nick looks at me: makes direct eye contact with the unkempt lunatic I have become. "Mate, I don't know you," he says. The information registers. The situation now makes sense. This really is another Nick Jones.

"Mate, that's a huge relief," I say, as the tension drains away. My smile is now genuine, and at last it is returned.

Photo: Nick Jones

16. Balearic Sea

The boundary of the Balearic Sea can be imagined as a net fastened to the Spanish mainland with the Balearic Islands as its catch. The net's attachment points are at Cape Sant Antoni in the Valencian region, and at Cape Sant Sebastià in Catalunya.

The Balearic Sea mainland coast is a gradual arc. The large bay that is formed is referred to as the Gulf of Valencia.

Much of this coastline has been developed. Tourism is a major economic driver, but there is also heavy industry, particularly around the major port cities – most notably Barcelona and Valencia.

The coastline of the islands has received more effective protection from overdevelopment. Ferries operate between them and the mainland. The island of Ibiza lies 90 km from the mainland. Menorca – 200 km offshore – is the most distant island. Stone monuments on the islands indicate early human settlement; and throughout history the ascendant powers of the Mediterranean region have looted, plundered, occupied or enslaved the islands and their residents.

The Northern Current flows down the mainland coast and an eastward-flowing Balearic Current travels across the north of the islands. Beyond the continental shelf – where the currents are more significant – the water depth is mostly between 1500 and 2000 metres.

Bluefin tuna spawn in the Balearic Sea region, and sightings of Fin and Sperm whales are sufficiently regular to assume that they are habitual visitors. Emblematic seabirds include the Balearic shearwater and Audouin's gull; and the mainland's coastal wetlands are notable for large gatherings – flamboyances – of flamingos.

Balearic Sea

extent and track

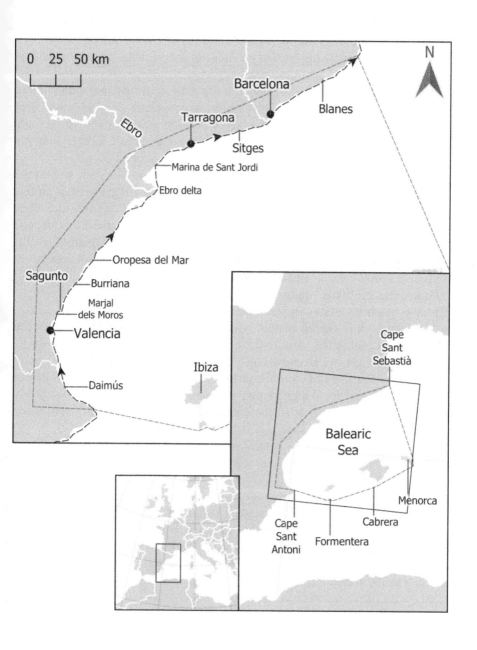

194

The Alien and the Astronomer

7-8 June 2018

My reliance upon *Puerto Deportivos*[23] since entering the Mediterranean conflicts me. On the one hand they are safe and convenient places to stop. On the other hand, they are segregated enclaves of wealth and privilege.

I know it is not that simple: that privilege is inescapable, and that wealth is not evil.

To an extent, the millions spent on floating caravans and rather more beautiful sailboats do drip down through an ecosystem of livelihoods. But nonetheless, the *Puertos Deportivos* serve existing wealth rather than society in any broader sense. In fact, their semi-public nature is just another example of the already rich taking a disproportionately large slice of the pie.

Those are my thoughts as the sun sets in a particularly mundane way at the Puerto Deportivo de Valencia. There is a bar – that I guess is a club – because there is a line of smartly-dressed would be patrons outside. They queue in anticipation of a ticket on a loop of ribbon. On the bar's outside premises the ticket wearers clamour for position to frame themselves for selfies against the flop-of-a-sunset backdrop. Only those who almost never witness a sunset would consider this one to be worthy of note.

I guess that all life is strange, but city life is truly bizarre.

I have nowhere to stay in Valencia. The board is in the *Puerto Deportivo* but access to it is barred at this hour, and I am told that sleeping in the compound is prohibited, despite there being acres of concreted empty space. "Can I at least get my sleeping bag?" I ask security, and that begins a chain of dialogues that ascends the hierarchy until port control – who had earlier witnessed my sail in – suggest that I sleep at their observation tower. My penthouse view is the best of the entire port – and once again I will sleep well tonight, as another of the privileged.

It will be a relief to sail away tomorrow. It will not make me free – I do not believe in free will – but it will restore a sense of liberation. After a few hours in a city I feel caged.

At sea I am often alone. Truly alone if I believe that the rescue beacon on my back is faulty – which of course it could be. I am a dot on the horizon that no-one would notice. With this isolation comes an understanding that actions have consequences; that "decisions made" will return me to land or drown me. It is the availability of – the dicing with – real consequence that brings a sense of being free.

---

[23] *Puerto Deportivo* ("sports port") is a dynamic term for what is in effect a marina.

***

My getaway is delayed. First there is a press call. I am getting better at these as I focus on the why. The why is the message. The message is that our planet is suffering and we need to put it first. This press call, it turns out, is a complete waste of time as there are a group of women on a boat about to embark on the "Ibiza Challenge" – a company-sponsored jolly where they sail a yacht to nearby Ibiza – and predictably the press are more enchanted by their made-up faces than by mine. Does that sound bitter? It is weariness, frustration, hope at a low ebb. The Ibiza Challenge – brand new and shiny-white in every way – is another cog in the machine of the insatiable economic system that is breaking our planet. I am tired of Valencia. It is time to leave.

***

The open water – when the plastic slicks can be avoided – is an antidote to despair. On this coast I have met several sunfish. They sunbathe on the surface and usually the first that is seen of them is a flopped over dorsal fin protruding from the water. For a moment the fin could be of a shark: perhaps injured, or drunk. Close up they appear to be missing a tail – but that is their natural form. Give them a nudge and the "casualty" swims away, fully alive and healthy after all. The sunfish I meet are all less than a metre in length, but they can grow to be bigger than any other bony fish.

A sunfish soaks up the warming rays

Just short of the industrial port of Sagunto there are a few kilometres of undeveloped coastline. Visible from the sea is a shingle bank topped by some spiky vegetation. Five-hundred metres offshore is a lone kayaker whose paddle strokes appear uncertain like the movements of the sunfish. I sail close-by to be friendly, and meet Amadeo. He is building experience and confidence to – another day – paddle round the moles of the port that block progress north. He is full of curiosity for my knowledge of the sea and also keen that we land to see over the shingle bank, to observe the wetlands and bird life on its inland side.

The Marjal dels Moros is indeed a lovely spot with shy red-legged stilts, dive-bombing little terns and many other species with names that for me never stick. We are scopeless, which Amadeo apologies for, though I do not understand why until invited back to his house for some food and rest. Here I learn that Amadeo is an astronomer and asteroid hunter. He is a man who does big scopes. Amadeo does not brag about his asteroid finds, but Google reports that he has several.

I like Amadeo. He has a curiosity with which I identify. Sometimes people think that I journey because in my life there is something that is missing. I am wished luck to find what I am searching for. But it is not that. My curiosity is like Amadeo's. It is for the joy of what might be found.

After some food I sail back to the Marjal. From the sea there is a glorious sunset of technicolour clouds that will never be repeated. I sail into the stiff headwind until the sun disappears. It will be a peaceful night tonight upon the shingle bank.

A red-legged stilt flies over the Marjal

Delta del Ebro

12-13 June 2018

The signs are there as I near the corner. The high wispy clouds. The occasional random gusts that chase away offshore. They pose no threat whilst I sail alongside the endless beach.

Before setting out I had scanned the forecast. It told of wind on the way: this evening maybe, most likely tomorrow. Today seems fine. A good day to get past the unknowns of the Delta, according to that casual glance.

I should have given the Ebro more respect. Of the rivers that empty into the Mediterranean Basin only the Nile is longer. The Ebro's source is in the mountains of Cantabria, whose snow-capped peaks I had admired whilst sailing Spain's Biscay Coast last year. The Ebro's plains are flanked by mountains that feed the river and funnel the wind.

The delta of the Ebro is an expanse where sediment from the river has created land. The estuary now extends far to seaward like a chevron tacked onto a smoother curve of coastline. Erosion has cut in behind the delta to leave an arm each side. To my left is the open water side of an arm: the

The beach on the south side of the Delta

endless beach.

For 15 nm this fringe of sand is my companion. Occasionally I roll in with the waves for an explore of the shoreline and a better view of what lies behind.

To be found are multiple realities that trigger conflicting emotions. Observed is a natural world: colonising vegetation, long views over the drying flats, distant flamingos standing tall as rightful custodians of ancestral grounds. Something perfect and in balance.

Simultaneously, the converse seems true. This is an ecosystem which is a sink for plastic. Its sun-shattered fragments have become part of the substrate. There is a scum of microplastic at the margin of the shallow pool from which the flamingos filter for crustaceans.

At each stop I inspect the scene. The macro plastic objects – fishing crates, bottles, buoys, laundry baskets, sandals – are half-buried like sculptures in the sand. On the inside of the arm are smaller items; and plastic fragments ever smaller and ever more numerous. In a handful of sand are colours that belong in a bucket of Lego, rather than on a beach.

**

The wind freshens some more as the estuary is approached. Clouds in the sky mobilise. I plane at full speed "down the line" – surfing – on small waves, in water just deep enough to keep the fin from grounding. Rarely does it get more magical. There are even fish in the waves: bass – that scatter in response to the threat from above.

Now the coastline slowly bends to the north. This is the corner. The angle to be sailed becomes tighter. I press the daggerboard down to set the board in upwind mode. A course parallel to the shore is no longer possible. The near shore bends away further, until it is gone. The manoeuvring sky is an ambush in the making. The cumulous clouds scatter, as the fish had done earlier.

The water is now estuarine – brown and muddy – and the wind has become strong. More downhaul makes the top part of the sail catch less wind. More outhaul leaves the lower part flatter and less powerful.

The water is shallow, and the chop correspondingly vicious. The current sweeps me further out. I am no longer sure where the nearest land is. The delta is so low that the distinction between land and water is blurred from sea level. This expanse is almost habitable and almost navigable, but in a practical sense it is neither. Shallow water forces me further from safety. The wind ratchets up. I now understand that this is not a typical – to be expected – local wind effect. It is the arrival of something big.

The board crashes into densely packed chop. Were it not for the river and its outflowing water then I would tack: get back in towards the delta. But it is too early – the angle would be wrong – even the tip of the delta would evade me now. I shall continue – cross the estuary first – then tack and make for the land that cannot be seen but that must lie beyond it.

The clouds fuse. They expand until a single mass dominates the entirety of the sky like an apocalyptic wave. The sight is at once beautiful and frightening. Strengthening gusts threaten to dump the sail on top of me. I tension it fully – maximum wind setting – battle mode – for the fight to reach land.

There is deeper water beneath me now. The chop – and how it is building into waves – confirms the ferocity of the wind. My hopes of reaching the delta are gone. I cannot tack in this wind and sea. A fall would be guaranteed. And having fallen it would be near impossible to resume sailing. After a few failed attempts exhaustion would begin to set in. Once exhausted it would be game over. In a few hours I would be in a monstrous sea far beyond the delta. Avalanche after avalanche of white water would roll the board throughout the night. A rescue might come – but when? It is certainly conceivable that I would not be alive come the morning.

Any breakage would be game over too. The mast is already flexed double by the downhaul load. The daggerboard creaks as it re-engages with unforgiving water after briefly gasping at air.

To the north of the delta, there is land visible ahead. It is not the shoreline – that lies beneath the horizon – rather it is the mountains that rise from beyond. The distant peaks offer a route to land that requires no tacks. I must fight the gale towards them. The tip of the delta from where I have lost contact is perhaps 3 nm away. That leaves about 8 nm ($\approx$15 km) to reach the land beneath the mountains. Hope is distant – in every respect.

I have screwed up. That pisses me off. It is gutting that having negotiated the entirety of Europe's Atlantic coastline my undoing is happening here: in the oversized pond that is the Mediterranean. All that good judgement, now without value. It was such an easy day, yet today is where it all goes wrong.

Fear is sensed near. Its closeness is motivating and soon my wallowing is done. New strength is found. More downhaul and outhaul are hauled on until both are taut as bowstrings. The mast curve is concerningly extreme. *Please mast, hold on for this one.* The sail is almost flat – just a few centimetres of belly. The trailing edge is loose like a flag, and it flogs like one as the gusts pass over it.

Maximum exposure comes midway between delta and mainland. I have never sailed a Raceboard in such wind. Much less so when far from land in an offshore gale. The chop has grown into close packed waves. The nose of the board smashes into them – sometimes completely through – and the collisions bring us to a near standstill. Despite the excess of power the board speed is much slower than in less brutal conditions.

It seems that the wind cannot pick up any more, but then it does. The gusts are seen coming from afar as tumbling balls of spray. The spray balls travel horizontally over the surface. From experience I estimate the wind to be in excess of 40 knots. Severe Gale force 9 according to the Beaufort Scale. A spray ball races towards me. Here comes the confirmation that I have fucked up. Gusts like these flatten windsurfers. The board will be picked up and flipped. This is game over.

The spray ball hits. I ease the sail. The wind tears at the cloth but cannot pull it from its carbon fibre skeleton. The leech screams: a revving fibrillation. The drag leaves us stationary. But in that moment the remarkable thing is that the board is not lifted and does not flip. It does not suffer the fate of a normal windsurfer. Instead it responds with the dignity of a seaworthy yacht. The weight on the bow can rarely be considered an asset, but today it may be considered a lifesaver. We come out of the other side of the gust. Windsurfer *Phantom* has delivered a message: We can nose into this for a few hours more. I'll get you to land.

Perhaps there is a lesson there, for the gloom I sometimes feel: Though it seems that all is lost we should continue to give it our all. Because we may be wrong – it may not be game over just yet.

Upon reaching land I am euphoric, wide eyed, almost deranged. A yachtsman named Alan sees me come in and is quick to offer a berth. The emotional stress and physical effort of this sail has been exceptional. The next day I suffer a migraine – a sure sign that mind and body need a time-out. For 36 hours the wind blows at 40 to 50 knots. I listen – from Alan's boat – as the wind howls through the shrouds.

Nerves that have a name

From my earliest memories to the most recent

This section is like a footnote. It has a link to Menorca and therefore also to the Balearic Sea. I include it because it might help others to recognise social anxiety – either in themselves, or in someone they know. Once social anxiety is understood it does less harm. In some contexts at least, it might be cured.

I was living my fourth decade before a diagnosis was sprung upon me. It made sense, but still came as a surprise. And I was dubious, as I had never known another me, and I regarded the acceptance of a clinical explanation as too easy and therefore as something to be guarded against.

However, from primary school age through to adolescence I was unable to prevent heavy blushing when the focus of attention or criticism. It was almost inevitable that tears would well, and the humiliation of crying made tears all the more probable. And as a young adult I had great difficulty initiating telephone calls other than with closest family. And I taught English for a while, but the anticipatory nerves led me to climb the walls and never lessened over time. These are examples from a much longer list.

I match the diagnosis in that my reactions to social situations are exaggerated and result in distress and avoidance. Not so much distress now, in fact. And sometimes I think that the avoidance is dealt with. Until – for example – yesterday, when I couldn't face a social Zoom call with friends and acquaintances, so made up an excuse not to join.

The psychologist put a name to my social anxiety. The day following our chat I went for a surf and for the first time observed my own thinking with real clarity. I wrote an account of that awakening. After reading it again there are parts that make me cringe. Or at least it seemed that way until a moment ago – before the re-read words came to settle.

Here is that account. It is nothing revelatory:

Menorca, 5 July 2016

I surf very infrequently now. My favourite location on the north coast has become popular and is always busy. Up until today I haven't properly questioned why I surf so little now. I just assumed that I don't like to surf when it is crowded. End of story. What else is there to know?

Today I am surfing on the south coast. The waves are really poor. There are only a couple of other surfers in, and there is lots of space. No competition for waves.

Conditions are so bad they are boring. I decide to finish the session and to get out of the water. But I don't. I change my mind because I would have to walk past a group of guys on the beach. I know the guys – they are windsurfers and surfers who I don't know well but know too well to not know. The important thing is that I can't just walk past them because that would be rude or odd. I would have to say a few words at least. I don't want to do that. Don't like that. So I stay in the water in the boring conditions.

But then I make a connection. I see that I have stayed in the water because of social anxiety. Staying in the water is avoidance of an anxiety provoking social situation. I see how ridiculous that is.

That helps me see then bigger picture. I surf infrequently now because of social anxiety. The problem is not busy waves. The problem is that I have some ridiculous thoughts that are not challenged.

This now seems very obvious, but at the time it is a completely new insight.

I stay in the water to clarify this thinking. I feel a new calm: that I am in control again. I can decide to walk past those people. I can decide to properly analyse and override the ridiculous thoughts that stop me doing the things I want to do. I can surf when the waves are sufficiently decent that others are surfing too.

And in a group of surfers I don't have to position myself a distance away from the group, where the waves are bad. I can be amongst the pack – who are all faces I recognise. Say a few words maybe. Not be anxious. Just, be.

And with this recognition I can recognise other parts of my life that I can change too.

The waves are still bad, but I have a conversation with one of the other surfers in the water. It isn't easy to say hello and start talking. But it gets easier. My anxiety recedes. The conversation is pleasant.

I catch a wave in – all the way this time – to the beach.

***

Maybe the account was too rose-tinted, or comes too loaded with assumptions that we should strive to change.

There are aspects of life that are fundamental to getting by and being functional. For example being able to make a phone call, or converse – even minimally – in a group of more than two, or state a musical preference. It really helps to tick those boxes. But there are other aspects of life that are more akin to optional extras. For me I would include in that category dancing or singing in public. Although I conceivably could overcome my phobic aversion to doing those things, there is no need to. The potential enjoyment I can foresee is so far outweighed by the cost of participation that I'll happily live without. To a degree, it can be better to just accept who we are, and to target our limited supply of effort more strategically.

In part, I have battled my way through social anxiety. Some aspects have faded over the decades – to the extent that sometimes I may lose sight that it is there, though experience tells me that it may be back. Importantly, I am now gentler with myself. I do not regret that recognition came late, but it would have been helpful had it come earlier.

Thank goodness that's over. Back to the windsurfing.

A moment of self-reflection, and the camera that took the pictures for this book

Tarragona, Sitges, Blanes

14-27 June 2018, from log entries

Tarragona

The last puffs of the now spent gale provide for a few miles of intermittent planing. They push me from Sant Jordi to a place of no wind.

A confused sea rebounds off the cliff. Familiar discomfort by now. More unnerving is a pilot boat from the port of Tarragona. It stands-off; with its tall bow locked upon my position – which is presumably a deliberate message for me to keep away. Without wind the port is most definitely a problem obstacle.

A first attempt to cross the entrance is aborted. A puff of breeze – and better timing between ships – helps for the next try. With that I reach the mole: 3 nm of giant concrete blocks that reflect the waves as if a chaotic sea were their design brief. A marathon pumping effort gets me past this protector of the industrial port. Darkness is falling as I near where the mole attaches to land. There is a yacht harbour adhered to its outer skin at this position. A mole on a mole. I take my chances in there and find a friendly Club Nàutic.

Sitges

A pleasant following wind gradually falls away to a trickle. Today my target destination is clear. I work hard to reach it by continually rowing the sail through the air. The fickle breeze holds for another six hours, sufficient to reach Sitges. My fingers are now inflamed and fat like Menorcan sausages. Fortunately, on the beach when I land are my two favourite physiotherapists: Rita – who is like family – and Bià – who I hope will one day be a windsurf expedition buddy if I still have the miles in me.

Bià's partner turns up later. Her family's apartment is where we are staying for this pre-planned weekend break. It also happens to be Gay Pride week in Sitges. There are some curious outfits on show.

On Saturday, Bià spends several hours restoring my back to full movement and wonderful comfort. The expert tune-up is long overdue. After some work on the hands I am also good for picking up beer. The seemingly permanent orangutang hook of my fingers is helpful for that.

On Sunday, Bià and I walk the gear to the friendly Club Nàutic de Sitges, from where it will be easier to make a departure tomorrow.

Suddenly we find ourselves in the middle of the Gay Pride carnival crowd. The only room for the board is above our heads on hoisted arms. All hands on deck. The current of bands, butt cheeks and noise sweeps us down the street. And then we emerge – wide-eyed and shellshocked – from this most surreal of squalls.

Blanes

For its proximity to and ties with Menorca, this part of coastline is like a homecoming. And for all that lies ahead, it is like a departure. Existing friends are met, and new ones are made on the hops to and beyond Barcelona. The sun shines. The water is beautifully blue. Though sadly there is much plastic to contemplate.

Approaching Blanes there are Raceboards on the water. We are a small and friendly community and some local sailors have already been in touch. There is a World Championship event starting soon, and organiser Luis persuades me to stay for a few days and perhaps take part. As the competitors arrive, I explain a hundred times over how the foam blocks on the back of my board are used to balance the sail when paddling. It is a genuine pleasure to share this time, and I am grateful to have been persuaded to stay.

With access to tools and materials there is also an opportunity to beef up the daggerboard. I drill its core and drive a half dozen fibreglass stakes through to traverse the cracked part. The result is not pretty, but it will certainly prevent the daggerboard folding.

I race on day one, though not as a genuine competitor. The committee then tell me to clear off – with every justification and touchingly good manners. On day two, as the competitors ready for their start, I sail away to what might count as a chorus of cheers. It is in any case enough to bring a lump to my throat. Friendships have been forged at this event. The important personal lesson here is to have time for people.

17. Mediterranean Sea Proper – Part Two

This part of the Western Basin – between Cape Sant Sebastià in Spain and the Ligurian coast of Italy – is outwith the bounds of a more specific IHO subdivision.

Cap Canaille sea cliffs

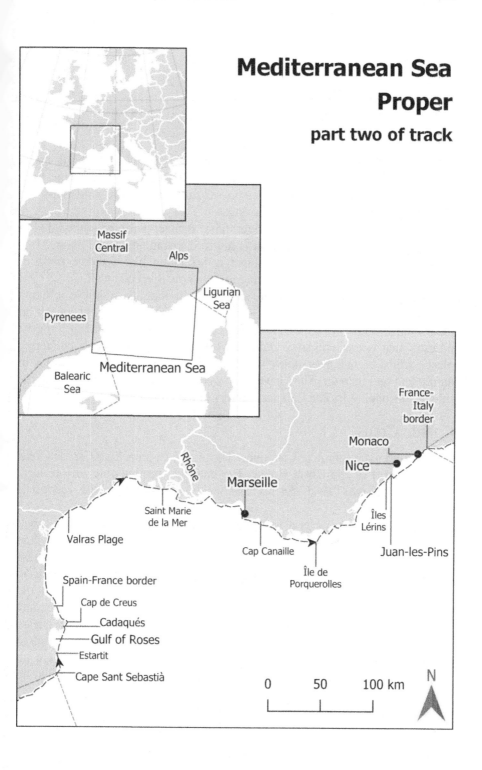

Mediterranean Sea Proper
part two of track

Massif Central
Alps
Ligurian Sea
Pyrenees
Mediterranean Sea
Balearic Sea
France-Italy border
Monaco
Nice
Rhône
Marseille
Saint Marie de la Mer
Îles Lérins
Valras Plage
Cap Canaille
Juan-les-Pins
Spain-France border
Île de Porquerolles
Cap de Creus
Cadaqués
Gulf of Roses
Estartit
Cape Sant Sebastià

0   50   100 km

N

Costa Brava

27-29 June 2018

Estartit

The Costa Brava begins at Blanes and runs all the way to the border with France. The outcrops to the north of the Gulf of Roses are a welcome find: much less exploited than the preceding Costas: where the wild parts are already small, under siege, and receding.

Most natural space that we might have contact with is not wild, but managed: curated, manicured. That is not to disparage managed nature. It is simply an observation that our planet is becoming like a theme park, or captive, or enslaved. It is difficult to envisage how that ends well.

In Alberto and Nuría I sense the stare of wild animals caught in a theme park. Alberto is a "marinero" at Estartit marina. The couple put me up on their sofa. In their work they suffer the contradictions of servicing a tourist industry that is too intensive. Outside work they kayak the coast collecting plastic whilst knowing that more will come tomorrow. They are connected to nature and feel its pain. They have open eyes, and would understand that the title of this book – In The Balance – refers to the natural world.

Cap de Creus

I land and overnight near Cadaqués. This area – approaching Cap de Creus – is the jewel of the Costa Brava. The coastline reminds me of the north coast of Menorca. "Real" Menorcans would think their island version is better, of course.

My selected campsite is a tranquil pebble beach outside the main town. Nearby, a family take an evening dip in the mirror flat sea, but other than that there is silence. It is perfect until a policeman turns up to remonstrate that I must move on. That does frustrate me. I would be happy to move 50 metres here or there, but cannot just disappear. It is a disappointment that the Spanish stage of this journey ends with an argument. The policeman threatens reinforcements and I invite him to go ahead. I offer him a coffee whilst we wait, which enrages him even more since he sees not a gas stove but a fire, and those are not allowed either. The reinforcements were an empty threat. The policeman loiters for a while; presumably realises that he has picked an unwinnable battle; and a while later is gone.

These are days that begin windless. In the morning I hear from and meet Lander from Bilboa, who is holidaying here with his family and has hunted me down by tracker. The policeman episode is already water under the bridge. Nonetheless, it is still nice to see friendly faces.

Later in the day, after rounding Cap de Creus – mainland Spain's most easterly point – I break away from the coast in a breeze that is correct and brisk. There is a perfect sailing wind to pass the Pyrenees in a single bite. A moody sky above the mountains triggers memories of Norway. An hour later, the foothills are already receding. The terrain becomes flat like Denmark. I finish the day deep into France, with the peaks now low and distant.

Tired of sailing with wet shorts, I tried a few hours without!

The South of France

30 June – 7 July 2018

Low land means clean wind and easy progress. The Tramontane – a north wind that blows from between the Pyrenees and Massif Central – is resting. And the Mistral – a northwest wind that blows from between the Massif Central and the Alps – makes only a short and half-hearted appearance. Both these winds can blow at gale force for days on end. My timing is fortunate.

The Local Contact network suggests places to aim for and stop at, and there are clubs and centres to head for too. France are doing well in the football World Cup and the mood is buoyant.

This stretch of coastline is quickly dispatched, and that is in large part thanks to the refuelling efforts that are made at every stop. I eat a mound of nutritious, real food every evening. Every person who supports at these stopovers gives a big helping push.

The aforementioned Mistral gives a moderate puff as I sail past the mouth of the river Rhône. The Ebro taught me to be cautious of deltas. This estuary is a simpler puzzle. I follow a sand spit for 4 nm before a 3 nm crossing back towards real land. The Rhône delta is another achingly beautiful world

Marseille, looking north from the Notre-Dame de la Garde basilica

where wildness can be felt: Vegetation grows unchecked; driftwood and plastic lay side by side as sculptures in the windblown sand.

Beyond the delta the wind continues to strengthen and lift the sea. The spirited conditions become a challenge. I zigzag downwind on the edge of control. Navigation is simple. A map in my mind has islands ahead that protect the city of Marseille, so I will tuck in behind those. Before that is possible, the sea state becomes quite horrendous. It bounces back – reflected square – off a 5 nm mole that protects the industrial port. The shores of the city are reached at the end of a 54 nm run. It has been an exhausting sail.

Next day the Mistral is blowing with gusto. A rough sea meets France's third-largest city and a blue-white corridor is alive with windsurfers who make big jumps with small sails. I briefly link up with Loïc, who bounds over from beach to an overflowing bar in time to see France win the World Cup final. Then Caroline and Jérôme rescue me from a second night of homelessness. Before departure the next day, this gentle couple show me their city from the heights of the Notre-Dame de la Garde basilica. The stadia and terracotta roofs of Marseille are laid out beneath us. To the west are the islands; to the north is the articulated arm of the industrial port; and to the south lies the coast of the onward journey.

The Mistral returns to standby mode. Back afloat, gentle breezes deliver restful sailing. The weather and colours are glorious. There is jaw-dropping beauty at Calanques National Park; and then France's highest sea cliff at Cap Canaille, where pale limestone and ochre-coloured sandstone layers stack upon each other to a height of nearly 400 metres.

Loïc celebrates a windy day and France winning the World Cup

Captain Pablo

1 July and 11-18 July

Pablo the sailboat captain lives on the Cote d'Azur. The boat in his charge – Sailing Yacht *Ellen* – is based in Monaco. Though his real passion is windsurfing – and particularly touring by Raceboard. It has been encouraging to hear from Pablo and sometimes useful to hear his take on progress. He can read a coastline from a chart, and understands the vulnerability of my craft. I can tell Pablo my location and perhaps my state of mind – and these make sense to him.

He is also a shipwreck survivor. Solo sailing across the Atlantic in the year 2000 his small yacht was sunk by hurricane Alberta. Good preparation for the possibility of that emergency saved his life. His attitude when I confide my near misses is to put them behind me. "You came through it," he says. "So you did alright."

It had long been planned that Pablo and I would sail a leg together, and that happened a few days back. Pablo's wife – Shona – dropped him off and we launched in the morning through a few small waves. We tacked upwind on a light breeze; it was a day that promised few miles. The water sparkled like glitter with shoals of tiny fish. The wind dropped towards late afternoon and the swell built some more. Inshore of us was beach, but without wind to propel us to shore the waves made landing inadvisable. We struggled to make the last mile to Valras Plage – where there would be a route up a small river mouth for a guaranteed safe route in.

With progress a mere fraction of a knot it became a long slog to the opening. The turn into the river was difficult: outflowing water, no real wind, incoming swells. After a while we aborted the attempt to sail up the river and went for the beach instead. I made it near to shore in a lull between sets, but was inevitably knocked off by the waves, and ended up swimming whilst being washed along by the longshore drift. A lucky surge bought sand under my feet and I hauled the gear clear. Pablo's swim began further out and ended with both of us hauling his sunken rig to eventual safety. Damage is avoided: We rode the waves like amateurs and our luck like pros.

The reunion with Pablo and Shona happens when I reach their home at Juan-les-Pins on the Côte d'Azur. The summer season is in full flow and space on land is at a premium: beaches near towns are elbow-to-elbow busy. The floating castles of the super-rich lie off the nearby Îles Lérins.

Pablo is away the first few days, so these are used for repairs to my ailing craft: epoxy injections under parts of the deck that have gone soft and crunchy. My host's Yellow House at the back of town is an ideal retreat. When I do head out it is with a bicycle: for spares from the chandlery, for bread from the *boulangerie*; and on one occasion to the beach, where my head spins at this world so crazy busy with people. I cannot help but project forward. Climate change will squeeze everyone tighter. The super-rich on their floating islands of oblivion will move further offshore. Societal collapse, when it happens, will come quickly. On a rosy day I give us a few more decades.

The beachgoers are the rabble compared to the super-rich, but they are wealthy by most standards. There is a buzz of excitement around town that momentarily I can sense. Lenny Kravitz blares out from a speaker somewhere. *Are You Gonna Go My Way*. I do, and there – round the corner – on a stage, is Lenny Kravitz.

The next stop is planned. Choreographed, almost. I am about to see real wealth. Shona drops me off. I sail round the Antibes headland, past the city of Nice – distant enough to notice only its airport traffic – and some hours later arrive at Monaco.

The harbourmaster prohibits me sailing in, so Pablo comes from the harbour with the launch that acts as tender to Sailing Yacht *Ellen*. He collects me from a jetty at Monaco's only beach so that the leg is completed without outside assistance. This seemed important at the time. My pride on this occasion almost costs Pablo a parking ticket from the watching maritime police.

SY *Ellen* is a 40 metre (132 foot) ketch. A beautiful craft and far more elegant than the much larger sailless vessels that are moored alongside. She is operated by a crew of five, and has four guest cabins. *Ellen's* owner is not on-board at this time – though he obviously has deep pockets and from what I can gather is an oligarch with interests in copper mining. Pablo is mindful to respect privacy. From the few comments that are made it seems that vast wealth brings the owner more isolation than happiness. A queue of gleaming Rolls Royce cars waits idle on the quay. My board sleeps on the deck of *Ellen*. There is an apartment on land for me to use.

We dine at a pizzeria. It is a good pizza – Italy is nearby. The streets and tunnels of Monaco are quiet, empty and fully monitored by CCTV. The principality blends the technological and modern with the historic and classic. The best way to get around is on foot. It is an easy place to be calm. Think of it like an environment-enriched hamster cage for some of the wealthiest hamsters on the planet.

Monaco: Sailing Yacht *Ellen* is second from the right with the dark hull. Windsurfer *Phantom* is there on the bow, resting on a bed of canoes.

I continue with the cage exploration next morning – up to the famous casino, through the iconic tunnel that is part of the Formula 1 circuit. As always, more is missed than is seen. On a next visit I would browse the Oceanographic Museum that stands out like a beacon to mariners. And – as a consequence of the research that has been involved in writing this book – I would know to knock on the door of the International Hydrographic Office. Perhaps they would accept a copy.

But now the day job beckons.

A strap for the barrel is missing. Every item is precious and losing anything is a frustration. Pablo provides a replacement and then we head out of the port by launch. I wonder if the strap is by the jetty where the pick-up happened, so detour there for a look. The strap isn't to be found, but the search for it – by accident – means that the leg begins on land, in full compliance with my own silly rules.

Afloat, there is a meagre headwind and a sea full of choppy rebound. The board is knocked about like a cork. Each nautical mile of zigzag progress requires over an hour of sailing. But the water is crystal clear and deep, deep blue. I am happy to be out here with my simple objective. A sunfish appears to be taking a nap – or at least is unbothered by the nudge of a barely moving windsurfer. Beyond a headland there is a bay where the wind stops entirely.

The surface of the water goes glassy smooth, and a ray cruises past in slow flight.

Inshore is France, but Italy is a trivial distance away now. A few kilometres with the paddle is enough to pass the border.

I land at a bay beneath a half viaduct that clings to a rocky hillside. Dinghies are hauled up onto the stones. A row of wooden cabins – fishermen's huts originally – sit at the base of the viaduct wall amid rampant vegetation. It is the prettiest of places to overnight, and quiet too, with no vehicular access, just the occasional passing train.

Pablo cycles over from Monaco to wish me luck for the passages that lie ahead. He also delivers the strap that I had assumed lost but that did in fact show up later. There is a sense of multiple chapters closing, and of a new voyage beginning. A goodbye isn't necessary. Voyages require good luck not goodbyes. In another port my captain friend and I will meet, and – on our voyages – we will sense that the other is keeping watch.

The occupants of one of the cabins say that I am welcome to sleep on their terrace, and soon we are drinking gin and tonic and being plied with fresh fruit. I return there later, but first we walk back into France for a pizza. Then Pablo cycles back to his ship, and I walk through the tunnel that leads back to the hidden beach. And that really is the end of the chapter.

The beach beneath the viaduct (Spiaggia del Darsenún)

18. Ligurian Sea

The Ligurian Sea is located at the roof of the Mediterranean's Western Basin. According to IHO *Limits* (1953) it is bound by an imaginary line from the France-Italy border to Cape Corse on the island of Corsica, and from there – via its outlying islets – to San Pietro Point in Italy.

IHO *Limits* (2002 draft) will – if adopted – expand the sea southeastward such that the southern limit runs from Cape Corse along the forty-third parallel – due east – to the Italian coast. This revised boundary is somewhat arbitrary. More logical would be to extend it a few miles further south to the island of Elba, as the Hydrographic Institute of the Italian Navy do in their definition of the *Mare Ligure*.

This book will remain consistent with the IHO *Limits* (1953) boundary. This meets the Italian coast where it transitions from a hard to a soft shoreline. North of San Pietro Point is uniformly mountainous, but in Tuscany – to the south – the mountains wander inland to become the spine of Italy, and sandy beaches predominate. For modern shipping the change is of minor consequence. But for smaller craft it does matter that the mountains of Liguria offer protection from strong northerly winds, and that the hard sides reflect rather than absorb the wave energy. By contrast, where waves meet sandy Tuscan shores they end their journeys. When the seas were originally described, such distinctions were the basis for the boundaries.

Where the Alps meet the sea they descend to a great depth. Their slopes produce abundant plankton and krill that attract cetaceans. In 2002 the 87,500 square kilometres Pelagos Sanctuary was established as a result of agreement between France, Italy and Monaco to "protect cetaceans and their habitats from all sources of disturbance." The Ligurian Sea falls entirely within – and indeed is dwarfed by – this designated area. Protection for whales provides umbrella protection for many additional species.

The main city of the Ligurian coast is Genoa – birthplace of Christopher Columbus.

Ligurian Sea extent and track

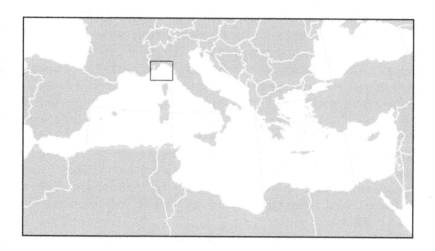

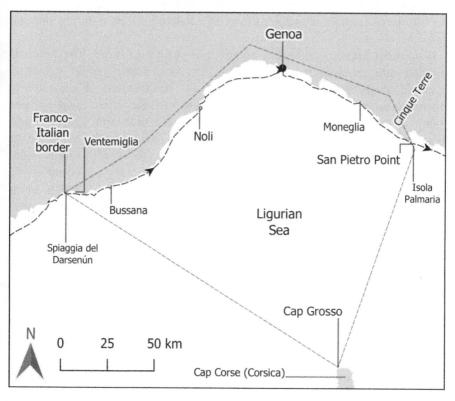

The Hobie Cat Brothers

19 and 21 July 2018

The sail plan is unmistakable even from miles away: a Hobie Cat. And it is so low in the water that it appears to be sinking. I detour a mile out to investigate. The catamaran is indeed semi-submerged. Its trampoline is covered in gear and amongst that are the two crewmembers. I assume they have come from afar. "Nooo!" the two boys sing, *"Oggi abbiamo iniziato il giro d'Itaaalia!"* – today we started the tour of Italy! From their smiles it appears that life could not be better than on a barely floating raft.

The boys are brothers – Giacomo and Francesco Galimberti. We end up at the same place that first evening and join culinary forces. Their beans are filling and nutritious, and combine well with my contribution of beer and crisps from a local supermarket. Beach sleeping in Italy is easy – no-one raises an eyebrow.

Two days later, once again we meet at sea. This time in no wind. My paddling system is more efficient than theirs, in that I have a paddle and they do not. Even without a paddle, life is still marvellous on a barely floating raft.

A storm is brewing. It would be advisable to get to shore. The beach is divided into multiple narrow strips. There is a single public strip and multiple strips that are commercialised by beach clubs. Each club is distinguishable from the others by the colour of their neatly lined-up sun-loungers and parasols. We land next to a beach club and Giacomo and Francesco introduce themselves, and me. The situation takes a while to explain – who's come from where, who's going where, who knows who. The beach club is a family run business that has been going for decades. We are given a warm and generous welcome. Kindness is a gift that is not a transaction. I appreciate that more now. And have greater understanding that it simply brings pleasure to allow stories to become enmeshed.

The boys have a bit of equipment "optimising" to do. The kitchen sink is surplus. Some paddles would be useful. For a few days we criss-cross, and then – one day – they offload the excess, the Hobie floats high, and they are gone.

Giacomo and Francesco will go on to complete their Giro – from Ventemiglia to Trieste – in 54 days.[24]

---

[24] The brothers will also beat me to publishing a book of their journey: Galimberti, G., & Galimberti F. (2020). *Una barca gialla. La storia della circumnavigazione dell'Italia su un HobieCat 16*. ViviDolomiti.

Noll, Genoa and Moneglia

19-23 July 2018, from log entry

Wind is in short supply on this sea. Long days are needed to make significant progress. Yesterday's half-metre short-period swell made it hard work on the legs, arms and fingers. The sea will be similar today. Having the Hobie cat brothers sailing the same way is fun and good for motivation. My board is quicker, but they sail in more comfort and are less troubled when the breeze dies away. So I forge a lead and then stop when it becomes too painful, but they keep going a few more hours and close the gap right down.

Having Giacomo and Francesco nearby is great for morale!

Noli was a particular highlight. There were friendly people at the Lega Navale Italiana[25], and I met up with contacts for a walk. We ascended Cabo Noli, an imposing outcrop that had been rounded the previous evening in failing light. The views – and in particular the colours – were spectacular. My guided tour was followed by pasta with homegrown pesto. *Delicious*! In the afternoon I sailed, and there was another meetup with the Hobie cat brothers. Then a thunderstorm cut our days short, which at least allowed for some more recovery time.

---

25 The Lega Navale Italiana is a public entity to which most Italian sailing clubs are affiliated.

Genoa tour with Alessandro

Yesterday I started early and squeezed sufficient miles out of the day to pass the long port of Genoa and reach Genova Surfing Club. Alessandro Portoghese (remember to sing the name) paddled out to intercept and guide me in, arranged for a place to sleep, and sent me for food.

This morning Alessandro took me for a guided tour of Genoa by moped. I loved that! We also explored by foot, had the best cappuccino and apple pastry thing I've ever tasted, went through narrow streets of old buildings, saw colourful markets, negotiated fillings for lunchtime paninis. City stuff. And so much experience and sensory input that my brain still buzzes.

After the fourth coffee my body was ready to sail. A very light headwind made for slow progress. Zero wind is preferable to a light headwind. The trickle of breeze died after about an hour, so I put in another 6 nm with the paddle (much better) to reach the impressive Portofino headland. A useful puff of favourable wind then allowed another 14 nm to be sailed, to an attractive little place called Moneglia.

Eight or nine hour days of sailing and paddling mean that I am permanently tired. Today's tea is *focaccio al formaggio*. There is an enclosure for small boats where I will sleep.

Despite the physical toil this section is a real joy! The Italians are great, and every day is a good one.

There was no sign of the Hobie cat brothers today. I think they are ahead.

Cinque Terre

24 July 2018

Just one more day's sailing is required to reach San Pietro Point where the Ligurian Sea meets the Tyrrhenian. The approach to the headland is magical, under the pink cliffs of the Cinque Terre national park, with a sea that is flat enough to permit sailing at touching distance.

I take my time – take it easy – and instead of aching fingers finish the day with a neck that is sore from gazing upwards.

Sleep comes on Isola Palmaria – under the sail, on a bed of pebbles.

Alongside the cliffs of Cinque Terre

19. Tyrrhenian Sea

The Tyrrhenian Sea – according to IHO *Limits* (1953) – is delimited on the east by the Italian peninsula: from San Pietro Point in Liguria, to Cape Paci at the entrance to the Strait of Messina. These two points are linked on the west by clockwise island hops to Sicily, Sardinia and Corsica, with a final imaginary line back to San Pietro Point.

By this definition it includes the Gulf of Spezia and the entirely of the Tuscan coastline. This matches the reach of the Etruscan people in northwest Italy, and corresponds with the modern day Tuscan coast.

The Greek term for Etruscan was Tyrrhenian, which is derived from Tyrrhenus, who was a founder of the Etruscan people according to their mythology. After the Etruscan civilisation became assimilated with the Roman empire the sea to the west of Etruria became known as the Tyrrhenian Sea. The sea name is therefore Greco-Roman in origin; and an approximate modern translation would be "Tuscan Sea" – although Tuscany only accounts for the northern part of its extent.

The Tyrrhenian Sea is relatively shallow in the north but has major basins in the south, with depths of up to 3800 metres. The south is also more geologically active. The islands west of Naples and north of Sardinia – for example – are volcanic in origin, and the island of Stromboli is still active. Other active-though-dormant subsea volcanoes are considered to be at risk of "major collapse from a single event." The occurrence of such an event would likely trigger a major tsunami.

The north and central part of the mainland coast is generally flat, and fronted by sandy beaches. Much of this coastline is devoted to tourism which in the summer months is intensive.

The Tyrrhenian is not particularly bountiful in terms of fishing – and subsequently its major ports deal more in the transport of cargo and passengers. Mafia related drug and arms trafficking at the ports is a historic and ongoing problem.

Rome was the world's largest city from around 200 to 500 AD. Through it flows the river Tibre which meets the Tyrrhenian Sea about 30 km downstream. The "Port of Rome" is in fact Civitavecchia – which translates to "ancient town", and is Etruscan in origin.

Tyrrhenian Sea
extent and track

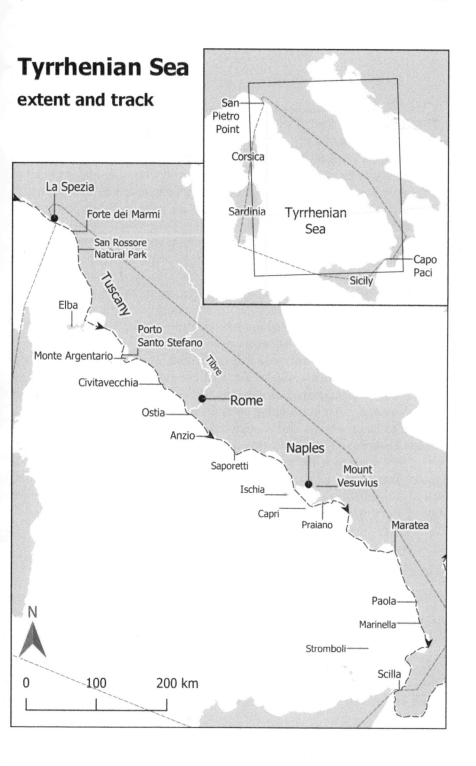

Matt

25 July 2018

This is holiday season. The beaches of Tuscany are covered by parasols – grouped by columns into garrisons – that collectively form a regiment – that stretches for 30 km from La Spezia to Viareggio.

I stop halfway along this stretch to meet a friend who is holidaying nearby. Matt – now Matt and family – is reassuringly nonplussed by the "glamour" of Forte dei Marmi. It has been years since we have met, but Matt is still very much Matt.

They flee back to their retreat in the mountains, and I continue south. Beyond the divide of a small estuary is San Rossore natural park. Here the beaches are as nature leaves them, rather than groomed to attract custom. Piles of bamboo and pine line the shore, and amongst the sun-bleached wood are what we have gifted to the sea: barrels, buckets, tubing, ropes, tyres, pots, crates. And plastic bottles to outnumber the breaths of a lifetime. And chunks of polystyrene to fill every gap in the latticework of wood and plastic. But green life still pokes through, and lizards forage. There is a forlorn beauty here that contrasts the shallow glamour of Forte dei Marmi beach. And it focusses attention – not on the self, or on bronzed bodies – but on our planet. It is nature reaching out to us with a message: Help.

I want to camp on this empty stretch, and do so before crossing the next estuary. Darkness falls, but night is delayed by the arrival of a helicopter. It hovers in a storm of noise and light then lands not a hundred metres away. It appears that I have camped next to a military base. No headtorch tonight. Best to stay quiet under the sail. I rise early next morning, and by dawn have slipped away unobserved.

Chris

27-31 July 2018

I cross to Elba – as Napoleon had done on his sabbatical from warring – that the history books record as exile. On his nine months on the island he built a road system and a theatre. During my stay I eat pizza. On both nights. The days are windless and sun-baked. To protect the sail from the cloth-crippling ultraviolet rays I cover it with *Posidonea oceanica* – Mediterranean Seagrass. The tape-like leaves of this aquatic plant are piled up on the shore. The top layer is dry, sand-hopper free, SPF 50+, and also comfortable for sleeping on. Additionally, *Posidonia* meadows provide shelter for marine life, sequester carbon from the atmosphere, and protect against coastal erosion.

The middle parts of the day are uncomfortably hot if not at sea, so it is best to be sailing if there is a breeze, and paddling if there is not. Space on land – particularly shaded space – is difficult to come by. Clear skies give a full appreciation of the arc of the sun across the sky: of the season, and the passage of time.

The cooking of the land gives rise to localised thermal breezes. Sailing past Monte Argentario there is glorious planing to be had, but within a few kilometres it is once again dead calm. I had messed up the previous day: started a cliff section as dusk approached and then had to retreat to Porto Santo Stefano in the dark, and then once ashore had neglected to remove my GPS from the boom. Unfortunately, someone else did that. My mistake. A more positive reminder of that night is the leather wallet bought from the town's market.

There is another lunchtime meet with another old friend: Chris, who is also now part of a family of four. Matt, Chris and I all worked together as sailing instructors. I ponder the divergence of our trajectories. The luck of it all. The many, many dice rolls that make it all unknowable. The authorship – of any of it – that is not there to be found. The day finishes at a delightful shack next to a shallow reef. The occupants offer a warm welcome and set me up to overnight there, and ply me with food. Octopus from the reef is part of the menu, though it shocks me that such small specimens are considered fair game.

Civitavecchia

1-2 August 2018

At night the land cools down so that by morning a trickle of heavy air falls out onto the sea. These land breezes are useful and will become more so as the effect strengthens further south. Early starts are required to benefit, and the best wind of the day may be over before breakfast.

The breeze is already gone as I paddle towards a friendly looking sailing harbour, having passed the main commercial port at Civitavecchia. A man with a smile so natural that his inner peace is self-evident beckons me in. No fanfare. Just a this-is-what-happens-here type tranquillity because he knows better than me that there will be no more sailing today. He helps me up the algae covered slope and introduces himself as Marco. The logo on his white polo shirt confirms this place as the Lega Navale Italiana Sezione di Civitavecchia.

There are a bundle of children from very small to nearly adult – a sense of family rather than of hierarchy. We gather under some welcome shade and Marco comperes a relaxed talk-through of my adventure. Endearing child voices politely address me as "Jonah-tan" with their questions. Their acceptance of me into their group is disarming. There are some other adults too. Letizia makes particular effort to ensure I am at ease. Letizia's daughter has the most strikingly beautiful blue eyes. Letizia's granddaughter – three years old and wearing arm bands – comes to find me when I am having a quiet moment alone by the sea. Her request: "Jonah-tan, will you swim with me?" melts my heart.

Marco tells me that Baron Arnaud de Rosnay was a previous visitor to the Lega Navale. De Rosnay will forever be a legend of windsurfing history – most deservedly for being a pioneer of daring crossings. Of aristocratic wealth, with every advantage in the world, and newly a father, he had no need to risk his life but evidently felt compelled to do so. He disappeared in 1984 whilst attempting to cross a hundred miles of sea from China to Taiwan. It seems that before this crossing he was consumed with doubt. Though alternative theories are offered for his disappearance, perhaps most likely – in my opinion – is that he was lost for want of a leash. It would have been interesting to know the real de Rosnay – beyond the headlines of his playboy years.

When windsurfing was still a young sport de Rosnay stayed two weeks at Civitavecchia, waiting for an opportunity to windsurf to Sardinia. But the wind never came.

My next day is truly windless. The smooth sea reflects back as a distorting mirror. Even here the waiting is not easy. My mind has ventured offshore. Acceptance into the group brings a lump to the throat, but it is not an anchor.

Perhaps the most remarkable thing about the welcome at the Lega Navale Italiana Civitavecchia is that it is not exceptional. In fact it is repeated at LNIs and other clubs as I proceed – southward – in a procession of sunset or night-time landings. The Italian way and the Italians are adorable.

A wave-off from LNI Civitavecchia with Letizia (at bow) and Marco (at stern)

228

Baia di Napoli

The beaches of central Italy are the easiest sailing of the journey so far. Despite this, there are still strategies to figure out to claw the miles when the wind is mostly light. Boredom is certainly not a problem. Though the straights are long, each part of them is never quite the same. And soon the next place has arrived.

There is more scenery to admire – more vertical dimension to the terrain – and more difficult sailing, around the Bay of Naples area. The bay, or gulf – either designation fits – is formed by two impressive headlands about 18 nm apart. The northern headland – Capo Miseno – has the volcanic islands of Procida and Ischia just outlying. There is a steady stream of boat traffic emerging from behind the Cape and headed to the islands. The motorized craft use brute force to overcome the resistance of the water. Most are in a hurry – which creates bigger waves, and adds to their already scandalous carbon footprint.

Crossing this maritime highway is fun, and reminiscent of the classic arcade game Frogger. The boats move fast; and I move slow and at right angles to the traffic flows. Two-thirds of the way across a rogue vessel forces me into last-second avoiding action. An instinctive backwinding of the sail prevents me from going under its bows. The board reacts immediately, as if acted upon by a bungee tether: full speed to stopped in just a few metres. The vessel churns past, close enough to swing a boom at. Astern – in its disturbed wash and fume laden air – I direct my anger towards the bridge, and an oblivious captain who has no appreciation of what almost came to pass.

Rather than detour into the bay I cross direct to the next headland. Wind blows into the Gulf – sucked in by warm air rising up the slopes of Mount Vesuvius. Naples itself sprawls in front of the volcano and its heat output perhaps contributes to the thermal wind effect. The open water crossing is soon complete.

At the south side of the Baia di Napoli the traffic resumes. This time it goes to and from the island of Capri that lies about 3 nm from Punta Campanella. Again the boats are not small dinghies. In fact, it seems likely that there has been an arms race of ever bigger boats to cope with the horrible mess of waves caused by ever bigger boats. The afternoon wind has whipped up a sea, and the heavyweight fleet has made it worse. And the chaos of the waves is reflected back into the cauldron by the mainland coast to leeward, and also by Capri itself that rises vertically from the water like the sword Excalibur.

On the south side of the headland the sea state becomes standardly lumpy. This is sweet relief compared to the mogul field just sailed through that bounced my brain and jaw.

The Amalfi coast lies to port. The cliffs tower ever higher – dramatically high – and further-on small villages cling to parts where the sides are less steep. There are few obvious places to land: few that I could get to without an appalling wind shadow. But I am tired and wish to reach land without risk of night reaching me first. The best option appears to be beneath Praiano. I will try my luck there, rather than at Positano, which is bigger – but in a windless nook. The majestic terrain ascends so abruptly that just 2 km from Positano is a ridge already higher than the summit of Ben Nevis.

A platform with orange parasols, just above sea level, is my target. A welcome finding is a ramp that simplifies the transition to dry land. The ramp is narrow and steep and has hairpin turns like a mountain road. Kayaks and small dinghies compete for space and their familiarity is reassuring – suggestive that this landing location is suitable. Adjacent is the platform with the orange parasols and – seamlessly – without skipping a beat – the Italian way – the family-like team from OneFire lido assume their role as hosts. OneFire is a fashionable place – at the exclusive end of the beach club spectrum. Perhaps because of this I had anticipated a snobbishness – a "Get off my lido!" attitude – but there is no hint of that. Rather I am welcomed into their family, and the sense of goodwill genuinely wished to a fellow human being is palpable.

There is a strong sense of family amongst the dozen or so employees young and old. Where does this sense come from? What nurtures it?

There are perhaps three or four hundred steps to reach the village of Praiano. I lose count. Somewhere around halfway up lives the cook, Mario. Not far from there is Maria. And undoubtedly the others live nearby too, or at the village where a public road passes. The challenging terrain obliges that community, family and work happen together rather than in isolation. Being cooperative makes for strong bonds. And strong bonds make us more cooperative. That is the way of social apes – and it seems to suit us.

Food is important too. I am far from being a foodie, but perhaps understand better its role now. Especially cooked food. Somehow cooked food is more than the sum of its parts. An offering of food that has received love delivers more than just calories. It nourishes more fundamentally.

Ilenia

14-15 August 2018

Breezes around these parts are timid. The afternoon thermals struggle to deliver a Beaufort force 2. The early morning land breezes can be more energetic. To catch these I sail before dawn. Where the wind falls out of a valley there may be a Beaufort force 4. In pitch black that is exhilarating. Then – as an orange sky turns blue – the wind falls away to nothing.

There is also wind beneath the cumulonimbus clouds. A storm is brewing as I approach the town of Paola. There are no lightning bolts yet and the beach is adjacent. Not too reckless, I convince myself. Then comes a loud crack of thunder, and the first big fat raindrops of a transition to a deluge. I curve-in to the shore, beach the board, and run for the nearest shelter. Serendipitous timing has landed me by a small sailing club – a modest hut and a few boats. It is the first evidence I have seen in days that anyone sails on this coast.

The wind blows moderately hard for a few minutes. The torrential downpour washes away days of encrusted salt. The group at the club embrace their voyager from Norway. The timing of the storm – how it forced a landing on their shore – is a curiosity to us all. Privately, shyly, we invest meaning in coincidence. The door is left ajar that – perhaps – it was meant to be.

Rodolpho becomes a mate. And there are half a dozen others from the club and the relations between them exceed my ability to work out who's who. Ilenia shows up with a camera and takes me aside to collect a portrait. Who is this girl? I think rather than say, more captivated by her dark southern European beauty than I believe is appropriate. Rodolpho's girlfriend? His daughter? She has perfect English improved by a perfect Italian accent, and speaks with words and intensity that flag a sharp intellect.

We talk occasionally – Ilenia and I – to this day, and she is an inspiration for me that there is hope: that it is worth fighting for change and a better world. Even the thought of her now inspires me to finish this book – because she is a reminder that the effort of writing is underpinned by a deeper motivation. We talk about grains of sand. Each of us is but a grain of sand. And yet each of us might make a difference. And that becomes more likely if we try – if we give our full effort. The result we see does not matter – it may be invisible to us – but we may touch others who in turn achieve something significant. We can be part of a chain of change.

This is not to deny fate or accept free will; the intrinsic motivation is entirely down to luck. We are fortunate if we apply ourselves, because it is easier to find satisfaction in a life with coherent purpose.

Ilenia's desire for coherent purpose is what now brings the next sea nearer. She – as much as I – wrote this chapter.

Storm Ilenia

A Look Back from Scilla

11-20 August 2018

Sicily had seemed a long way off but now it is coming into view. The Tyrrhenian Sea has been kind though resistant. The people have shown instinctive, unfiltered kindness. There has been the puzzle of making miles without wind. The varied coastline has been sometimes spectacular – particularly in the south, where small towns perch upon mountain plateaus.

Many names are missing from this section. Help comes daily. And many people offer oceans of help. If the help on this journey were all told, the account would run to many volumes.

It bolsters my humanity to be with people, but it is also effortful. Restoration happens when alone. Aloneness in nature is communion with the natural world. It is very different to being lonely.

The shag is a bird that has been seen on most days of this journey. A shag is often seen on a strategic rock – resting up and drying its wings. I also am on the lookout for a location to conserve energy and get the gear back in condition.

An opportunity presents itself at Maratea – a port village, nestled like a pearl in a rugged vertical coastline. A quiet cove becomes a workshop to repair longitudinal cracks on the deck of the board. First the wounds are opened up. And while they dry in the sun, I forage bits of bamboo from the beach and shape these to fit over the cracks like elongated bridges. Finally,

Mountain villages south of Maratea

epoxy glue is used to plug the holes and affix their bamboo roofs. The repairs are a success – and the same technique is used many times subsequently.

I enjoy the day of mending and relative anonymity. That qualifier is needed because the fire and rescue service know I am here. They patrol the mountainsides from a boat, and yesterday – on my crossing to this coast – had wanted to rescue me from a lull before an approaching storm. The storm never arrived, but later on a beer did – sent my way by the boat crew who had also headed straight for the nearest bar upon reaching land.

The subsequent days tick by. It is sobering to find so much plastic – not just in the sea, or washed up, but also abandoned in the forests by campers and day trippers. It would be easy to despair at humanity for this, and sometimes I do, but bad habits are not inevitable.

Wholly uplifting is an evening when birds fill the sky. A reminder that we already live in paradise, and that nature's wellbeing is our own wellbeing.

Stromboli becomes clearly visible. A drift of smoke rises from its crater. Its outline, 30 nm distant, could not be any more volcano-like.

Though Stromboli is a detour too far, the Pylons of Messina do become a target. It seems that I sail towards them for days. One of the pylons lies on the eastern point of Sicily and the other is on the Italian mainland. Each is 232 metres tall and the gap between them is 3.6 km wide. The cables they

Heading out for some space and some miles. Photo: Matteo Cundari

once carried have now been removed, but the pylons remain as historical monuments and are rather beautiful from a distance.

Close to the mainland-side pylon is Scilla – an ancient port settlement that in a literary sense is the entrance to the Strait of Messina. The name Scilla derives from the nymph-turned-multi-headed-monster Scylla, who nearly did for Homer's Ulysses, and is said to live beneath the town's castle. The other monster of the Strait is Charybdis, who generates whirlpools to swallow her prey. The mythology is based on the currents of the Strait of Messina. I stop at Scilla – long enough for a coincidental second overlap with a French family I had met some weeks back.

The monsters and the crowds persuade me to move on. A quiet beach beneath the pylon becomes home for the night. It has been another day of heat and still air, then of fierce gusts and the torrential rain of a thunderstorm, then of calm and nothing much at all. The sun sets over Sicily. At these latitudes it plummets. The pylon across the water is silhouetted by a sky that fades from orange to the inky blue of nearly night. In the foreground is the Strait of Messina. It is a sea of irregular swirls: the turbulence of Charybdis, who writhes in the deep.

Sicily's Pylon of Messina and Capo Peloro Lighthouse

An early start

20. Ionian Sea – Part One

From west through north to east, the Ionian Sea is mostly bounded by: Sicily, the sole of the boot of Italy, Albania, and Greece. It is connected to the Tyrrhenian Sea at the Strait of Messina. It shares a maritime limit with the Adriatic Sea between Capo Santa Maria di Leuca which is the stiletto point of Italy, the island of Corfu, and Albania's Butrint River. Its southern limit is between Capo Passero of Sicily and Cape Matapan of the Greek Peloponnese.[26]

A seafarer who passes from Tyrrhenian Sea to Ionian also passes from the Western Basin of the Mediterranean Sea to its Eastern Basin.

The name Ionian may come from Greek mythology, though several alternative explanations exist. It may derive from the Albanian "Joni", in which case the meaning would be Our Sea.

The Ionian plunges to remarkable depths. Calypso Deep is the deepest point of the Mediterranean. It lies about 35 nm southwest of the Greek town of Pylos, and reaches 5267 metres below the surface. The name Calypso means "she who conceals", and originates from the goddess nymph Calypso who delayed Odysseus for a few extra years in the Odyssey.

In relative proximity to the Greek mainland are the seven Ionian Islands. If smaller islets are included then the island count is much higher.

Major gulfs include the Gulf of Taranto – the hollow beneath the boot of Italy, and the Gulf of Patra – that connects to the Gulf of Corinth.

In 1893 the Corinth Canal was opened. The 6.4-kilometre-long channel cuts though the Isthmus of Corinth. The canal turned the Peloponnese peninsula into an island and offers a shortcut from the Ionian to the Aegean Sea. Most modern shipping is too wide for the channel, but it is used by yachts to save a chunk of miles and hard sailing.

---

[26] In IHO *Limits* (1953) the Ionian Sea meets the Peloponnese at Cape Matapan. In IHO *Limits* (2002 draft) the Ionian reaches further east – to Cape Maleas – where it begins a common limit with the Aegean Sea. For a more elegant chapter structure, content for the Ionian and Aegean seas will be organised according to IHO *Limits* (2002 draft). This is more fully explained in "The Ionian Sea – part 2".

Ionian Sea extent and part one of track

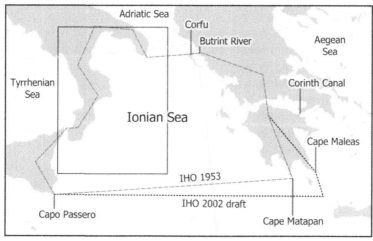

Stretto di Messina

The Hobie Cat brothers had a wild ride through the Strait of Messina. Charybdis tripped their banana hulls and pitched them forward in a tumble of bubbles and distorted sound. The video was later posted online.

My paddle through, by way of contrast, is windless and tranquil. Tidal currents in the Mediterranean are usually negligible, but in the Stretto they are significant: the result of the Ionian and Tyrrhenian being out of phase. When the Ionian is relatively higher a current runs northward. When the Tyrrhenian is more elevated the flow goes south. The direction of the current changes every six-and-a-bit hours in rhythm with the lunar day.

This morning the stream runs north. But close to the shore there are favourable countercurrents to glide along with. Patrolling the Strait are the swordfish hunters. Their boats have tall ladder-like masts for the spotters, and long bowsprits for the harpooners. Ferries depart for or return from Sicily. The city of Reggio Calabria glides past on the left.

Captain Pablo sent a message earlier to suggest I should try to get beyond Reggio today. It has a reputation for being a rough place. In 2012 the entire government of the province was dismissed over links to organised crime. Messina – on the Sicily side of the Strait – is also a mafia stronghold.

The populations of Reggio and Messina also face an underworld threat from shifting tectonic plates. Throughout history, earthquakes and tsunamis have impacted the region. The last major quake was in 1908 when 90,000 people were buried or drowned.

As I paddle past there is nowhere simple or inviting to stop, just the concrete and steel of commercial port.

***

The gentle swirls of the Strait are tranquil for some hours. I will use the time to explain to the reader the source of my funds and free time. Experience tells me that people are curious to know. And for completeness I am happy to include this information.

Inside the rucksack on my back – inside two further waterproof layers – is a laptop computer. The computer allows for work from home. Home is under the sail. And in bars and cafés with good cake and internet access.

Funds arrive from writing updates for *Surf Magazin*; and there is a monthly fee for some website management work. And there is a trickle of income from my first book. And some donations through the *buy me a coffee* link on the website.

Before the journey's start I had a few thousand euros saved, bolstered by the sale of my van. My apartment in Menorca is rented out which covers the mortgage and most expenses on that. I have enough to have freedom.

I also have a generous mother and stepfather. And I could protest more vociferously about their habit of topping up funds. My protests are instead rather meek. I am tremendously fortunate and – yes – privileged.

Whatever we achieve in life is the result of privilege and good fortune. Any achievements we are credited with are not ours to claim. I'll pass on pride: do without that. And I'll pass on guilt about opportunity, and guilt about mistakes, too. We neither choose nor play the hand that we are dealt.

These savings, incomes, and donations – combined – are sufficient to allow me to continue the journey. I do not need or desire more cash. In my mind there is no work-life balance to be struck. And in this blessed life drudgery is absent. A "working day" of eight hours afloat seems about right. Some days require overtime, but rest is a necessity too.

The sailing gear is mostly provided free, and the tracking is donated too. To the companies that are helping – Starboard, Severne, Stohlquist and YB Tracking – thank you.

I declined sponsorship from an alcoholic drinks brand because I do not wish to promote drinking. Later, another brand offered sponsorship, but after careful consideration I turned that down too:

If I am too well funded – I reason – then that would be isolating. It would complicate the acceptance of genuine charity. And if I could not accept charity – help, support – then I would miss out on that which is truly nourishing: the sharing of food and shelter, and the warmth of human companionship.

At present, funds are limited enough that I must be frugal, but money is not so tight that it is a dominating concern. This represents a financial goldilocks zone.

A further reason for caution regarding sponsorship is the public message of this journey. My hope is that blog and book encourage more thoughtful rather than more prolific consumption.

***

Most of the Strait is behind me now. Punta di Pellaro is a short distance ahead. I ponder transparency whilst paddling.

To see clearly, and to be in sight, can be intimidating. I learnt to sail – aged ten – in murky waters. I liked it that way. The beasts imagined swimming beneath my plastic Topper dinghy remained hidden. Perhaps I was hidden too.

But later – when clear waters had become my normal – I realised that it is better and safer to have the underworld in sight. My fear of seeing and being seen dissolved away. That preference for murkiness had been nothing more than a habit.

Finances are usually kept private. I think that is a bad habit. The world would be more equitable if all financial matters were in plain sight – like the residents of a coral reef: where the water is clear, and it is more difficult to cheat, and the sharks cannot hide. Financial privacy is a habit that does not serve a collective good. Where an individual has a reason to be coy is where society has a greater need for clarity.

A random fact retained from Norway – a more equitable society than most – is that the tax returns of Norwegian citizens are public.

***

A headwind has filled in now. The mind is occupied by navigation. I sail the last miles to Katanhouse – a windsurf and kite centre – and make landfall shortly before the afternoon storm. There is support here organised by my contact Robby.

Once again, I am in the best of hands. We eat as a group in the cool air of the night. Prompted, I talk: Of seas that are now far away. Of the cold, white Arctic landscape. Of Atlantic swell. Of moments when nature accepted me as part of her. Of anxiety and fear. Of hospitality and warmth. Of humanity. Of family – my niece and nephew – who reveal to their uncle his own humanity. And of the challenges ahead.

Daggerboard and fin show through a transparent Ionian Sea

Calabria

22, 26 and 30 August 2018

Much of the Ionian side of Calabria is undeveloped. Some is so pristine and wild that I have to stop so that the memories that are formed have texture from every sense. The flood of experiences is relentless. Here are some days based on log entries at the time:

Bova

Around dusk – eking out the last of the breeze – a brief alien visit: the hum and the red LED of a drone, 1 nm from the coast.

Landfall in the gloaming at Palizza Marina, where drone pilot and local windsurfer Bruno shows up. He apologises for the intrusion and offers an invitation to visit Bova – his family town – visible from here – that sits upon a mountaintop.

Wonderful and fascinating. Bova is centre of Greek Calabria, where a dialect of the ancient Greek language maintains a foothold. 850 metres up the air is clear and cool. The intoxication of the mountaintop is the same as that of the open sea. From the highest pinnacle I would stay forever: between the lights of the stars and those of the coast. Bruno and wife Daniela are perfect guides. Another favourite day is added to an already long list.

Soverato to Crotone

Sisters Beatriz and Francesca arrive early at the sailing club with croissants and matching wetsuits. Yesterday I had landed here for a short break that became a longer one. I joined the Gallelli family for good food and wine, and possibly confessed some oddness that prompted Beatriz to share a truth that made me smile. *"Da vicino nessuno è normale!"* Up close no-one is normal!

We are in convoy for a few minutes before my companions gybe and head back towards land. I continue – a downwind course on an open and increasingly bumpy sea. The colours of the Ionian are stunning. A green canopy of vegetation over a white strip of sand and turquoise water. After 25 nm, when the kink in the coast at Capo Rissuto is near, the wind is howling. I hang on a for a few zigzags more, on the promise of protection in the lee of the outcrop.

Now – at that kink – the wind gallops seaward. I follow the coast round into calm sea and air. That had been quite an effort. The next point of land is closer. "What's the point?" I ask myself, as if ready to throw in the towel. The joke never fails and I laugh once again.

An isolated and soul-nourishing coastline somewhere north of Crotone

There is a Doric column on the headland. I sail past the corner. The board seems slow. I could do with a rest so hook into the first available cove. Sure enough the slot flusher has partially detached.

A repair is needed. I prepare the surfaces, apply the glue, then pile sand-filled fishing crates upon the rubber strip to apply pressure. Then I go for a wander while the glue dries.

The point – on this occasion – is Capo Colonna. The Doric column is from a Greek temple: a navigational beacon from ancient times. A closer look always reveals something of interest. Perhaps that is the real point.

Later, I reach Crotone, and Fabrizio from the Lega Navale. There is a bed to sleep in. 50 nm for the day! Crotone is nice. Pythagoras was born here. He invented the triangle – a shape later perfected to become the pizza wedge.

Golfo di Corigliano

Sleep isn't happening – and there is a generous moon – so I decide to sail and am away by 3am. There are the lights and sounds of working fishing boats. Distances are difficult to judge. The scent of the air gives clues as to the origin of the breeze.

It is calm at Capo Trionto – the southern limit of the Golfo di Corigliano – so I paddle through the dawn. Then sail against a tiny headwind to Al Risparmio da Raffaele, a modest but likeable town, where early-rising locals line the beach, angling for tuna. Now sleep is irresistible. The locals are friendly too and bring coffee, chocolate and water whilst I doze.

A slight breeze arrives and that carries me towards the midpoint of the Gulf where two currents collide to form a sand spit. The going is hot and slow. I slouch over the boom like a drunk at a bar. Then the sonic boom of a military jet makes me jump like a startled cat.

I eventually reach shore on the north side of the Gulf. The shaded forest – next to the lidos – had been appealing from a distance but up close it is rubbish-strewn. And there is flat-pack furniture being traded from the back of vans that could easily swallow an unguarded board. Shattered, I rest in the shade until dusk, then struggle upwind to a spot that feels safer.

Sadly, it was not unusual to find a scene such as this

Brunella and Cataldo

2-4 September 2018

The coastline of the Gulf of Taranto runs for about 400 km. Most has been sandy and pleasingly undeveloped. Winds have been gentle. The sailing clubs I have stopped at – without prior announcement – have welcomed me as they would welcome their own.

This morning began at Basilicata Vela. Filippo had taken me to visit a turtle nesting site before I set sail. WWF volunteers ensure that the eggs remain undisturbed, but we are a day or two early to see any hatchlings.

Taranto itself occupies the northeast corner of the gulf. I cut the corner – so am far from the city – and sail through a shoal of tuna that turn the water white as they feast on smaller fry.

Beyond Taranto the shoreline is rocky, and near to the city the small coves are busy. I look into an inlet where a contact has suggested a stop, but the crowds are overwhelming, so I decide to continue. A mental note is made to send Cataldo a message to explain that the day held more miles.

I sail parallel to the craggy shoreline. Conditions are easy and it is pleasant to be in open space. Movement on land catches my eye. A lone figure standing on a rock – a tall and thin outline – facing seaward in my direction. An arm waves a gentle wave. So shy and gentle is the wave that it might not be a wave at all, but it is insistent enough to beckon me in.

A turtle: *Caretta caretta* (photo from the Greek Ionian)

There is no obligation to stay, but it is an easy decision to do so. Cataldo's character is as kind and gentle as his demeanour had suggested. We forge a bond in Italian-English and Spanish. The language barrier is insignificant when there is nothing but good intent.

Cataldo and his partner Brunella have a little boy – Guiseppe. He knows the names of all the dinosaurs, whilst I only know a few. I soon feel a part of their family. A break is welcome after eighteen days of sailing. I stay three nights.

Brunella is wonderful. She feeds us at home and guides me around the local area. A walk at the WWF reserve of the Mar Piccolo ("Little Sea") helps replenish batteries and it is a welcome change from being on the sea proper. We visit the city of Taranto. The main sites are indicated, including the infamous steelworks that is the largest by area in Europe. Air pollution from the plant is chronic. Brunella explains that warnings are issued to close windows when the wind blows from a certain direction, and that child mortality is 21 percent higher than would be expected.[27]

That may be depressing, but the stay with Brunella and Cataldo is uplifting. They are my new favourite people of all time and I hope we will meet again some day.

---

[27] In 2021 the Italian state were convicted by the European Court of Human Rights for failing to protect the health of Taranto's population.
https://www.dw.com/en/italy-taranto-residents-rise-up-to-stop-air-pollution-claiming-local-lives/a-49050350

Preparation for a crossing

5-7 September 2018

Inner reserves are replenished. The barrel is well stocked with healthy food. Pockets are overflowing with protein bars donated by friends of Brunella and Cataldo. All will be helpful for an upcoming crossing that is already being eyed.

In four days' time the wind will turn northerly. Not too strong and not too light. My intention is to sail over the horizon to Albania. There are miles to cover before then. On the last day of the run-up I sail beneath Capo Santa Maria di Leuca, and into the Adriatic Sea.

Capo Santa Maria di Leuca – the tip of the stiletto heel of Italy. The town is also home to Smaré sailing school who generously donated some repair materials.

Heading to the Adriatic

21. Adriatic Sea

The Adriatic Sea is the body of water between the Italian peninsula and the Balkan countries. In antiquity it was sometimes considered to reach as far south as the Peloponnese, but since Roman times its southern limit has been placed at or near the Strait of Otranto. The IHO (1953) limit is shared with the Ionian Sea: from Capo Santa Maria di Leuca, to Corfu, and then to Albania's Butrint River.

The Adriatic is approximately 850 km long and 200 km across at its widest. At the Strait of Otranto the minimum crossing distance narrows to 73 km.

The coastline on the Balkan side is rugged and has many islands, especially further north. The Italian Adriatic coast is much smoother.

The name of the sea likely derives from the Etruscan city of Atria which now lies some metres beneath the modern town of Adria in northern Italy.

The Adriatic is a shallow sea in the north due to a far extending shelf. In its southernmost third it descends beyond 1200 metres. Rivers and subsea springs that discharge into the Adriatic account for a third of all the fresh water that enters the Mediterranean. The diluted waters sink and travel far into the Eastern Basin.

More than 3.5 million people populate the coastline of the Adriatic. Farming, manufacturing, shipping and tourism contribute to pollution that enters the sea. Overfishing is a recognised problem. Surface currents rotate anticlockwise and contribute to an accumulation of relatively more polluted water on the Italian side.

The Adriatic has been of strategic importance since antiquity: the Romans moved eastwards via the Strait of Otranto; during WW1 the Allies blockaded the Strait to prevent Austro-Hungarian access to the Mediterranean; during the Cold War the sea was in effect the Iron Curtain; in 1999 NATO vessels stationed in the Adriatic intervened during the wars of the former Yugoslavia.

Adriatic Sea

extent and track

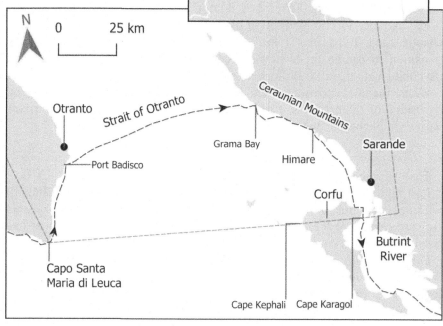

The Crossing

7-8 September 2018

Beyond the lighthouse at Capo Santa Maria di Leuca there is nowhere to stop. Limestone cliff has replaced sand. The air by the cliffs barely moves and the deep water is a graveyard of decaying jellyfish. Further out – where I sail – the lurching swell is uncomfortable. The afternoon sun is low in the sky.

Towards evening the wind may die away further. I work hard because time is precious. Cramp has invaded my arm muscles. Each pump moves a scoopful of air and in exchange the board joggles forward. Each effort is a gamble of balance. The board has the stability of a log.

Sunset happens and strengthens motivation to maintain the work rate. My phone – in its waterproof pouch and a struggle to hold still – provides glimpses of progress. 2.4 knots. 3.8 knots. The readings swing about as wildly as the device itself.

Twilight proceeds through its phases: civil, nautical, astronomical. Before night proper descends I strap a headtorch to my forehead. The lighthouse is now 15 nm to the south. That leaves 4 nm to go.

The entrance to Port Badisco is black and windless. Its outer reach has a chaotic chop. Exhausted, I fall – and curse – and almost fall apart. The transition to paddle mode in these conditions is physically awkward and psychologically painful. Belligerence gets me through.

Where the inlet narrows the sea becomes calm. The sail balances easily on its bridge of foam blocks. Composure is restored; and satisfaction arrives with a simple beach landing.

***

That was the real work of today's crossing.

Last night I met up with Andrea – who is a friend of Tino from Galicia. It was a planned link-up and Andrea delivered some spares that had been sent forward. Amongst these items are a GPS unit to replace the one that had been stolen, and a cosy Sealskinz hat. Both will be useful today.

Port Badisco is a quiet and charming place to finish the Italian leg, and Andrea is the nicest of guys to have signed-off with. We had a pizza at the local tavern where Andrea explained that in Port Badisco valley are caves with paintings from the Neolithic period.

Andrea is a teacher: the sort who involve their students with nature; the type who if we were lucky as kids we might still remember. We said our ciaos and our crossed paths became a memory. And then a flood of sentimentality welled as a I realised that Italy – the Italian leg of this journey – had come to an end.

I rested under the sail. Over the sea were the flashes of a distant storm. Sleep was fitful: disturbed also by night-fishers, and night-owls keen to pair up, and by a mind that had found a second wind.

***

The alarm sounds. The anglers and lovers are gone and the storm has cleared. I must have slept. Breakfast is porridge and coffee – generous portions. Camp is broken under the light of headtorch and according to routine. Coordinates are triple-checked. The GPS batteries are loaded, and pockets filled with various bars. The board carries extra water, for it cannot be taken for granted that any will be found on the other side.

A final check on the weather forecast. The general situation is unchanged with a northerly airflow through the Strait of Otranto. The green shading of the map suggests average wind speeds in the 11 to 15 knot range. Though I am savvy enough to know that Beaufort force 4 could easily end up as a limp force 2 or an arm-wrenching force 6. Regardless, there is no doubt that this is the day for the crossing. I note that the wind may veer northeast later and decide that it would be wise to keep north where the crossing is shorter.

Port Badisco. Farewell Andrea and farewell Italy

The work of getting to the water is done. Soft sand and warm water caress my feet and legs. I clamber aboard and lift the sail. The only witness to my departure is a rising sun.

I am not particularly nervous. Not full of fear as I had been before setting off to cross the Irish Sea on my journey round Britain. It helps that the target is not a lone dot in the ocean, as it had been when I had sailed to Lundy Island. There are options even if pushed wildly off course – for example a forced reroute to Corfu or nearby islands. A full day ahead lends confidence.

The GPS rests on the harness line and is held steady by an elastic. Coordinates are set for a small cove on an otherwise inhospitable Albanian coastline. The display has large numbers and a direction arrow: Heading to target 79 degrees; distance to target 46 nautical miles, or about 85 kilometres. I sail a few degrees north of the rhumb line [required constant bearing] in anticipation of the forecast wind veer.

Near to land there is a trickle of north-westerly breeze. The sun's rays are warming. The sea is quieter than last night, and to begin with its splashes barely reach my shorts. Sailing across the wind is easy – effortless – compared to the downwind slog of yesterday. That effort was pre-payment for today's favourable angle.

The wind freshens and sometimes there is enough to sail from the footstraps in planing mode. Other times the mast-track is slid forward and my weight is more central. There is a near miss with a turtle on the port side. I look back. Port Badisco has sunk below the horizon and Italy has become an island.

Offshore, the sky turns overcast. It is lonely out here. I had imagined coastguard or military boats patrolling this Strait and gateway to the European Union.

It is also cooler. The drysuit can be accessed, but while the going is fast I prefer to sail on than squander the minutes that would be needed to suit up. Thick wetsuit boots and my newly delivered fleece-lined hat are defence against the chill.

The wind has gradually veered but now does so more severely, as had been forecast. Now if I sail from the back footstraps my course line is too far to the south, which puts land much more distant. In response, the daggerboard goes down to achieve a more north-targetted course. The board speed is slower and the ride harsher – colder and wetter – heading against the wind and waves.

The change of mode gives rest to the body. For a moment it seems possible that ahead is an outline of land. But it is hazy, perhaps it was cloud. I raid the energy bar supply in my pocket as a boost for the muscles and to keep the brain alert.

One ship crosses. And then another. I pass astern of both and that is the shipping lane negotiated.

The outline returns. I had expected Albania to rise from beneath the horizon, but – in fact – her Ceraunian Mountains are revealed by a thinning of the haze. It feels good to be heading for land, however distant it may yet be.

When 15 nm remain the mountains have grown in stature and definition. The upwind sailing has placed me well to windward of the original rhumb line and the angle is now correct to charge at full pelt towards shore. Windsurfer *Phantom* sails a controlled broad reach – fast and wet but without the nose trip hazard of a true downwinder. Soon my thighs are burning. I blink away spray from a sky that has rediscovered colour. The sun is once again brilliant.

A hundred flying fish leap from the water to evade the predator that has chanced upon them. They have the brilliance of kingfishers and the synchronicity of a murmuration of starlings. Their flight path and mine will surely collide. I instinctively duck and the flock bank hard and pull up. We miss each other in the nearest of misses. They climb further and then flow beyond the leech of the sail like the breeze itself.

And then, the wind stops. Really stops. Just 2 nm short of land and 3 nm short of my objective. There is zero wind, but still a breaking sea. It is impossible to paddle because the waves tell a story of a solid force 5. It is

The Ceraunian Mountains ascend to over 2000 metres. This picture is taken from a vantage point above Grama Bay

time to eat and be patient and accept the warmth of the Mediterranean sun. The coastline is majestic and untouched.

Occasionally a gust arrives. These are messengers of downdrafts from the mountains that will crash down with increasing ferocity. The gusts are unpredictable and arm-wrenching but allow bursts of progress. Two hours later I reach the opening and force a way to paddle the choppy, swelly, windless last few hundred metres into the cove. The landing is at Grama Bay. It is a wild and wonderful place. There are no roads that reach here.

Though it seems unlikely, at the corner of the bay is a shack. On a busy day the beach bar restaurant might serve six beers. Today, a travelling windsurfer will be their first customer.

The post-sail come-down is particularly wonderful today. This arrival is the culmination of days of effort. The surroundings are a fitting reward. I notice a stowaway – a ladybird – a companion who had been with me at the start of the crossing – and who I had written off as lost at sea.

Grama Bay. The pleasantly unobtrusive "beach bar restaurant" is right of centre

Albania

8-11 September 2018

If a gulf can divide then a strait is a greater division still. The Albanians I meet are subdued. They note with sadness the advantages – enjoyed by me as a European Union citizen – that they are denied: a whole continent of opportunity, a relative absence of corruption and crime, a mostly enabling state. Their welcome is quiet rather than gushing. I am taught the crossed hands eagle gesture that is a symbol for ethnic Albanians across the globe. I also learn the word *"faleminderit"* – thankyou – and witness again – not for the first time – that a small amount of effort can go a long way.

Most Albanians are poor, but not all. A powerboat pulls into Grama Bay that has nine-hundred horsepower of outboard motor on its transom. If contraband were your thing that boat would do the job.

During the communist era, Albania was denied the economic expansion enjoyed by western European countries. Its people suffered, but from the point of view of the natural world it was saved. The country could be declared a National Park and perhaps it should be – from what I have observed of the Mediterranean it is a refuge of nature unique in scale.

The onward sailing is a trial – because northerly winds in the Adriatic leave the sea rough but the coastal fringe in the lee of the mountains is windless. My objective is a passport stamp. The port of Himare finally arrives after two more days of toil.

The entry process requires a full day. Moored up alongside the quay is a Turkish registered galleon. The crew of this theatrical looking vessel are able to advise me where to head for. I patiently wait around where the first mate has indicated, and knock on doors and windows, but there is no-one to be found. So I return again later for another loiter and this time a uniformed officer eventually shows up and I decipher that the relevant person is taking a coffee. An hour later I return again and wait some more until finally the same officer shows up, casts me a glance, and opens the door. It turns out that he was the border official all along.

The Venn diagram of our respective language skills has minimal overlap. It will be best to keep my story simple. I say that I arrived today, from Otranto, by boat. That is what he is expecting.

The man also expects my craft to have papers. I am ready for this so deploy part two of the explanation. "My boat is a windsurfer. Very small. No papers." I raise my hands and pull on an imaginary boom – a universal sign that has worked elsewhere – but that this time draws a blank. Charades is not his forte. The term windsurfer is unknown to the man, and to the forms on his computer screen.

"Like a kayak," I say. Time appears to have slowed down. But then comes a distant echo:
"Kayak." Finally, we have a word in common. The computer is ancient, and its operator's keystrokes land with the frequency of a long range Atlantic swell. Eventually, progress is confirmed: "Name of kayak?"
"Windsurfer *Phantom!*" We are on a roll! And with minimal extra fuss I am documented.

I return to the galleon, triumphantly brandishing a stamped passport. Now that I am documented the day can be enjoyed. The boat's young Turkish skipper has many questions and is excited for me that I will visit his country later on the journey. The boat's owner – also Turkish – and an Albanian deckhand complete the crew. They have come from working the tourist season in northern Italy. This strange craft has bare masts and no sails, but does have plenty of space for parties.

Later in the afternoon I walk past a seafront café and hear my name called. The official who had processed my entry is sat at an outside table where he is obviously a regular. He beckons me over – not because there is a problem but because he wishes to invite me to a coffee.

The following morning we meet again. This time my request is for an exit stamp. Having received that, standard maritime practice is that I must now complete the departure in a single hop. The Albanian authorities were seemingly unaware of my arrival, but it is possible they will watch as I leave, so I will make every effort to comply.

There is a gentle breeze to begin with. The coastline is typically wild. Military gun emplacements are nestled into the jagged shore and blend-in as seamlessly as the goats that somehow scrape an existence on such terrain. Later in the day the wind dies completely. It seems unlikely that departure will be achieved, and a building chop makes it increasingly difficult to move anywhere by any means. Once again it is very uncomfortable. I have been many hours afloat and am tired. Eventually, just before nightfall, the wind that is pushing the sea finally arrives. In no time a solid force 4 develops. I race downwind until the city of Sarande lies to port, and then lunge a further 7 nm to the Greek island of Corfu, and the familiar security of the European Union.

First glimpse of Himare (arrival completed by paddle)

22. Ionian Sea – Part Two

After a few days of the Adriatic I dip south back into the Ionian to begin the voyage down its eastern margin. This is the route I will take to reach the Aegean Sea, rather than the shortcut through the artificially excavated Corinth Canal. I enjoy finding shortcuts, but only those that would have been available to mariners of old.

According to IHO *Limits* (1953), the Ionian and Aegean Seas are close neighbours at the Greek Peloponnese but do not share a boundary. Instead, the Laconian Gulf – between Cape Matapan and Cape Maleas – is sandwiched between them.

In IHO *Limits* (2002 draft), the limits of both the Ionian and the Aegean are adjusted. The proposed changes situate the Laconian Gulf in the Ionian; and provide a common limit for the Ionian and Aegean. This new shared boundary for the seas extends from Cape Maleas to the island of Antikythera.

For a more elegant chapter structure, this book will borrow from IHO *Limits* (2002 draft) for the Peloponnese region. The Laconian Gulf will be considered part of the Ionian; and the crossing to the Aegean Sea will happen at Cape Maleas.[28]

---

[28] Consult the "Seas of Europe" map for clarification that IHO *Limits* (1953) locates the Laconian Gulf in the Mediterranean Sea Proper, Eastern Basin, without further subdivision.

Ionian Sea part two of track

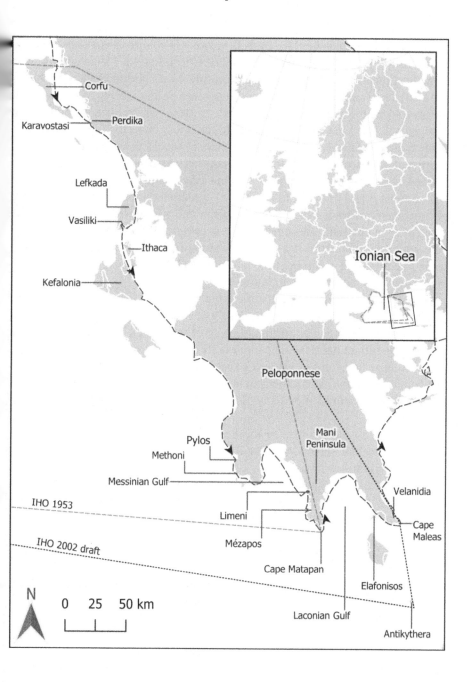

Corfu to Kefalonia

12-22 September 2018

The conservationist Gerald Durrell wrote *My family and other Animals* about his idyllic childhood on the island of Corfu. Later a TV adaptation was filmed on location, and I remember from my own childhood viewing being captivated by the flora, fauna and vivid colours of that world. At that age my dreams – and sometimes nightmares – were of wild and biodiverse ecosystems. But I never thought I would feel them underfoot and inhale their scented air. And much less did I imagine that I would voyage to them.

Coincidence sees to it that I make landfall close to where the Durrell's resided – at a small cove north of Kalami Bay. I am sure that Gerald would have known it and perhaps he – like me – squatted on the sand here. I do my best to leave no trace when answering the call of nature. The paddle is of great help to this end and enables the excavation of an impressively deep hole with minimal effort. A wash in the sea suffices to clean up afterwards – so no paper is used – and the hole is refilled. I hope this level of detail is not more than the reader wishes to know.

Corfu city is impressively fortified but presents as a complicated stop. Positioned off the city is Sailing Yacht *A*, owned by Russian billionaire Andrey Melnichenko. The form and scale of her monochrome, silvered hull is more sci-fi than nautical. The alien craft appears dormant, for now. Later the wind is strong for a while as I streak downwind in long zigs and zags. I make sunset landfall where the ground is low and prosperity has bypassed. A rising sea level would inevitably flood the land here and make the people destitute.

The following day I cross to the mainland side and a scenic spot called Karavostasi Beach. The beach has a lifeguard tower and is patrolled by two lifeguards: Yannis and Lazarus.

Both guys are warm and friendly to me but there is a tension between them. I later learn why: a swimmer died on their watch yesterday. It is a time for searching questions to be asked, and normal that those questions might be pushed away.

At the end of the lifeguarding day, Yannis invites me for food at his digs in Perdika, which is reached after a hundred hairpin bends of mountain road. The food is home cooked, delicious and nourishing. Then we take a tour of the town and its little taverns. I have the sense that Yannis is the embodiment of a sane – healthy – person.

Two days further on, at Lefkada – the main town on the island of the same name, Guy and Justine host me on their catamaran. They have also sailed a long way. Our first mutual sighting was at the Isles Cies in Galicia, and we exchanged a few words at Cascais in Portugal, and now – at last – we meet properly in Greece.

Hospitable friends are also found on the south of the island, at Vasiliki, which is a popular windsurfing location. Despite paddling into the windless night I cannot quite reach the village in one hop, and set camp with about 3 nm to go.

The next morning – before emerging from my sleeping bag – a search and welcome team arrives. First on the scene is Mark on his SUP. He comes bearing croissants – and has already organised a few days rest and recuperation at Ocean Elements windsurf centre – so the least I can do is get the coffee brewing.

Vasiliki is well known in the windsurfing world. I like the village and the vibe. The much-hyped wind makes a semi-appearance one afternoon, and – yes – I borrow some gear and clatter a few miles there and back, there and back, there and back, until my knees suggest it is time to stop.

Ocean Elements – managed by Doug, a friend from Minorca Sailing days – lend their workshop to build-up the mast where it has become worn. There is an opportunity to write an overdue next article for *Surf Magazin*. And it is a pleasure to share my experiences during an informal chat with some trainee watersports' instructors.

There is also time to kick back with professional relaxers Andy and Polly. Over the brim of our iced frappés we observe the activity in the bay, and guess at the wind conditions between here and the islands of Kefalonia and Ithaka.

The 10 nm crossing is a simple one, and once in the Ithaka Strait – with a wild and depopulated island either side – the sailing is reminiscent of Norway – but without the cold hands.

In Homer's *Odyssey*, Ithaka was the kingdom of Odysseus. The tale describes his perilous ten-year-long voyage home. But Ithaka is not my quest, and since there is no obvious fresh water on offer I choose not to stop. However, the island is significant, in that it encourages me to be interested in Odysseus and – later – to read and be moved by Cavafy's *Ithaka*. On any complicated journey that poem helps to settle the mind.[29]

Next day, after camping with some friendly dogs on a pebble beach on Kefalonia, I paddle to the south of the island. The colours, white sand coves, and crystal-clear water of the coastline are mesmerizing. That leaves a jump to the mainland of about 20 nm. I start early the next morning, and thankfully there is a breeze for the crossing. On the way I meet a turtle that fits in the palm of my hand.

---

[29] A translation of *Ithaka* can be found here:
https://www.poetryfoundation.org/poems/51296/ithaka-56d22eef917ec

Pylos

24-30 September 2018

I depart under a full moon to make use of a breeze that falls from land to sea. The wind stops around dawn and then I paddle until reaching shore. Then I walk to find a second breakfast. A message arrives from Hans. He makes the breezy prediction that I will easily reach Pylos today. Maybe. We'll see. The miles do not count until they are behind me.

Back on the water I notice an adult turtle. It swims for the bottom and stays there. Then the going becomes lumpy and uncomfortable for a while. And then for the last 10 nm a decent wind comes in. I pass through the choppy gap at the north end of Pylos bay into the quiet waters inside – tired and happy to have reached this spectacular natural harbour.

Hans is Dutch and lives on his boat, SY *Zephyr*, at Pylos village. He is a septuagenarian eco-warrior with a healthy disregard for what other people think of him. He favours bikes and shuns aviation for climate reasons. He is vegan – for health and climate reasons – and figures that he will die in 35 years' time, aged 108. Not that age matters. He is good at seeing through bullshit, and admirably principled. Maybe he is a bit "on the spectrum", which could be a reason we get on well, because maybe I am too. I study Hans and wonder what my own future looks like.

If you would like to meet Hans, then look him up. He welcomes visitors. In fact, there are apprentice sailors on board when I arrive.

Heavy weather is brewing: a tropical-like cyclone, or medicane. Hans makes a convincing case that I should stay until the threat has passed. Pylos is a very agreeable place to wait some days: a pretty square, bars, bakeries, and a rugged castle on the headland.

On Saturday morning, a pulse of swell warns of the medicane's imminent arrival. An easterly wind causes no problems, but then it swings north – onshore – strengthens to hurricane force, and lashes the town with a biblical quantity of rain. Rarely have I witnessed such fierce weather. Pylos loses power and the place is awash with debris. A pair of yachts find themselves tied up at the wrong place in a cauldron of jumping waves. The boats become entangled. They take chunks out of each other in an ugly, heavyweight bout of steel versus aluminium. Fortunately, *Zephyr* is better hidden; and my board and sail are also safely stowed.

The medicane had spun into life very close to Pylos and been intensified by the warmth of the Ionian. After it tracks over land it soon loses its potency. The waves and swell it generated are also short lived – to the extent that the next day it is safe to sail. I round the headland at Methoni. All the boats there are tossed up on the shore – high and dry – as if the tide were out.

Of course there is no appreciable tide here, and the boats had been stranded by the surge of wind and sea.

Later in the day I take on the westernmost prong of the Peloponnese. There are three peninsulas to negotiate, and it turns out that this one is the tamest. Having rounded it, the wind inside the Messinian Gulf is also rather kind. Hans' lentils power me for a total of 40 nm. That is further than my arms wish to sail, but enables an end of day rendezvous with family friend Moira and her sailing-instructor granddaughter.

Pylos. Tangled yachts as the medicane departs

The Mani Peninsula and Cape Matapan

1-3 October 2018

Round 1

The south of the Peloponnese forms a trident of peninsulas. The middle of these – an extension of the Taygetos mountain range – is the Mani Peninsula.

It is a pleasant, gentle day when Moira and Zoe wave me off. The wind comes from behind and gradually awakens. It has personality today. 20 nm from the calm of Messini beach, and 5 nm from the craggy cliffs of the peninsula, it blows with gusto. Its game is no secret. It will continue to build. At the tip of the peninsula, a further 20 nm from here, it would flick me away to Africa.

I harness the wind's strength and favourable direction. The board tears downwind. My thighs burn, but that is good because it is a drenching ride, and I could do with the heat. Goose-pimples stand proud on my drenched skin. I should have worn the drysuit. It is easier to continue the charge than remedy that error. A hat warms the head and insulates the ears from the howl of the wind.

Navigation is complicated – not complex – just difficult to do with so much spray, and prune like fingers, and a requirement that both hands be on the boom. Ahead there is a bulge of coastline: a growth with steep sides, about 10 or 15 nm from here. It looks awkward, and it will be.

Stopping at sea is problematic too. The sail is weakened from sun damage and may not withstand a mauling from the waves. But fatigue and cold are setting in and calories are needed. It is better to stop now than delay. I sit, and chew, and contemplate – and a feeling of wellbeing returns. It is majestic to be out here where the white horses gallop. A wayward equine tumbles through board and sail. A signal that my five minutes are up.

I continue for another 10 nm, but eventually reality bites. That the wind has built gradually does not make it any less windy now. It is no longer possible to sail as deep as is needed. The result is that instead of gradually closing on the peninsula the gap to it is widening. The outcrop's jagged, central spine reaches into blue sky. But where rock meets sea is obscured by the curve of the earth. It is disappointing to backtrack, but retreat is the best option.

Behind me and to leeward there appears to be a settlement. I gybe and head that way. The nose of the board dives. Sinews are strained in the effort to wrestle it from Poseidon.

It is useful to have had some experience of this. Few are the days that cannot be compared with something similar or worse! Today is a difficult and wild ride. But Svaerholt to Honnigsvag was more difficult and wilder; and the Portuguese coast had its moments... Nonetheless, it is still a relief to reach Limeni bay.

The Mani Peninsula has a coastline that is mostly low but sheer cliff, or shipwreck-hungry rock. At Limeni – fortunately – there is a concrete slipway to haul myself up. A local photographer documents my dishevelled arrival. I begin shivering, and without delay throw wet clothes off and dry ones on. The photographer is gone a few moments and then returns with food: big bread rings and feta, and then cake. *Efharisto!* – thank you! I had been chastened by the retreat. But now I open my eyes to this place and this kindness, and the disappointment is gone.

Round 2

A young German couple provided lodging and spaghetti bolognese last night. Limeni is stunningly pretty in the morning sunshine. The air is still. I repair the daggerboard gasket that had been partially ripped from the board during yesterday's exertions. Today will be the second attempt to get past that bulge of rock.

Near to shore the water is turquoise. Further out – where there is a slight breeze – it is deep blue. It will require patience to reach the wind. At the limit of the bay a turtle and I meet – like drifting logs – in the gentlest of collisions. *Caretta caretta* live into their sixties. They are vulnerable to boat strikes. This animal has a carapace of nearly a metre, and weighs probably 150 kg. The old mariner has wisely chosen an empty sea. I am happy to meet this way: by chance, without noise, without stress.

On open sea proper there is a trickle of headwind. Residual slop bounces off the cliffs and bangs into the nose of the board. Each vibration is felt: slap, slap, slap! Progress is painfully slow.

After four hours of toil the bulge of rock is before me. It is a natural fortress: there would be nowhere to cling to under its towering cliffs. I sail at it for a further hour, but am forced to accept the maths of average speed and daylight remaining. Once again I must retreat.

The best – and in fact, only – option is to head for Mézapos – where there is a tight inlet that leads to a narrow beach of white shingle. There is also a natural bowl shape in the cliff-line that just about counts as a harbour.

I land on the shingle beach then go in search of food. The few houses are mostly ruins, but one professes to be a tavern. A knock on the door finds the owner, who opens up his front room for long enough to overcharge for an underweight Greek salad.

It's difficult to reconcile this place with being in Europe, and really a wonder how this desolate peninsula provides to support anyone.

Round 3

The bulge of rock plays its last card: a wind shadow that extends far downwind. A full detour to avoid it would be lengthy. A compromise course shortens the doldrums. Eventually I hook into some turbulence, and moments later pop out into a flow of solid breeze.

The 20 knot headwind is bruising but welcome. I am properly dressed today and push the board so that it smashes through the waves. Two hours later the bulge is behind me. A spirited breeze now rips across the peninsula from east to west. Another narrow inlet provides an opportunity for a brief stop. I refuel, reconfigure clothing for full battle mode, then relaunch. The tip of the peninsula is 6 nm from here.

The wind comes from behind now and the gusts are more vindictive. It used to be thought – some still do think – that the gods control the wind. Aeolus is enraged: I ignored his warnings and broke through his defensive headwinds. Gusts from the north are hurled my way like a challenge from Aeolus himself. "You think you belong here? You think you can hold on?" Cape Matapan is the most southerly point of mainland Europe. Libya is the next stop downwind, across 400 kilometres of open sea. I must hold on. To the sail, and to this rocky spine of peninsula that is my lifeline.

The end of the headland is where the exposure is greatest: the wildest sea, the fiercest gusts, the most tenuous link to safety. I pass the lighthouse and am detached from the continent. Upwind zigzags claw me back. But the sea is rougher this side and there is nowhere to stop. I smash into the wind and waves for another hour. Gradually, the threat diminishes: the wind moderates, and once again I am alongside the peninsula rather than hanging on to it by aching fingertips. Three days of stress drain away. I look back at this middle finger of the Peloponnese. Out of defiance and admiration I flick it a middle finger of my own.

The troublesome bulge of rock, finally dispatched to leeward

Cape Maleas

6-7 October 2018

I detour into the hollow of the Laconian Gulf. Headwinds mean that a direct crossing never presents as viable. It is quite lumpy as I head to more sheltered water, and difficult to get clear of land when hemmed in under high ground.

Some days later I turn back southward towards Cape Maleas. Offshore winds blow into, over or around the mountains. 25 knots here; zero knots there; and in some places going round in circles. I have to sail more separated from the land than is comfortable. By mid-afternoon the terrain is lower and has the warm hue of sandstone. Sailing at speed over flat, turquoise water is joyful. Suddenly a dark barrel-shaped object blocks the way. Instinctively I backwind the sail so that it fills from the wrong side. A collision is averted and a startled turtle swims for the sand a few metres below. An apology is due but difficult to communicate. Shortly after I land upon the island of Elafonisos, The island and its waters are the definition of picturesque. I decide to slow up a little; live life at the pace of a turtle. Connected to the main village by a walkway is an islet with only a church, a few trees and a sandy beach. Perfect for sleeping. Dinner is a knockout octopus and pasta dish. My under-sail campsite is blissful.

The Cape itself – over 500 metres high – would have been fearsome in yesterday's winds. It is renowned for treacherous sea conditions. In the Odyssey it is where Odysseus was blown off course by a storm that further delayed his return to Ithaka. Another legend of the Cape involves an English sea captain who became the "Hermit of Cape Maleas" after shipwreck on the outcrop and the drowning of his beloved. Tomorrow's forecast is for lighter winds. It would be a good day to cheat my way round.

There are 13 nm to the Cape. I start early, begin the day paddling, then slog upwind in a trickle of breeze. At the Cape the breeze has no exit plan. It hits the towering obstacle and flops into incoherent uselessness. The surface of the water is a mess of reflected chop. In search of wind and an angle to pass I stay on port tack all the way to the shipping lane before tacking back to starboard. I pump the sail continually – and with the regularity of a heartbeat – to create wind where there is sometimes none. The effort is exhausting, but each little surge of power lifts the angle of the board a few degrees. Two hours later I scrape past the lighthouse and into the Aegean Sea.

The trickle of breeze is now unobstructed. It is sufficient to push me to the ancient hillside town of Velanidia. This is a remarkable place – remote, shoehorned onto a mountainside, with streets as wide as a wheelbarrow. Back down at sea-level there is a bar that does food, and a little church inside which I end up sleeping.

Cape Maleas. The white building is a church. A tiny dot nearer to the end of the cape is a hermitage. Further round (not visible in this shot) is the lighthouse.

23. Aegean Sea

The Aegean is an embayment of the Mediterranean that lies between the mainland of Greece and the west coast of Turkey. It is a sea with many islands and islets: 1400 of them is an oft-quoted estimate.

The boundary in the south traverses from island to island, and in doing so forms a curl from the Peloponnese to the Anatolian peninsula. Crete is the southernmost of these islands and also the largest of the entire Aegean.

At the Peloponnese, IHO *Limits* (1953) brings a boundary to the island of Elafonisos. IHO *Limits* (2002 draft) proposes a revised boundary – shared with the Ionian – that makes landfall at the actual cape of Cape Maleas.

The Aegean Sea witnessed the birth and decline of two bronze age civilisations: the Minoans of Crete, and the Myceneans of the Peloponnese. These were advanced civilisations who traded over a huge area, produced vibrant art, and used complex writing systems. The reasons for their collapse are unknown.

Following the subsequent Greek Dark Ages, political and cultural development allowed Greeks to settle across the Mediterranean and Black Sea regions. These advances led eventually to the Classical Period. The political, philosophical, scientific, and cultural advances of the Classical Period in turn influenced and allowed the expansion of the later Roman Empire. As such, it is accurate to consider the Aegean Sea region as the birthplace of Western Civilisation.

There are a number of suggested etymologies for the word Aegean. Perhaps it derives from the mythical Aegeus, who drowned himself in the waters off Athens because he believed his son to have been killed by the Minotaur. Or maybe it derives from Aegea and her tribe of warrior women.

A name used in antiquity for the Aegean was *Archipelago* – meaning "chief sea" (ἄρχι-, *arkhi-* "chief" and πέλαγος, *pélagos* "sea") – and from which derives the modern term for a grouping of islands.

The gyre of the Aegean runs anticlockwise. It is maintained partly by water arriving from the Black Sea via The Dardanelles, and partly by a current from the Mediterranean that flows up the Turkish coast.

The Etesian – or Meltemi – wind is a dominant weather influence in the Aegean basin. It blows from the north through most of the summer, often for days at a time and at gale force strength. The word Meltemi is thought to be a loan from the Italian *mal tempo*: bad weather.

Aegean Sea

extent and track

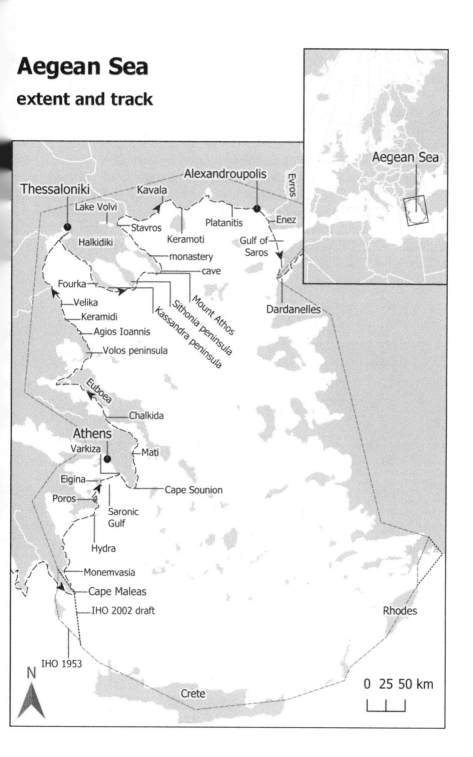

The Greek fishing fleet is large in number, although compared to most EU countries the average boat size is small. Commercially important species include anchovy, sardine, hake and red mullet. Overfishing has reduced catch and there are EU incentives for fishermen to scrap their boats.

Tourism in the Aegean is a major industry for both Greece and Turkey. Less frequented coastlines are also a favoured habitat of the endangered Mediterranean monk seal.

The region is seismically active. Devasting quakes and tsunamis happen several times per millennium according to historical record.

There has been a Greek state on the Aegean coast from 1829 onwards. During WW1 Greece gained control of the territories to the north of the Aegean and by 1930 its present day mainland borders were established.

However, Greek-Turkish relations remain strained on issues relating to territorial waters. Greece is a signatory to the UN Law of the Sea, but Turkey is not – and has a differing interpretation of maritime law.

An octopus of the Aegean investigates my paddle

Life's Generosity

8-12 October 2018

I read my notes; it has been a while now since the Aegean was sailed. Memories surprise me: episodes that I do not habitually recall and had in some sense forgotten. An intended recipient of my first book was my mother – it was a way to tell her who I am. Or who I had been at that time. An intended recipient of this book is my older self. Documented memories become like Post-it notes on a fridge. Perhaps these reminders will help me stay mindful of life's generosity.

My mental state is in a good place as I sail the Aegean. Gone are the nerves of the opening seas. Passed are the stresses and occasionally harrowing experiences of the Atlantic coasts. Previously – to fill the void – might have come rumination about the past. But in this present the mind wanders unburdened. This is an epoch of personal freedom. I sense a consolidation of learning – as islands of knowledge begin to form a landscape.

***

This sea is replete with untold stories. Imagine how many! In the subset of those that relate to my footnote of a voyage, people demonstrate that we all have it in us to make a difference in the lives of others. Time and again I am humbled by kindness.

Xenia is an ancient Greek concept of hospitality. In *xenia*, the bond of friendship is recognised as a two-way honour: Hosts to guests must be hospitable, and guests to hosts must not be a threat or burden. That is how it has been understood since antiquity. There are multiple examples of *xenia* in the Odyssey, and *xenia* is a recurring feature of this voyage too. The Greek people are historically and culturally literate. Perhaps their hospitality is a legacy of Odysseus. It feels that way – as if I sail in his stern wake.

***

Kate and the gang from Monemvasia demonstrate *xenia*. In need of friendship they give me laughter; in need of nutrition they provide food; and in mutual appreciation of quirky language they offer "a sea like yoghurt."

When I depart this ancient town, the Aegean has none of the glassy calm of yoghurt. The meltemi is back in and its waves push a river of trash southward. Nature has a neat trick where she concentrates junk, and here it is squashed against the east side of the Peloponnese, soon to be launched Africa-bound from the tip of Cape Maleas. The stream is continuous – a kilometre-wide highway of our detritus. Despite this blemish, the scenery is majestic, and the sailing invigorating.

The replacement sail – that was new when received in northern Spain – is already old. Its laminate films are now crispy and brittle. Recycling is the best thing for it. Given that a plastic bottle is said to last for 450 years, there is an irony that a plastic sail is so ephemeral.

Some days later, a fall onto the weakened sail punctures it. This obliges a stop on the island of Hydra. The tear will be taped up once the sail dries. The main town is some distance away and my pebble beach is quiet and peaceful. Hydra is entirely unspoilt and has no cars. I decide to stay, and in the afternoon hike up to the central spine of the island to enjoy a beautiful mountain-top sunset. The peak experience is appreciated as such: That we have some moments of existence – and that we can be awed by that existence – brings a flood of gratitude.

Dinner is a bowl of posh spaghetti: fresh tomato sauce, basil and parmesan. The food is delicious, but I cannot pay – or even thank who has paid – because they have already slipped away.

Sunset from a peak on the island of Hydra. The island also agreed with poet and songwriter Leonard Cohen (see *Days of Kindness* [1985])

The Saronic Gulf

13-23 October 2018

Galatas

Galatas is on the south side of the Saronic Gulf. I have a contact here – Manos – who is a friend of Hans *"Zephyr"*, from Pylos. Opposite Galatas is Poros, where I have a contact named Tasos. Try saying that after an ouzo.

Manos has offered lodgings. This lovely man is good to his word. He arrives with a pickup to load the board in, and delivers me to an apartment for the weekend.

In the adjacent room are two Dutch cyclists. Pietr and Edmund are both retired and Pietr is in his 70's. They usually rough camp. The only comfort they miss is a shower, so sometimes they take a room to get clean. On this trip they have already been touring for five weeks. Last year they cycled the Sahara. Their big smiles are encouraging proof that life can deliver spectacularly in our later years too.

Before Pietr and Edmund depart, Manos invites us for a meal at his house. The table is full with 15 different plates of hospitality. His visitors are clean, and clean shaven, and Manos for the first time is without his trademark blue overalls. I feel very honoured to have been at that table.

I stay on one day longer, and liaise via messages with Tasos of Poros – a windsurf coach for the Greek windsurf team. We meet on the water and put in a loop of his island.

There is something delightfully ridiculous in that shared loop. Look closely – it's there on the map – and you'll see the joy of windsurfing. And I'll pretend we went round *widdershins* – meaning anticlockwise – because that word is a favourite and too good not to use.

Varkiza

Varkiza is on the north side of the Saronic Gulf. It is reached via an overnight on the island of Eigina. On the first leg I dodge island-hopping hydrofoils, and on the second leg there are container ships heading to and from Athens.

At Varkiza, preparations are underway for a major youth windsurfing regatta: the Techno 293 European Championships.

The event becomes a whirlwind of social networking. The UK team of coaches and parents act as foster family. Some of them have arrived bearing gifts: of footstraps, and downhaul rope. All of the team include me in their plans: I eat at their tables, sleep on their sofas, and spend many happy hours in their company.

The Spaniards have arrived too and amongst them are Billy, Alvaro and Toni from my local club in Menorca.

Another familiar face is Patrik. We met in Spain at the event in Blanes. Patrik is filming the event and conducting interviews, so he knows most people. Through him I also meet Tatyana – from the Russian coaching team – who is captivatingly beautiful, fantastically encouraging, and married – Patrik helpfully tells me.

The vibe at the event is inclusive and heart-warming. These are lucky kids, and adults.

And when racing finally gets underway, so do I.

Techno 293 European Championships opening ceremony

Bedtime Stories

23-25 October 2018

Varkiza had been continually social. The next few days alone are restoring for their solitude. There are stiff headwinds after emerging from the lee of Cape Sounion, from where the Temple of Poseidon looks down. The onward sail is cold and bruising. I land at a quiet spot and make use of the shelter of a small sailing club for sleeping. Only later – after a carful of policeman show-up and aim torches at my face – do I realise that the club has CCTV surveillance. I retrieve a passport for inspection and am eventually allowed to get some shuteye.

The following day I see a bloodied fish lobbed into the air. At first glimpse I think that the animal beneath it must be a shark. Subsequent glimpses confirm that it is in fact a Mediterranean monk seal: my first sighting of this endangered species.

Impending darkness leads to a stop at Mati, where a windsurfer called Nick says hello, and confirms it will be no problem to sleep under the boat shelter. I'd seen lots of burnt buildings whilst paddling. Apparently, wildfires swept through the neighbourhood earlier in the year with considerable loss of life.

The following morning is too windy to sail. By afternoon it has softened enough to set sail in pursuit of miles. After sunset the wind dies away. I struggle on past uninviting rock to a gentle sand beach. There are some facilities here. It is kind of like a holiday camp. Amongst the trees are some lights. I head in their direction in search of food.

There was a Butlins camp at Clacton when I was a kid. That was a strange place, and here is odd in a similar way. There are no people about. but then it is the off season, and it is rather late. I go into a building where there are lights on. There is a corridor and a canteen. This looks more promising. *Pizza? Pita souvlaki?* Then I realise that I have landed within the grounds of a military facility.

I have some more explaining to do. This set of uniformed interrogators speak better English. They are from the Hellenic Navy. This is some sort of training centre. Thankfully – since it is dark – my deportation is by road. We detour via the beach, where I derig the gear and load it into a supplies truck. The landfall adjustment undoes a portion of today's sail. That suits me fine. The navy dudes dump me at the roadside, and we pose for a moonlit timelapse selfie.

Nickolas of Chalkida

27-28 October 2018

I take advantage of a sheltered water route up the inside of Euboea. The island is closest to the mainland at Chalkida, where I have a contact – Nickolas – who had said:

"Good morning from Sunny Greece!

I will have prepared for you a lot of cold beers.

I will be happy to sail together when you come to my town."

Yesterday I sent Nickolas a message. There has been no reply yet, but there are Optimist dinghies on the water from the sailing club he had mentioned, and there is a trainer in a RIB alongside the sails. Like a mother duck and her ducklings. It is a glorious day. The coach comes alongside. He has a broad smile and knows of my journey, but this is not Nickolas

Chalkida looks nice, I would be happy to stop here if it were later in the day. But there are still good miles to be had. Nonetheless, I would like to pass on my regards to Nickolas. I ask the coach if he knows him, but it's like he hasn't understood the question, so I ask again, and again no reply is forthcoming. The coach's smile is absent. His expression is as if he has seen a ghost. Then he turns to me and the words come:

"Nickolas is dead. He died of cancer, earlier this year."

I should have stopped. I wish I had stopped. To pass on my condolences.

***

The northwest coast of Euboea is breathtakingly beautiful: a searingly blue sky punctured by craggy, clouded peaks; mountainsides of forest and scree-slope; wavelets that tumble the sun-bleached pebbles where my board takes a brief rest. I try to live this place rather than just collect a photograph.

The Volos Peninsula

2-6 November 2018, from log entries

2nd November – Agios Ioannis

The local forecast these next days is for feeble headwinds. But the Meltemi will blow across the central Aegean and send swell this way. The sea is already stirring. 12 nm is measured quickly, but with all the gear, and a rigged sail, and a trickle of headwind, on an open sea, the paddle is a tough one. I sometimes measure progress in terms of marathons – full or half. Today's "half" is a decent effort that gets me to a proper port.

After landing, I learn that Severne Sails are building a replacement sail. Great news! I like to make the gear last, but the current sail has now truly reached end of life. Its fragility compromises my route choices and landing options.

More great news: Agios Ioannis marks the end of the (open) tavern drought! Dinner is red mullet with roast aubergine and garlic, and chips. I shovel in the calories. There is a decent-sized swell hitting the beach by evening.

3rd November – no sailing

The next safe landing – disregarding another small harbour just round the corner – will come after another 14 nm of hostile shore. My subconscious – perhaps with awareness that conditions for sailing and for paddling are terrible – guides me instead to do some proper patching up of the sail, and to observe the evolution of the day, so that the clock runs down. There is a window of a couple of hours where progress could have been made.

Back to the Taverna Posedonia for more aubergines.

4th November – Chorefto

A four-egg breakfast to fortify me for the pain I know is coming. I manage 4 nm before the wind becomes so light that there is no power to drive the board through the confused sea. The sound of board being slapped to a standstill reverberates through me. Seasickness rises from within. I try to paddle, just to confirm what I already know: that significant forward progress is impossible. I claw some extra metres but at this rate it is futile. Retreat is the only sane option. A knot or two of following wind eases the pain. I belch my way back to the small harbour. The ask to get beyond this section of cliff is now 12 nm.

5th November – Keramidi

The day dawns still. Even if a breeze does come in, I know it won't last. And paddling with the rigged sail in this sea is just too impossibly difficult. And the sail is too fragile to survive a de-rig once afloat. Options are to either wait it out until conditions change, or organise on land to paddle the whole stretch with the sail derigged. It is worth a try. I set to the task, tie everything down securely, and then set out for beyond the shelter of the harbour wall.

With so much top-loaded weight the instability is perhaps even worse than with the sail rigged. Imagine a Weeble – the egg shaped children's toy – balanced upsidedown. But at least the waves do not catch at the boom. And with the previously front-stowed bag positioned instead as a central seat the board can be used like a sit-on-top canoe. And where the rebound is less severe – if I maintain hawk-like concentration on the waves – it is also possible to stand up paddle.

The first milestone is where I had reached yesterday. The average speed has been encouraging. Inevitably, the Weeble wobbles and I do fall down. Fall in. And the board rolls into an effortless capsize. The load – however – stays tight, so that the board is easily righted.

At 4 nm there is a tiny beach. With a rigged sail, and zero wind under the cliff, it would be a totally unthinkable landing site. But configured like this I can tuck into the most protected corner and make landfall for a short break.

At 8 nm there is a small cut in the rocks, allowing for another reconnect with solidity, and a second brief rest. The next stop will be at a habited place, so I ditch all the water I am carrying to lose a few kilos. For the final third to Keramidi port the slight headwind at last falls away.

Fatigued, but well satisfied. A survey of the "town" finds nothing open, so dinner is mountain food: re-hydrated spag bog. Then comes bed. Excruciating cramps around the rectum and pelvic region attack me through the night – presumably a result of the intense balancing effort throughout the day.

6th November – Velika

An early start today, because there is some movement of air forecast for the morning, and only 6 nm to cover to before the cliffs descend and beaches return. Now that I am further north the swell is also smaller, and its angle is more from behind. The fading breeze pushes me to the next harbour. The air goes still. There is nothing open here either. Later, a weak sea breeze develops, sufficient to reach Velika. At this town there is a shop for supplies. And I go for a beer and a pizza at Hliaforas Bar, where the proprietor kindly offers a shower and a bed. My first shower in two weeks.

Thessaloniki

12-14 November 2018

Thessaloniki – jammed up in the northeast corner of the Aegean – is Greece's second largest city. Had it not been for the encouraging messages of Thomas and Theodore, I would have straight-lined across its gulf and it would never have become a stop.

Instead, by accepting the detour I enjoy a magical overnight on a sand-dune spit; then cross 12 nm of open water under sail; then cross 6 nm more – under paddle – through "a sea like yoghurt" made thick by a bloom of comb jellies. These animals are translucent; and – up close – rather pretty, with lines of cilia that refract light like a rainbow.

I follow Thomas's directions to the Thessaloniki SUP club, and there it gets a bit confusing. Kostas shows up: he's been sent by Thomas. And Odysseus shows up: he's from the Hellenic Rescue Team – a volunteer network who assist with mountain and sea rescue. My rule about double bookings is to go with the first offer. So I say goodbye to the board, arrange for a meet with the HRT tomorrow, and get in the car with Kostas.

We drive until I am disoriented, and then stop for food. I tuck in. If this is a hostage situation then better to face it with a full stomach. Our respective nerves settle. Kostas is too nice to be a hostage-taker anyway.

More driving, to the centre of Thessaloniki. I meet Thomas and his wife Stavroula, and a bunch more amazingly welcoming folk. They put me in a hotel – I don't need a hotel I tell them – but for the first two nights that is how it will be. We go for more food. Much more food!

The following day I meet with Odysseus and Harris – from the HRT – who take me for a tour of Thessaloniki. It is a standout day. It is fascinating: to be within history; to witness the layers – the physical layers – of the city from old to new. My guides are as knowledgeable and patient as I am ignorant and awed. There is so much to be seen and heard. At last I fully grasp the obvious: for most of history Britain and the west coasts of Europe have been a far flung nowhere; *here* is where the action of history really happened!

We walk and my teachers gently educate, building in time for stops in cafés. The physical evidence of the past is beneath our feet and in the fabric of the city.

The Greeks, the Romans, the 500 years of Ottoman rule; the arrival of Spanish Jews expelled from the Iberian Peninsula, and the extermination of their descendants by the Nazis. It is necessary to know a little to realise how little one knows. Walking round Thessaloniki with Odysseus and Harris I reach that threshold.

In the evening I show some pictures from my journey. The audience is a full room of HRT volunteers: outdoorsy type people. I am typically nervous, but their interest is so sincere that the talk is easy and enjoyable. Their questions flow and so do I.

Thomas has been busy making things happen. The following day I am interviewed twice on Greek TV. The first interview is for a local channel and the presenters allow a proper conversation to happen. Their questions are sensible because their interest is real. The second interview is for a national channel. It is glossier, but the questions are vacuous.

I pop into an optician. Not just any optician: this is Theodore who had also put a pin on the map here in Thessaloniki. He is concerned about all the UV my slate blue eyes receive. The UV dose is also something I am aware of. In fact I do have a thickening of the coat over the eye, and a permanent redness. Theo prescribes – and provides free of charge – a pair of Cébé sunglasses that are in his professional opinion the most optically correct and protective.

Thomas and Stavourla have a windsurf shop – "Stonero"[30] – in the city, but their real home is at Lake Volvi about 60 kilometres away. The large open plan building by the lake is also a café and windsurf club. After the fast pace of the city it is a place to unwind, and Stavroula's mother's cooking is memorably tasty.

Lake Volvi is just a few miles from the coast. Tomorrow we will drive back to Thessaloniki, and I will begin the sea voyage back towards the lake's nearest coastal town. This will require a 150 nm (≈280 km) detour round the three peninsulas of Halkidiki. The last of these peninsulas could be awkward – but we will come to that later. Comforting for me is that it will be a temporary departure. The objective will be to return – back towards the friendship, warmth, nest-like security, and fresh baking of Thomas' family; back towards Lake Volvi and where feels like home.

---

[30] From the Greek *Sto nero* (Στο νερό), meaning "in the water".

Halkidiki and Mount Athos

15-23 November 2018, from log entries

Each of the Halkidiki peninsulas are noteworthy. The Kassandra peninsula stands out for night-time arrivals and phenomenal support from the HRT. The team from Fourka make a maritime interception and guide me in through the blackest of nights. They diligently care for me over a number of days whilst bad weather and mild illness pass through.

I cross to and camp on the very tip of the Sithonia peninsula, where a sand isthmus connects to another almost-island. It is a magically wild and empty camp spot. As darkness falls a vehicle bumps down a track and parks in the distance. I do not see the man until he reaches me and flicks on the bright light of his torch. In his other hand is a speargun. Later in the night the fisherman reappears with a rack of honey to donate. Wonderful! But awkward luggage.

The easternmost peninsula is the Monastic Republic of Mount Athos. The peninsula is home to Orthodox monks and has been under self-rule since 972. Unauthorised public access is prohibited, and there is a blanket ban on access for women. Mount Athos itself it a colossus that rises steeply from the sea to an altitude of over 2000 metres. It is the focus of this section because I underestimate its challenge.

20th November – Landfall on Athos

Honey decanting issues mean that I am slow and rushed to get away. I also skip the routine tightening of footstrap screws. A mistake. There is a strong headwind. The port side beating straps pull out! But luck is on my side, as the layline [correct angle] to clear this middle outcrop is already passed. I tack, and a few miles later can free-off into protected water, and then stop at a beach to re-affix and tighten the straps.

From here the crossing to the Mount Athos peninsula is 15 nm. I proceed in upwind zigzags. Longer zigs and shorter zags, comparatively. I am aware that failing light could be an issue, but speed is good.

A damned big hill this! Majestic too. With the distance closed to 5 nm it seems that already I have arrived. Of course that is premature. This is still very much open sea. Low cloud adds to the dramatic views. Monasteries are discernible. Those at sea-level altitude are potential landing points. I have no permission to land. I decide to push on to the south facing tip. There is stronger wind – a solid force 5 – at the first corner. Good! Solid breeze is needed to scoot round the next corner – just 5 nm to the east – and then quickly reach away to safety. My bet is on finding an increasingly favourable wind angle. A bad gamble! I head south, out to sea, looking for the required wind bend. I tack back, and moments later am severely headed. Damn it! The wind has shifted – but it has swung the wrong way – and the last half-hour of sailing has delivered no gain.

Cloud base descending. Wind dropping. Progress slower and slower. The board moves drunkenly in the sloppy sea. What had I been thinking? 5 nm sounds nothing – but in these conditions that distance is an ocean. The metric that matters is time, and there is no chance of reaching safety before dark. Some curses to release the stress:

Damned honey! – because it made me late

Damned social anxiety! – because I know that it was that which sailed me past those beaches by the monasteries.

Damned phone! – because it is new from Thessaloniki, and navigation is still a challenge.

This mess is a screw up on multiple fronts. "Fuck it!" At last a proper swear word. That gets it out of the system.

In parallel with these recriminations is an awareness of the incredible beauty: The mountain draped in cloud; the shocking scale! It is an exhilarating fear.

I recheck the GPS for options. There is a red marker on the screen. Red is my code for "Don't go there / terrible option / emergency only". It appears to mark a kind of port behind the lighthouse on the east corner of the cape. Bingo! There's my target, and at a reachable 2 nm. But even if I can claw that distance sailing, the final few hundred metres will have to be paddled, and converting to paddle mode in the waves and in the dark will be immensely difficult. So I must set up for paddling now.

Thankful now for the countless refinements – and hundreds of repetitions – of this operation. I paddle on my knees against a headwind and sea from all directions. Thankful now for the blinking lighthouse. Jarring slaps vibrate through the board and stop it dead.

A full moon behind cloud offers no illumination. But the sea is full of phosphorescence. Paddle strokes light up the sea, and waves bleed white where they ascend jagged rock. The lighthouse is eventually reached, then passed. I search for the entrance. None can be discerned. But GPS says it must be here. It is noisy. Water sloshes and echoes off the high sides as swells carry me deeper into this tight, black corner. Then my headtorch picks out stonework about three storeys high, and the entrance itself – wide enough for a rowing boat, and in I go.

The converted cave could – at best – be described as offering a fair weather landing stage, but that will do. Sloshing water echoes. A roll of swell pushes us further in and instinctively I follow up into a landing.

The cave is damp and loud. The interior is lined with smashed-up fish trays carried here by sea and wind. But there is a route out, and a path, upon which I sleep, beneath the light that has guided me to "port".[31]

21st November – Vatopedi Monastery

Porridge and honey for breakfast. There is no wind or space to sail out of this corner. And the swell has picked up overnight, though its more southerly direction compensates for this added complication. I set up the gear in paddle mode, launch it into the gulley, then scamper round the rocks to board on the bow. Successful launch.

Further out there is a gusty on-then-off following wind. Mightily awkward with this swell. I topple in, have to load the boom excessively on the fall to protect the oh-so delicate sail, and the connection between board and rig fails. A replacement for that worn-out mast extension is long overdue.

Next – after a break during a windless period – the uphaul line breaks, sending me toppling in backwards, with drysuit zip wide open, which allows the Aegean to flood in.

The wind comes and goes. Between puffs, I sit and wait to recover energies – patiently playing the long game. That delivers gradual but useful progress. Past the first of the east coast beaches and monasteries.

Around mid-afternoon a coastguard launch shows up. Apparently they have had some calls about me. Friendly guys. They say I should stop at the next port, and can stay at the monastery there. Technically I need a permit, but the coastguards say they can't leave me out at night and will arrange everything, which they do.

The monastery is like a micro-civilisation. I eat well, have a comfortable room, and the people are very kind. The monks mostly keep to their routines. Some are young, under their beards. This monastery also has some outside visitors. Conversation is limited in scope. "Orthodox? Anglican?" they ask. "Atheist" is not the correct answer, so I flip to "undecided", which is – on reflection – probably a more accurate description of my belief.

22nd November – Akra Arapis

Breezy for the first miles. Then less wind but a lurching, choppy sea. Later, the wind makes a reappearance so that I can bounce along to the target promontory. I pass inside a small island for the shelter it offers. There is a near miss with a plump fisherman in a brown wetsuit. It takes a moment for

---

[31] Some history and pictures about this location:
https://athosweblog.com/2018/11/24/2028-arsanas-prodromou/

me to register that the swimmer had been a monk seal. The protected habitat of this peninsula is good for them, and nature in general.

In the shelter of the hook of land there is flat sea and a beach perfect for camping. A campfire provides welcome warmth. During the night my slumber is disturbed by the prolonged vibration of an earthquake. Later, reference to seismic records confirms that the epicentre had been nearby.

23rd November – Stavros

An easy day to complete this section. I cross a small gulf, then gently finish the 20 nm run to the pretty town of Stavros. Kostas is already here. We load up and head off to nearby Lake Volvi for the weekend, to meet up with Thomas, Stavroula and the Thessaloniki crew.

With (left to right) Thomas, Stavroula, Tzeni, Chris and (behind the camera) Kostas

Eleftheron

28 November 2018

Autumn turns to winter. The wind is either a chilly easterly, or absent. Support along the northern Aegean continues to be rock solid.

It is necessary to go with the flow. Sometimes I have no idea who I am with or where I am being taken. At Eleftheron a thunderstorm forces me to land, and then robs me of all heat. A couple with a cliffside house had almost called the coastguard but instead wrap my hands round a mug of warming tea. A contact – another Tasos – somehow tracks me down. Maybe I had a plan with this guy, or maybe not. I cannot keep up with the to-and-fro of messaging.

An hour later I am in a four-by-four. Either side of the main beam it is pitch black. Tasos and Christos are up front. The windscreen wipers swish at full tilt. We ascend a forested valley. The vehicle's headlights illuminate unguarded security gates. We splash through a river. Next come the graffitied walls of abandoned buildings.

We pull up next to and enter the shell of another building. Christos undresses and dons a fluffy bathrobe. The alarm bells in my head sway, though do not quite ring. My outfit is a travel towel. I wear it like a miniskirt. Back to the four-by-four we go. More driving. More rain. We re-cross the swollen river and bump down a dead end track. The end of the road.

Sulphur is in the air. Our headtorches pick out steaming geothermal pools. "In you go!" I am encouraged, so in I drop, and stay for a 30 minute soak. Wonderful! The water is a steady 42 degrees Celsius. It is an almost perfect end to the day. Only let down by the discarded rubbish – a blemish so often observed that it no longer surprises.

The sherpas – their work done – leave me at a room of the squat. I am warm to the core. Dinner is powdered mash and tinned fish "cooked" on my camp stove. Before the flickering candle burns away, I am asleep.

Alexandroupolis

1-16 December 2018

The edge of the European Union – a hard border – is nearing. There is another rendezvous with Sherpa Tasos at Kavala – this time with his family. The normality of helping their little boy with his English homework is a treat. Further on there are multiple linkups with the ever vigilant Hellenic Rescue Team.

Yannis – the lifeguard from Karavostasi beach – and his brother come to meet me when I am near to their hometown. We go for *pita souvlaki* – Greek fast food – meat, salad and chips in a pita bread wrap. Yannis tops up my honey supplies. Dimitris wasn't dealt the best hand in life, but he does have Yannis as a brother, so in another sense he lucked out.

50 nm later, Nikos exemplifies *xenia* and is ideal company for some low-key days. My sleeping bag gets a wash and tumble dry. The refound fluff doubles its warmth. We study maps. I process an e-visa for Turkey.

On the beach the next evening a dog befriends me. Dogs are usually spooked when they find a human in a sleeping bag. This one cries a startled "What the woof is this?!" but then decides I am friendly, and snuggles up in the warmth behind my knees. Later in the night another dog stumbles upon us. "What the woof is this?!" it exclaims, before being barked into chastised retreat by my possessive companion.

With Nasos at Alexandroupolis

At Alexandroupolis I have a proper bed, courtesy of Nasos, who installs me in the sailing club. Nasos even arranges for a shower to be plumbed in.

The new sail from Severne has cleared customs and is ready to pick up. At last! It will be a huge relief to no longer have to nurse the sail. The films of the new sail are flexible and strong. Nasos's friends help to get it logoed up with a WWF Panda on the top panel. On a lower panel go the flags and Windsurf Round Europe translations – in Turkish, Georgian, and Russian. The sail looks and feels great.

Alexandroupolis is the last significant port on the Greek mainland before the border with Turkey. The border itself is the river Evros. Tomorrow – before departure to cross the Evros delta – it will be necessary to get an exit stamp in my passport.

Nasos accompanies me to the port building for a chat with the relevant authorities. I explain my route, and let slip that I had crossed to Albania – and then back into the EU – without obtaining the required exit and entry stamps. This is my first realisation of that oversight. The room goes quiet. Fortunately, I am given the opportunity to rephrase an explanation of the route sailed. The essential details are a crossing from Italy and a landing on Corfu. No entry and exit stamps are required for that. For all of us it is a much simpler passage.

We formed a bond

Enez

17-19 December, from log entry

From Alexandroupoulis in Greece to Enez in Turkey – across the Evros delta – is about 12 nm.

Deltas are places to be wary of. They are wind corridors that have no distinct land-water boundary. For the mariner they are featureless and disorientating. The thought of near disaster at the Delta del Ebro intrudes. This morning has started gentle, but a stronger wind now funnels out of the delta. The angle to Enez is tight, but doable as a single leg. A tack inshore would make no sense. For a while that leaves me exposed and offshore in this no-man's land between countries. Though the sea is a tumble of whitecaps, the new sail remains reassuringly tight and silent.

At this speed the distance is gobbled up. I sail by GPS heading, until a bump on the horizon becomes unequivocally my destination. Mid-crossing the fetch had been significant, and the water choppy; but now the "weather shore" [land on the upwind side] is nearer, and the water flatter. Eventually the sea becomes groomed and flat like a speed strip. As a precaution I had sailed a little higher than necessary. That now leaves the final miles more open – as a flat-out straight line blast to Enez harbour.

Bordering the harbour interior is a vast expanse of concrete. Squashed into one corner are tatty craft suitable for navigating the channels of the delta. Moored at the opposing corner is a coastguard cutter. The space in the middle – where I haul my gear onto the concrete plain – is empty, cold and grey. The wind blows across the unforgiving surface such that the board will not settle.

In the government corner there is also a coastguard building. I walk to its gates and show my passport and e-visa. To enter Turkey most yachts would sail to Çanakkale before presenting their papers, but for me that port is still several days from here. I hope to get a passport stamp here, in Enez. Instead I am told to wait. They tell me that a storm is on the way – which is true – and we agree that I will not sail during the storm.

A coastguard official comes to take a picture of the gear. I ask about moving to a more sheltered spot in the harbour, closer to the smaller craft. Mime helps to fill the language gap. "Sleep. There. OK?"

"No!" comes a reply. "There not OK." He struggles for the words and turns to Google Translate for help. I read from the screen, "There smugglers," and the man nods his head.

A lone upturned boat offers some limited protection from the wind. I get comfy in my sleeping bag and enjoy the start of hibernation. After an indeterminable time my slumber is disturbed by the offer of a glass of tea. The offer comes from Murat.

Murat's job is to monitor the port. He has CCTV and a good-sized window. He works for Fisheries Control to keep an eye on a non-existent fishing fleet, and – I guess – the smugglers. It is warm inside his little room. We also communicate via Google Translate. Before clocking off, Murat opens a shipping container and indicates that I can sleep inside.

***

The next two days are windy and cold. Seawater is whipped airborne and onto the concrete plain. My original campsite is awash. My dorm – the container – has no insulation but at least it is dry. Puddles of rainwater are frozen solid. Arriving vehicles are snow covered. Dogs shelter where they can. I wonder how they do not perish. By day the animals scavenge for food: crunching on mussels that grow on mooring lines, and squabbling over feathers.

Murat and I drink tea through the day. The police call by every few hours. They also like the warmth and the tea inside Murat's little room. I ask for a passport stamp. They say they are unable to provide one. On day two the policemen bring food and offer a pocketknife as a gift.

Later, the coastguards send a car and I am taken to their compound. They seem disposed to find a solution now. I am cleared to sail to Çanakkale to be processed. The wait has not been a delay. I was going nowhere in this weather. There are worse things to do than look out at a storm – from behind glass – whilst drinking tea.

Enez harbour with Murat (right) and friends

24. Marmara Sea

The Sea of Marmara (the Marmara Sea) links the Aegean to the Black Sea. To its north is the European part of Turkey, and to its south is the Anatolian Peninsula – the Asian part of Turkey. The Marmara has a maximum width of about 40 nm (≈74 km), is approximately 150 nm (≈278 km) in length, and reaches a maximum depth of 1400 metres.

The Sea is named after Marmara island – which is a rich source of marble and itself named after the Greek word for this valuable rock. A name used in antiquity for the Sea of Marmara was *Propontis* – which in that period would have carried the meaning "before the Black Sea".

The Marmara communicates with the Aegean Sea via the Dardanelles, and with the Black Sea via the Bosphorus Strait. The extent of the Marmara Sea includes both of these straits. The city of Istanbul – population 15 million in 2020 – is bisected by the Bosphorus Strait.

The Sea and straits are strategically important. The Dardanelles straight was the focus of the WW1 Gallipoli campaign; the outcome of which was half a million casualties, a hundred thousand deaths, and an eventual allied retreat.

Surface currents flow north to south in both straits, and in deep water there are currents that travel in the reverse direction.

Istanbul discharges most of its wastewater – untreated – into the deep water of the Bosphorus. "1100 tons of organic matter, 130 tons of nitrogen and 20 tons of phosphorus, and a wide spectrum of settleable solids, chemicals and hazardous materials" are discharged daily. A mixing of the layers means that much of this effluent is returned straight to the Marmara Sea.[32]

Pollution from this and other sources is literally choking the Marmara. During 2021 the sea became clogged with the mucous slime of an algal bloom that penetrated into the depths and suffocated marine life over widespread areas. Fishing catches were decimated, because the fish had died, and their rotting corpses were further reducing the already critical oxygen levels.

In the colder winter months the Marmara recovers – somewhat – but experts agree that it is already too late for the Marmara to recover fully. The Marmara needs a rescue package now. It is the story of our planet on a smaller scale.

---

[32] "Will the Marmara Sea Survive? The Struggle Against Pollution" – Prof. Dr. Derin Orhon – Government Gazette March 2014

The Marmara Sea

extent and track

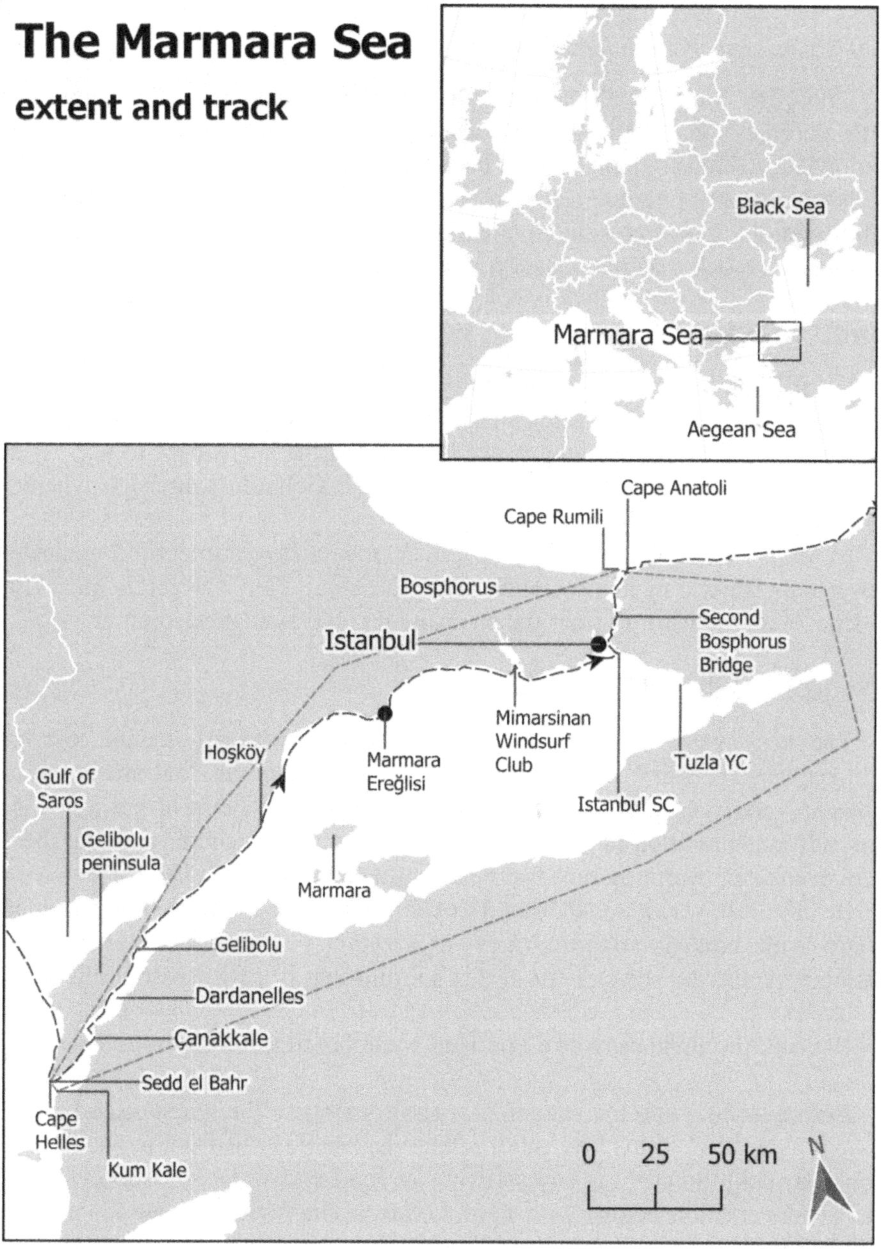

Black Sea

Marmara Sea

Aegean Sea

Cape Anatoli

Cape Rumili

Bosphorus

Istanbul

Second
Bosphorus
Bridge

Mimarsinan
Windsurf
Club

Hoşköy

Marmara
Ereğlisi

Tuzla YC

Gulf of
Saros

Istanbul SC

Gelibolu
peninsula

Marmara

Gelibolu

Dardanelles

Çanakkale

Sedd el Bahr

Cape
Helles

Kum Kale

0   25   50 km

N

Gelibolu (Gallipoli) Peninsula

20-22 December, from log entry

Upon first contact with the Gelibolu peninsular I reflected on its suitability for a coffee stop, rather than the tragedy of war. Only later was a gap in my knowledge filled so that Gelibolu become Gallopoli.

Normally, my overdue research starts with Wikipedia, but in Turkey this indispensable resource is not available. President Erdoğan's government has imposed a block – on national security grounds.

Gulf of Saros

From Enez the wind – though bitingly cold – is of an ideal strength and from a perfect angle. A direct crossing of the gulf saves a much longer detour. Regular arm swinging is needed to bring the hands back to life. After the open water there are easy landings on the Gelibolu peninsula, where I stop for coffee from the thermos flask.

In total, 33 nm are sailed. What a difference a favourable wind makes! I overnight on one of many empty, sandy beaches. This is a gentle, peaceful place. With the warmth from the campfire it could almost be summer.

Sedd El Bahr

The sea-level has dropped overnight – indicative of an increase in atmospheric pressure – to create dry reef with rockpools that are home to shrimps and fish and crabs and whelks. I regress to being a kid and lose myself in exploration of the pools. The day is windless, and once afloat there are even some warming rays for the tranquil paddle to Cape Helles.

In the clear water are thousands of jellyfish: the common, bowl shaped type with pinkish-coloured rings – *Aurelia*. Though all jellyfish have stinging cells, the sting of *Aurelia* is so mild that it isn't usually noticed by humans.

Beneath the lighthouse of Cape Helles the board glides into the Marmara Sea.

Before turning into the Dardanelles strait, I stop on the spacious and sandy shore at Sedd el Bahr. The small village has spilled out from a large castle upon a rocky outcrop. My objectives are food and water – a shop. That is how conversation begins with Farouk and Sovinc, who are out for a stroll with their dog.

They offer a place to stay, and dinner that includes Dardanelles sea bass, and the opportunity to get clean and wash clothes. Faruk tells me about the Commonwealth war graves, and explains that he sometimes goes to have a drink with the soldiers at the cemetery behind the beach.

Lest we Forget

In the morning I read up on history and visit the memorials. This strategic peninsula is where the 1915-16 Gallipoli campaign unfolded, the objective of which was to restore a supply line to Russia. There are now a number of cemeteries that commemorate both the Commonwealth and Turk forces. My camp location yesterday had been next to Anzac Cove, landing site for most Australian and New Zealand servicemen.

A late breakfast with my hosts is a beautiful table-full of goodness. Looking down towards Helles Beach, I think back to the steps of the tall monument, inscribed with the words "Lest we Forget." A confusion of imagery comes to mind: humans crated like animals, and animals crated like humans – on their journey to the slaughterhouse of Gallipoli. Lest we Forget. I realise that the inscription relates not to the heroism of men, but to the horror of war.

Departure happens early afternoon. The perfect forms of jellyfish glide alongside and all about. The wind dies off until the board barely moves. In my thoughts the jellyfish become the souls of men. I am grateful to pass so delicately through their waters. Defying gravity – liberated and at peace – is every soul from every battle.

The Martyrs' Memorial commemorates Turkish forces and commands over the entrance to the Dardanelles

The Dardanelles has a strong current flowing out to the Mediterranean. The air is still so I paddle. Sometimes there is a helpful countercurrent close inshore, other times I must paddle hard to make progress. Çanakkale proves beyond reach. I sleep on a quiet beach that faces the city. Overhead there is a full moon. The groan of engine noise from passing shipping is continuous, and intermittent washes peel along the shore.

Çanakkale

A gentle following breeze to reach this small city. I cross the shipping lane at the narrowest part, where the current is strongest, so that it pushes me back into the wind, and a Beaufort force half becomes a reassuring force 2. An easy crossing. I sail to the port police and with their help ascend the dock, and an hour before nightfall have my passport stamped.

I sleep rough in a park, where it is busy through the night. Not a good sleep.

***

In January 2020 the Turkish courts deemed Turkey's Wikipedia block to be unconstitutional, and full read and edit access was restored. #WelcomeBackTurkey.

Jellyfish blooms are often related to excessive nutrient levels. When the blooms go bust the decaying medusae contribute to a hypoxic environment that other marine life is less able to tolerate.

The Dardanelles Strait at Çanakkale

Picking your Battles

24-25 December 2018

The remaining 20 nm of the Dardanelles strait become a duel against the elements. A tailwind blows from the south and steadily builds until I can barely hold on.

The Dardanelles at this point is approximately 2 nm wide. It is too enclosed to develop ocean-like swells but plenty large enough to raise a difficult sea if it blows hard – which it does – and if the current is opposing – which it is.

The day had begun with long downwind zigzags. For a while I had measured progress alongside a tugboat that was also going north. Later it became too wild to sail mid-channel where the opposing wind and current were strongest. Now I sail close to the tame coastline on the west side of the strait. The sail is downhauled to oblivion. I hold the boom with both hands up by the mast so that it flags open to spill the excess power. Still the board planes down the faces of the waist-high chop. The crazy joyrides are difficult to control. A hundred metres out it is already too wild and somehow I must execute a gybe and then zag back shoreward. Many times the nose spears, or I fall, or both. Adrenaline is the fuel for countless of these zigzags.

With energies spent I stop in the lee of an outcrop to eat, consult a weather forecast update, and consider options. Windguru indicates that there are gusts of 44 knots! No wonder it is a struggle to get downwind – board and sail are about three times too big. There is another rainy cold snap on the way. Though my body says to stop and camp here, in a north wind there will be no shelter. It makes sense to push on to Gelibolu town, 8 nm from here.

The pummelling continues. Staying close inshore has its hazards too. While sailing at full tilt the fin belts a rock. In the resulting fall the board overturns and I see that the fin has been split open like a peeled banana. In another fall that dodgy mast extension releases once again. The clothes beneath my worn out drysuit are soaking wet. It is hard going, but it is not a hard decision to keep going, because what other option is there?

Gelibolu town sits on a little outcrop. I crash land onto the boulders of its unprotected side and haul the gear to safety at cost of some minor damage to the board. Later – when the wind switches north – this will become the protected side of town.

A beachside carpark is the best campsite on offer. There is a patch of grass, and I am overlooked by a hotel which provides a sense of security. In the night, the wind switches to the north, the temperature plummets, and snow-rain beats on the sail.

Christmas day dawns with a howling wind. There is no question of sailing or reason to get up. My gift to self is a lie-in watching fierce gusts groom the carpark's puddles. Entirely unprompted, the hotel people bring out coffee and some breakfast pastries. That is just a kind act, not festive spirit, because Christmas in Turkey – a Muslim country – goes unnoticed. Later, I find a bar to loiter in and repair the fin.

An upturned board shows off its damaged fin

To Istanbul

26 December 2018 - 1 January 2019

On the seaward horizon the island of Marmara is visible. On the near shore there is farmland and white plastic sheets that on closer inspection are snowdrifts. I stop in small, empty places. The few people I meet do not speak English – but they may offer a glass of hot tea and that is most welcome.

At the fishing town of Hoşköy I haul the board ashore next to a closed-up restaurant terrace. Inside the structure are the restauranteur and his fisherman sons huddled around a wood stove. It is polite to establish contact. An icebreaker question says: I am humble, and I am not a threat. Communication is a wonderful thing. An offer of floorspace inside follows. And knowing that there are friendly eyes watching over the board enables me to head into town for a lamb kofta dinner. Later – back with the group – there is more food: fried fish, and sips of warming wine. Then we communally sleep in the radiated heat of the stove.

There is a larger town at Marmara Ereğlisi. This has a more western feel: with cafés, and internet that works. Some aspects are macho and cheesy: like the punchbag machines that play *Rocky* theme music on repeat.

The following day is windless. I paddle past a huge oil refinery and for safety choose to stay close-in rather than roam offshore and be a shipping hazard. I get past seemingly without incident of major note, but an hour later am apprehended by a coastguard boat because the refinery area was a prohibited zone. I show my papers and eat humble pie and it seems that sanction has been avoided. The boat turns back and I breathe a sigh of relief. Ten minutes later the boat bears down upon me again. Had I counted my chickens too early? No, the return visit is simply to take a picture.

On New Year's eve I reach the hinterland of Istanbul. Once again it is perishingly cold, but a huddle of people light a fire on the beach and invite me to join them to see-in the New Year. These are professional people – teachers and journalists – from Istanbul. We drink wine and eat *kokoretsi* – lamb offal wrapped in intestines – grilled over the fire. Tastier than it sounds. They have disdain for Erdoğan and the increasing Islamization of their country. This beach outside of their city is an escape where dissent can be voiced without fear.

On New Year's day it is gearing up for another cold snap, so I sail early, hoping to beat its arrival. Dolphins join me for much of the journey. We punch upwind in convoy. It is an uplifting sail. A huge milestone has been achieved. I have reached Istanbul!

A place to land is already organised. My contact Mert has done the groundwork and cleared it to leave the gear at Mimarsinan Windsurf Club. Mert and friends provide the warmest of welcomes. We leave the gear snug, and my guides take me to central Istanbul. It is comforting to be in safe hands. The sights whizz by and we take rests in different restaurants for local cuisine. When it becomes late I am booked into a hotel.

Drifted snow behind the shoreline of the Marmara Sea

Winter Pause

9 January 2019, from log entry

This is not the time of year to be sheltering under a sail in the Eastern Med or Black Sea region. There is no warming effect from the Atlantic this far east.

Although I had wanted to make this expedition as continuous as possible – one expedition rather than a set of connected legs – that hasn't happened. The first break – 2017/8 winter – became necessary for health reasons. I'd become run down and then flu wiped me out in a big way. I was already in Spain so headed back to Menorca for recovery.

This winter I've been more careful to eat well, stay warm, and generally not push quite so hard. There have been no health problems so far. On the first day of 2019 I reached Istanbul: a mega-city with twice the population of London, that straddles both Europe and Asia. Istanbul could be considered an edge of Europe – so perhaps journey's end – but the original idea had been to windsurf Russia to Russia – so I'm not done yet.

Next up is the Bosphorus – a strait that is complicated because of strong currents, maritime transit, and permissions obstacles. That needs planning and some luck with the weather. Beyond the Bosphorus lies the Black Sea and its winter storms. Whilst no doubt it would be possible to push on regardless, it might be quite a miserable experience.

So instead I've adjusted my expectations to allow myself a second winter break. Rather than fight nature I'll be flexible as she demands, the way it has historically been for seafarers.

My Turkish visa allows for 90 days in a six-month period. If I waited in Turkey for better weather those days would be ticking away, becoming eventually insufficient to sail the coastline to Georgia. So once again the decision was made to hop on a plane. That has paused the count-up; and is also – I admit – a convenient opportunity to see family and generally regroup.

This pause will also be used to source replacements for safety-critical worn out parts – notably drysuit, mast extension and fin. And to research and prepare for the route ahead. In theory that is to Russia, but I will consider other options too.

A Plan to Close the Loop

10 February 2019, from log entry

From the outset of this journey it has been my target to reach Russia, or at least her border. The day to day of making miles I am accustomed to but the official hurdles are burdensome. Authorizations are time consuming to research, costly to apply for, and riddled with uncertainty. They hang over me like a cloud.

Parallel to the Russia to Russia objective – also from day one – I have privately harboured an ambition to "close the loop". To – somehow, someday – arrive at where I had departed from. To convert this wandering into a circumnavigation of sorts. Would that be possible?

Well, kind of. There was an Irishman – Miles Clark – who circumnavigated Europe by yacht, linking Barents Sea to Black Sea by a route through the White Sea and rivers including the Volga and the Don. That was in 1992, which were perhaps easier times politically. And unfortunately poor Miles died soon after completing the trip, possibly from toxins ingested whilst navigating the Russian waterways.

I studied this and other potential routes. An interesting alternative looked to be Ukraine's Dnieper river then other waterways to the Baltic, from where the White Sea could be reached. But – ultimately – the hours on Google Maps and Wikipedia failed to inspire a practically realistic plan: the distance would be too far to sail and paddle in one summer season, and the inevitable Russian winter too bleak. This, and the realisation that I don't have an appetite for the administrative obstacles, allowed the idea to founder.

Having abandoned waterways, other options could be considered. I happened upon the EuroVelo 13 "Iron Curtain" bicycle route that terminates at the coastal border of Norway and Russia. That happens to be the exact same location that I started sailing in May 2017! An Excel sheet later and a new plan was born.

To recap, Russia's annexation of Crimea rules out an approach to its border via Ukraine. The Russian border situation with Georgia/Abkhazia is not quite as tense – but is still complicated. I will therefore maintain efforts to reach the border with Russia – and perhaps cross to Sochi – but I will be realistic and accepting if circumstances do not allow that to happen.

The details are yet to be ironed out, but when the sailing is done, I will transition to pedal power, and "close the loop" by bicycle.

The Bosphorus

15-28 March 2019

The Bosphorus is policed like a motorway, and a windsurfer upon its waters would generally be as welcome as a bicycle on the M25. Going from the Marmara to the Black Sea there is also a very strong current to battle against. The difficulties seem insurmountable until Edhem gets in touch.

Edhem is positive, helpful and kind. He also happens to have a degree of celebrity inside and outside of the sailing world. He has pride in Turkey as a maritime nation, and the sea runs through him like it runs through the Bosphorus.

For all of the above he fully understands that the continuity of the track is something I hold dear. He pledges to help me reach the Black Sea under sail. On my behalf he negotiates with the Turkish coastguard and navy; and then gets back in touch with the good news that we are ready to go.

On 15th March I arrive back in Istanbul, and the following day solo sail to Istanbul Sailing Club – near to Fenerbahçe, on the Asian side of the Strait. This is a good place from where to enter the narrows. The six-hour-plus sail in light winds is a slog rather than a cruise. There must be a hundred tankers moored up outside Istanbul.

Tuzla Yacht Club becomes base for the next few days as we wait for a southerly wind. There is a little jetty with clinker built National Twelve dinghies. It is a pleasant and privileged place to be. Sometimes I have a guide, but other times I take a bus and ferry to reach Istanbul. To see the suburbs this way is in some ways more eye-opening and enriching than keeping to the famous sites. During independent travel I keep a low profile where possible, and usually walk even though a taxi might be wiser. On a lonely and dimly lit street I witness two men load rifles into the trunk of a car. They obviously hadn't seen me.

I give a talk at the naval school. I have overprepared – with too many pictures – and a majority of the adolescent audience are not obviously appreciative. By midway through the presentation I am dying inside as I race towards the end. The end – is death – but then Admiral Chem explodes with enthusiasm! "Amazing! Fantastic talk! Thank you so much Jono!" I could have hugged him. Admiral Chem Gürdeniz is our contact who has made it possible to attempt this sail through the Bosphorus. What a great guy.

Edhem and I look ahead to find a suitable day but there are no southerly winds on the horizon. We will have to try with a northerly wind instead. We pick a day when a stiffer breeze is forecast in the hope that I can beat the current.

We have a TV crew for the launch from Istanbul Sailing Club. A swirl of wind sends me swimming seconds after I go afloat: impressive for those spectating. Poor Edhem must wonder what sort of a disaster he is about to preside over.

A white-hulled coastguard boat motors gently upstream at a respectful distance. Closer by are Edhem and crew in his grey launch. The board moves rapidly through the water, but actual progress is more gradual. I zigzag between crisscrossing ferries. On the far shore is the Hagia Sophia. What a privilege to sail through the centre of such a historic city!

Maiden's Tower – 200 metres from the Asian side of the strait – is slowly hauled in. The current rushes past such that the tower appears to be being towed upstream. I try a longer zigzag – to mid-channel where it feels like there is more wind – but the net result of that is negative progress. Although near to shore there is less current, the hard, vertical walls of the Bosphorus mean that there is no escape from its pull

As the strait narrows further the current strengthens. My zigzags now are limited to no more than 50 metres. Each tack has to be perfect to minimise the distance surrendered downstream.

There comes a point where progress is no longer being made. The net result of the zigzags is stalemate. Edhem gives the signal to cross to the European side of the strait.

The board is swept downstream as if it has no daggerboard. There is nothing to do but persevere and accept the loss. A kilometre later the board hooks back into firmer water. The board glides into a calm spot in the lee of a bend on the European side of the strait. The wind is fluffy but the current is also relatively slack. A few more zigzags situate me under the first of three suspension bridges that span the Bosphorus.

The basic strategy is to sail close to one bank until the current becomes too strong, and then cross to the other and try again. The outsides of the bends are where the current is strongest. It seems that I tack a thousand times. Without today's good wind it would be a futile task. I wonder how ships of old beat this current. My guess is that there were systems to tow from the banks. After four and half hours of sailing, bridge two is hauled in. Edhem then sends me to the jetty of a waterfront residence. Apparently the toughest part is behind us. We wave goodbye to the coastguard boat crew. The grins of our joint selfie confirm that two bridges are a victory!

Edhem shoots off downstream and leaves me to settle in at my new home. The usual occupier is a TV channel owner who is away this week but has lent me the house, and also his staff: Hasan and Sonja, who couldn't be more lovely. The garden reaches down to the sea and there is never a dull moment watching the Bosphorus: the stream of water, the tankers, a Russian submarine, the stream of traffic over the suspension bridge, dolphins jumping beneath it.

Turkish TV spread the word of my journey. A Whatsapp group of sailing club contacts is created. Notifications ping to let me know of welcomes that await along the Black Sea coast.

We wait for another day of fresher breeze to complete the final turns of the Bosphorus. Edhem and the coastguard boat are in contact at the beginning. Then the coastguard boat peels away, leaving Edhem and I to cross under the third suspension bridge in splendid isolation. Where the strait widens it is time to bid goodbye to my dear friend and pilot. What a guy! What a team! We did it! Released from the pull of current the board finds another gear. It spears the waves powerful like the dolphins. I look back. Edhem is still there. He is doing what all mariners do: taking some last gasps of space and solitude, prolonging the escape just a few moments longer. I look back again and he is gone. Now there is the hazy outline of a tanker about to thread the needle between Europe and Asia. And around me are the waves of the Black Sea.

The third Bosphorus bridge and beyond it the Black Sea. Photo: Edhem Dirvana

25. Black Sea

The Black Sea connects to the Sea of Marmara via the Bosphorus. It is often considered to include the smaller Sea of Azov, though the IHO *Limits* treat them as separate.

The coastline of the Black Sea is formed by Turkey, Georgia, Russia, Ukraine, Romania and Bulgaria. The Georgian shores are the easternmost of the Atlantic Ocean. To the ancient Greeks, Georgia – Colchis – was the end of the known world. In classical literature, Colchis is where Jason and the Argonauts voyaged to in search of the Golden Fleece. Greek colonies eventually settled all of the Black Sea coasts.

Early Greeks used the name Póntos Áxeinos – Inhospitable Sea – to refer to the Black Sea. This was often euphemised to Eúxeinos Póntos – Hospitable Sea – to ward off ill omens. Modern names that translate to Black Sea date from around the 13th century, and by popular supposition relate to the murky weather and water.

The northern shores of the sea are plains that have a far-extending continental shelf. In the south it is mountainous with subsea canyons. The sea descends to over 2000 metres and the water column is highly stratified. Only the upper layer has oxygen. Deeper than about 100-150 metres the only life to be found are specially adapted bacteria. Drilling of the seabed has found some significant oil and gas reserves.

Historically, the Black Sea has been a productive fishery – notably for anchovies and sturgeon. For decades it has also been one of the most overfished.

Major rivers that flow into the Black Sea are the Danube, the Dnieper, and – via the Sea of Azov – the Don. The deep current from the Bosphorus is another river-like tributary and is sometimes called a subsea river. The rivers and ports of the Black Sea are important for trade.

Increases in population, agriculture and tourism have generated vast amounts of raw sewage and run-off. This pollution reaches the Black Sea via its rivers, and has in turn led to enormous algal blooms. In the nineties, the arrival – in ballast water – of a non-native species of comb-jelly became the trigger for full ecosystem collapse: fish stocks were reduced to a fraction of their previous levels, the anchovy catch fell by 95 percent; stinking slime clogged the shoreline; and some bathers caught cholera.

Biologists introduced a predatory species of jelly that now helps maintain a healthier balance. And with accession to the EU many of the polluting countries have cleaned up their sewerage systems. Better fisheries management is also beginning to reap dividends for some fish species.

Black Sea

extent and track

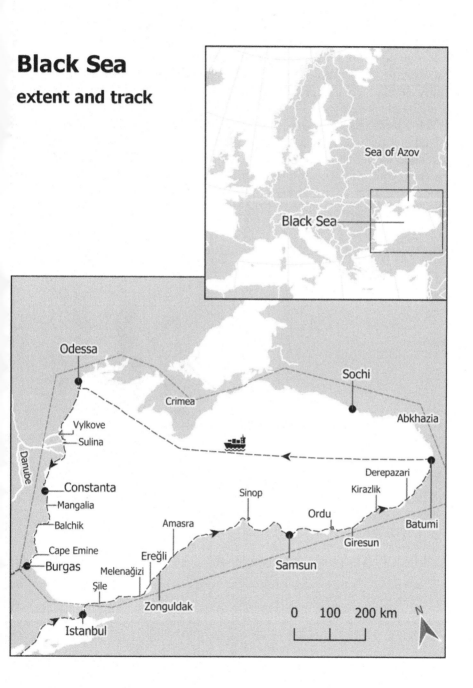

In the north, the Crimean peninsula separates the Black Sea from the Sea of Azov. Crimea was annexed from Ukraine – by Russia – in a 2014 invasion. At the time of writing Russia is massing its forces along the Ukrainian border – threatening another smash and grab.[33]

Winter conditions – particularly in the northeast – are harsh. Temperatures can drop to -30 degrees Celsius and the sea ices over. The Turkish coastline enjoys a relatively milder climate. Winds are mostly from the north and there is an anticlockwise gyre.

The Black Sea has few islands, and most are very close to shore. Snake Island – a relatively distant 20 nm from the Danube delta – was famously defended by defiant Ukrainian solders in February 2022. "Russian Warship, go fuck yourself" they told the *Moskva*, the then flagship of the Russian Black Sea fleet. Two months later the *Moskva* was sunk by anti-ship missiles.

Paddling over the Black Sea. Photo: Giresun coastguard

---

[33] At the time of publication, war is ongoing.

Launch, Sail, Land, Repeat

28 March - 3 April 2019

Between Istanbul and Batumi – in Georgia – there are 700 nm to sail. An equivalent straight line distance is the Isle of Wight to the Faroe Islands. The mainland coast is now on the starboard side. "Land on my right," I tell myself – with a nod to a book of the same title that tells of a round Britain sail in Laser Dinghy.

The re-introduction to open sea is a reminder to exercise caution. During a fluffed launch in a punchy shorebreak the board is pitched vertical and falls down upon my back, the spray deck tears, and the fin – a replacement – snaps at the tip. Earlier, I had passed the Russian cargo ship Natalia that lies broken-backed on the rocks. Later – in bruising conditions – I will reach the safe harbour of Şile. Then come three days of sheltering from harsh northeasterlies like an honorary seagull.

The flat spell when it comes is short-lived. A gentle onshore allows for useful progress but by early evening it has died to a trickle and the swell has risen from nothing to about 2 metres. The landing – after 42 nm of sailing – through a river-mouth with breaking waves – is desperately difficult and hazardous. An approach gets me near, and then autopilot takes over: I attack the entrance, realise that the next set of waves threatens a demolition job, round up and head seaward towards the teetering peaks, climb over those, about turn again, and attack again – giving it everything. The next set of waves to arrive will either fell me or propel us into the river. Thankfully it is the latter.

The dramatic entrance had been witnessed and brings instant celebrity. Melenağizi is a small, agreeable place and the local fisherman are hospitable. Across the river is a yard where trees are being turned into fishing boats.

Most days I meet someone kind and interesting. Today it is Selçuk, who gives me a ride in his Lamborghini tractor. Yesterday it was Volcan who insisted I hop in his monster truck for a lift across the beach. Tomorrow it will be Sitki, who believes that life – for most people – is enslavement. My take is that it is theoretically possible to find contentment in any situation. We will drink Raki.

A Legal Alien in Eregli

4-6 April 2019

A direct line to Ereğli sends me offshore all day, and the last 5 nm are paddled. The town's coastline and industrial port is protected by two moles. Within the harbour is a sailing club. While the club members await my arrival DJ Metin provides the tunes. Upbeat music carries far over the calm water. The volume cranks up when they see the sail, and the mix transitions to a dance version of Sting's *Englishman in New York*. With the paddle I find my rhythm!

There is an immediate sense of connection with this group. They lend me a bike to get around. The kind doctor does the usual thing of offering whatever drugs might be needed. We go and eat together. It is no good saying that the clubhouse floor will do for a place to sleep because the hotel is already arranged.

The following day has a full programme. First there is a talk at a local school. The kids and staff are so delightful that my heart overflows with love for humanity. Giving back is what gives meaning to life. And receiving kindness is itself a kind act. Life is astonishingly simple really: Take opportunities to give, and do not be too proud to receive. Oh, and cast off all expectation.

Next, I am handed a bunch of flowers to present to the new mayor. According to a local newspaper report Ereğli is the city of love, peace, and friendship. That fits.

In the afternoon we go biking. DJ Metin and Erdinç lead the way to some viewpoints overlooking the coast. It is a bright day with cool air. The Black Sea is invitingly blue. The winterized vegetation will soon take note that summer is around the corner.

Tea in Turkey is served in small tulip-shaped glasses and punctuates every activity. After the bike ride tea stop we visit a cave where there is direct access to the underworld and the dead – or at least that is how it goes in Greek mythology. This "gate of Hell" is where Heracles (Hercules) tamed a ferocious three-headed dog. In a literal sense that was a Herculean task.

Erdinç joins me on the water the next morning before a thick sea fog swallows the coast. The guiding sound becomes the horn of Ölüce lighthouse.

Zonguldak

7-8 April 2019

Zonguldak is a city built around coal mining from where I have memories both happy and sad.

The happy is Ferruh and his family, and particularly the lazy Sunday morning breakfast we enjoy in the midday sunshine. *"Kahvaltı"* in Turkey is spectacular: lots of fresh salad stuff, exquisite tea, various jams and honeys, cheeses, and – my favourite – *menemen* – which is a kind of spicy scrambled eggs with tomatoes and peppers, with a taste far superior to the sum of its parts.

The sad is the pollution in the water round the city. Plastic pollution on the Black Sea coastline is everywhere where the wind blows it, but around Zonguldak there is so much of it in the water too. This is to be expected given that waste disposal is simply landfill piled high. In some places the dumped waste has become the new shoreline. And as the waves eat into the landfill they pull the waste into the sea. The plastic pollution also says nothing of the invisible pollutants. Or the periodic foul smelling outfalls. The thought of falling-in is stomach turning.

There are many other locations where subsiding landfill falls into the sea, and the Turkish Black Sea coast in its entirety is littered with plastic – though much of this will have arrived on the prevailing northerly winds from the European side. The coastline remains beautiful, and at a distance we could choose to ignore our impact. Satellite and drone photography – though spectacular – enable us to be in awe of nature without the discomfort of a close-up look.

Amasra, Sinop, Samsun

9-23 April 2019

Many more sailing clubs and individuals make it their business to provide support.

Amasra is amazing. A fluke of geography made it a natural harbour and it has prospered ever since. It has a treasure trove of historical artifacts from the Greek, Roman and Ottoman eras. The sailing club, on the gentle curve of a shallow shelving beach, is a low-key volunteer-run affair, similar to Gunfleet Sailing Club where I learned to sail.

At Cide I meet Erdin, who founded a sailing club because he wished to learn how to sail. We go for a coffee and when rain beats down on the café window I succumb to the offer of another hotel room, and another meet with another mayor.

It rains a lot on this coastline. Wind is often in short supply or has a habit of stopping, to leave me stranded on an uncomfortable sea. Often there is just an hour or two to sneak some cheap miles. It is satisfying to make progress on these stubborn days.

A day of reliable wind allows a sprint to İnceburun Feneri – Sharp Point Lighthouse – which is the most northerly cape of Anatolia. It has been a dreich day at sea, made happier by the company of porpoises and dolphins. The low, grassy, empty headland – and the weather – remind me of Scotland. The rolling swells are of a fun size, and with the knowledge that round the corner is protection it matters little that darkness will soon arrive. This is a summit to savour.

The following day I round a more imposing headland and arrive at Sinop: another geographically privileged, historic maritime city. Özden from the sailing club guides me round. I stretch my back out in the mosque and can understand the attraction of the temporary time outs that calls to prayer offer. The hotel is a favourite: old style with wooden panelling, and crisp cotton sheets.

Sinop to Samsun is a two-day hop. The first of these runs is more wild than sensible – with a following wind that increases to a solid Beaufort force 6. Anticipating difficult conditions I had loaded light at the front. The sail is downhauled to extinction. I sail well – for 33 nm – and get away with just one major submarining incident. Exit from the sea comes at a well-protected fishing harbour. I am dripping with sweat and pumped with adrenaline. These wild days are not sought out, but they are enjoyed once safety is reached! It is another day with rain.

At Samsun I am distracted from the demands of making progress by pretty translator Gülşah. A couple of nights out are fun and that I can only talk with

Gülşah is a bonus, though perhaps also a regret. At 3am. we go for *işkembe çorbası* – tripe soup – which is apparently a hangover remedy.

Before departure the next day Gülşah translates a Q and A with the Oppie [Optimist dinghy sailing] kids from Samsun Sailing Club. Our miniature audience are attentive and endearing. We made a good team. Another overcast and cold sail becomes good for 25 nm. I select a sheltered camp spot to hunker down in readiness for bad weather tomorrow.

Water supplies are low and food supplies boring. Rain runs from the sail roof to refill empty bottles. There is a stretched out settlement here, but in terms of amenities only a brace of mosques. Horses and cows wander about. The contrast between city and rural is a time warp.

Two nights pass. The sky awakens refreshed, clear and blue. A green fade paints the sea, and it is brushed by a child's breath of wind. Once afloat, snow-capped mountains provide a backdrop to deciduous trees still in winter browns, but which up close are being resuscitated by the slow explosion of spring.

Sailing Clubs of the Black Sea have offered unwavering support.
This pic: Samsun Oppie kids with trainer Gökhan and translator Gülşah

Reflections on the *Karadeniz*

25 April 2019, from a contribution to Surf Magazin

The Black Sea

Sailing the *Karadeniz* – the Black Sea – reminds me of the Barents Sea. It is usually lonely, grey and cold. There are many seabirds: grebes, terns, divers, gulls. The marine mammals here are bottlenose dolphins, common dolphins, and harbour porpoises. Fishing boats are typically industrial-sized. Outside of harbours, no pleasure craft have been seen. It has also rained a lot. Sometimes it has vibrant colours like the Aegean, but darker and moodier is more frequent.

There have been occasional days to raise the pulse: either because of waves or stronger winds. Neoprene mitts and fleecy hat are standard dress. The Black Sea is given the full respect that all seas deserve. But I am not the same sailor who sailed round Britain back in 2015, or who set off from Norway in 2017. Much sea has been sailed. I have been scared on occasion – and am mentally toughened as a result.

A gulley with a stream provides a perfect camp location, though it is shared with plastic bottles and polystyrene from broken fishing crates

Water quality is poor near to the cities of the coast

A sadly unmissable feature of the Black Sea – and enclosed seas generally – is plastic. The stuff is everywhere. In Turkey is it not helped by poor infrastructure. At places the waves are eating into sea-cliffs of refuse. Near to fishing harbours it is normal to find polystyrene chunks from broken fish crates. Near to beauty spots is it normal to find trash from picnickers.

The apathy towards plastic pollution is dispiriting. What hope then for the bigger issue of the climate crisis? But in Turkey – as elsewhere – I have also met educators and young people who are the start of a wave of environmental awareness that will only grow. I choose to remain hopeful, for what other option is there? We either fight for our planet or give up on its future. We must react in voice and vote, else the Human Era will be a short and cautionary tale.

People

I look back and laugh at myself: for the trepidation experienced before sailing outside of my European comfort zone. We pick up fear of the unknown and carry it. It conditions our attitudes and can undermine our humanity if left unchallenged. People here have the same good intention as people elsewhere. I enjoy reflecting upon historical migration, trade routes, discovery and conquest. We are a genetic tangle – and that's fantastic!

If there are religious tensions these go unnoticed by me. The mosques issue their call to prayer five times a day just as municipal clocks mark the passing hours in European cities.

***

The sun is out this morning – the earlier description of a grey, dour Black Sea no longer fits. The café where I am writing this plays jazz music and my sleeping bag is airing nicely in the gentle breeze. Time for *kahvalti* – breakfast – and a few more glasses of tea. The journey continues to be a huge privilege. It can be sensed that Russia is drawing near.

The terrain is more mountainous in the east

The Three Amigos

1-2 May 2019

The sea has gone windless and sloppy so I bank the miles at Kirazlik. The small boat harbour is separated from its town by a dual carriageway road. Three teenage boys show up. I try to be generous with my time and offer an explanation of what I am doing. The sail sticker has a schematic map, flags of the countries sailed, and a few words of explanation in Turkish. These boys have almost no English, but they show genuine curiosity. That makes it a real shame when the dominant friend of the group mistakes me for a money tree. He cuts short a potentially more meaningful interaction.

To be sure of the request – and exaggerate the paucity of his English – and buy me time – I ask the lanky teen to speak into the Google Translate app of my phone. Sure enough, he is asking for money. I am not quick witted with put-downs, but am quite practiced at playing stupid. "Very kind," I respond. "How much money would you like to give me?" Google Translate converts and then reads back in machine voice Turkish.

Earnest misunderstanding is an unfair but easy tactic. The lead boy becomes unsure of himself. His backup duo become sheepish and abandon their friend. They snigger behind him, and he is the butt of their joke.

It is a sad episode really. There is no pleasure in causing humiliation. Before the boys skulk off I encourage them to learn English. Those with language skills become mobile and prosperous. Those without will have fewer options for bettering their lives. There are honeypot towns that grow, and dead-end towns that decline.

To reach the town – and a shop – there is a narrow tunnel under a motorway's width of road. Or a dash across the carriageways. It is difficult to envisage that prosperity will come here.

I feel sorry for Kirazlik – until I think harder, and realise that would be patronising. There are plenty of less fortunate places.

In the morning I notice an old man and a little girl. He holds her hand tenderly and is patient as together they make smalls steps on a walk to the sea.

The mayor shows up – with an English speaker borrowed from the town's school. They are happy I stopped at their town, and wish to present it in a good light. It is the same story as everywhere: people doing the best they can.

Arrival Georgia

11 May 2019

Much of the remainder of the Turkish Black Sea coastline is lined by a dual carriageway, that itself is buttressed by a rock-armour wall. Only the occasional outcrop remains in an untouched state. Most coastal towns and villages are therefore separated from the sea. Road noise is a regular companion. Inland, there are attractive hills and mountains. Dark-green tea country has replaced lighter-green hazelnut country. Snow-capped peaks lie behind.

Progress into light headwinds barely provides a return. The paddle brings many miles. Help continues to come my way, either planned or spontaneous: fish soup, a covered place to sleep. These contributions are sometimes very humbling. Every town has a harbour, so there are frequent stopping opportunities even on days when there is an awkward swell.

With a few days to go until the border with Georgia I step up my attempts to attain permission to sail into Abkhazia, which is self-governing having declared independence from Georgia. Abkhazia borders Russia. I reach out to embassies and specialist fixers, and it slowly becomes clear that my idea to cross to Sochi – or even to reach the Russian border – had never been viable. Avoiding misunderstanding where there is conflict is paramount. There is no sea traffic from Georgia to Abkhazia or vice-versa. The situation now is calm, but the border remains a tense place after more than 12,000 deaths during this still unresolved conflict.

Over a few days I move to and settle on a revised plan. From Georgia I will catch a ferry to Odessa, Ukraine in order to bypass the politically complicated north-east corner of the Black Sea. Then I will continue to Burgas, Bulgaria – from where the return cycle to Norway will begin.

The final leg of the continuously windsurfed part of the journey is a border crossing from Turkey to Batumi, in Georgia. It is a suitably effortful day, part-paddled and part-sailed. Ten hours of hard slog. Cramping muscles at the end. The mountains give way to a river delta and, a plain of flat land, and then a modern clean city.

The continuous track from Norway to Georgia has been 15,846 km. A broadly similar distance is later ratified as a new Guinness World Record for "Longest Windsurfing Journey".34

---

34 The previous record of 8,120 km was held by Flavio Jardim and Diogo Guerreiro, who travelled from Chui to Oiapoque on the Brazilian coast between 17 May 2004

Batumi. Photo: Georgia coastguard

Maybe I have underplayed the effort. My notes at the time – for that last day – are these:

"Go to customs at 8am. (after the last expedition porridge of the current batch) and am cleared to go at 10.45am after 5 signatures... Have 18 nm to make to Batumi in Georgia. Try to sail but futile in light headwind. Resort to paddle. With occasional attempts at sailing when a bit more wind (still slower but gives a rest to muscles; also allows eating). Border @10 nm. Cross border and am intercepted by Georgia coastguards, so have to make it to Batumi – no option to stop short now I have coastguard shadow. Paddle into headwind. Attempt to sail. Not enough wind (soon drops below threshold). Paddle. Repeat. etc. Make progress but really EXHAUSTING. Finally, conditions go good for paddling and settle into rhythm. Georgia already has nice scenery: a lower, delta region. Pick up gentle tailwind. Coastguard boat change. The first signs off with a toot. Friendly! Pump like a demon until wind expires on corner of city. Have done it!! Paddle in last bit. Really DESTROYED after that. Great end! Really HARD last weeks

---

and 18 July 2005. My sail is recorded by Guinness as being 14,454 km, meaning that a chunk of distance was lost somewhere.

with so little wind. City (Batumi) is spectacular. Officials take me away for processing formalities. Stay on fishing boat (thanks Vaxo). Am fed tea bread salami butter. WONDERFUL, though am almost too tired to eat after so much effort. Physically spent. Night a bit painful with overtiredness and cramps. Play it well (water, no alcohol) to avoid migraine next day."

The expedition porridge referred to above is to a secret recipe developed by Børge Ousland, who the reader may remember I met on Mannshausen island. The recipe was passed on to Helene during preparation for her coast-to-coast Greenland ski journey. Helene shared the recipe with me on oath of secrecy.

It seems that there were not many tracker watchers today, but Helene sent a message of congratulations.

Odessa

12-22 May 2019

Batumi tourist information keep an eye on the board, and at night I sleep close to the office until the ferry arrives. A pram base – purchased from a market-stall vendor of second-hand junk – provides mobility to wheel the gear to the ferry port. After boarding comes the release of finally being able to relax. Two nights on the ferry provide uninterrupted and restful sleep.

The ferry passes within 9 nm of the Crimean Peninsula. Even at this distance it has an impressive vertical component. I look out from the cold, blustery upper deck. Crimea is not Russia, and I am on a ferry. The voyage was not completed on its original Russia to Russia terms. I am at peace with that.

The sun shines for our morning arrival at Odessa's seaport. It is not without complication manoeuvring my extra-long pram through the gangways of customs and passport control. With a few bends and hurdles remaining I catch sight of Max and Aleksandr, my contacts in the city. Their smiles and relaxed demeanour are instantly calming. And they know how to tie a roof rack strap, which confirms that I am in good hands.

In fact, with Max and Aleksandr I am in the best of hands.

***

Uncertainty about the onward sail takes some days to resolve. The Ukraine-Romania border is at the Danube delta. But there are no ports of exit on the Ukrainian Black Sea coast that are nearby. Max and I investigate, and hope we have an acceptable solution. We submit a request to the appropriate Colonel for permission to exit from Vylkove – a small port on a Ukrainian branch of the Danube. If processing at Vylkove is permitted, it will be possible to complete the exit from Ukraine in a single hop.

During this time I take up lodging in Aleks' flat in a suburb to the north of the city – about an hour from the centre by bike or bus. The infrastructure and housing here – tramways and tower blocks – are partly familiar from memory of cold war era cinema. Endlessly-long main throughways are wide like football pitches. Mature trees separate the lanes for pedestrians, motorised traffic, and trams. The ten-storey tower blocks are basic and not pretty, but there is sufficient space between them to see the sky and breathe clean air. The population of Odessa is in excess of one million people. Communist planning has done a reasonable job from what I can judge.

The transport systems are daunting to an outsider. Buses, trams and trolleybuses are filled cheek to jowl. With no room to move, fares are paid by shoulder tapping and Chinese Whispers. Cash is passed along the chain and eventually the change arrives back. With coaching and instructions from Aleks I eventually manage some journeys on my own.

The centre of Odessa, by contrast, has French architectural influence. Linden trees provide shade along generous avenues. I have the pleasure of a walkabout with Max's mother, who explains many historical aspects of the city, and opens doors to favourite courtyards. Odessa has reserved elegance, as does my guide. We finish with a dram in a discreet club. Inside there is wooden panelling and fine upholstery, and more Scotch whiskys than I knew existed.

Aleks organises for us to go beneath the city. The mining of the limestone from which Odessa was built created a network of tunnels over 2000 km in length. These are the Catacombs. During WW2 they were used for shelter or hiding, and during the cold war they were to be used as nuclear bunkers. The underground museum is a chilling reminder of these horrors.

Back above ground – in beautiful sunshine – we join with thousands of cyclists to claim the streets on Cycling Day. As a mode of transport the bicycle is only bettered by the windsurfer. There are EU flags in many places. Odessa looks west.

Rolling down a sunny boulevard on Cycling Day

On the way back home I am introduced to Sergiy Naidych, who as a younger man circumnavigated the Black Sea by windsurfer, and is the current holder of the Guinness record for Longest Windsurfing Marathon. 71 hours 30 minutes is a long time to be standing up.

My Odessa guides Max (left) and Aleks (right). The city and its people are a joy

Danube Delta – Part One

23-27 May 2019, from log entry

The Danube

The river Danube is Europe's second-most major river after the river Volga in Russia. The Danube delta covers over 4000 square kilometres, most of which lies in Romania. It hosts 23 natural ecosystems, and is one of the least populated area of temperate Europe.

The Volga – incidentally – empties into the fully enclosed Caspian Sea, which has no link to the World Ocean. The IHO *Limits* make no mention of the Caspian Sea.

Odessa to Vylkove

Odessa to Vylkove requires three days of upwind sailing: 30 nm, 20 nm, 20 nm. These are long days with a nice expedition feel and a very empty coastline. The factor that limits autonomy is fresh water supply.

At a camp spot before another long empty stretch, holidaying Ukrainians invite me to join them for breakfast. The homemade ravioli is a perfect start to the day: nourishment for body and soul.

Later, a thunderstorm provides dramatic skies and then sailing in the rain. An uncomfortably close lightning strikes forces a stop, and soon after it is night.

Everything seems to happen for a reason. The beach where I stop is a barrier to an expanse of fresh water. A bridge over the lagoon is a perfect vantage point for a close up view of several "pods" of pelicans.

After these days comes a mercifully easy sail to the edge of the delta, before pushing against the current of Danube tributaries for another 8 nm. At most places there is wind, and by keeping out of the main streams it can mostly be sailed. Where there is no wind I punch through with the paddle. The bird and plant life is spectacular – everywhere is an explosion of life. The river appears to be clean and in good health. There are dragonflies, damsel flies, swimming snakes, fish, frogs, otter, and birds of all sizes everywhere. I imagine the Danube as the Amazon basin of Europe. The rampant plant life must be inhaling significant amounts of carbon dioxide. The natural borders, home to so many species, are also such sensible flood and erosion defences. Wild habitats like these are life support for the planet.

At Vylkove – the Venice of Ukraine – I spend my remaining currency on beer and hotdogs. It is late when I return to my camp spot. Discarded beer cans have appeared, and there has been a failed attempt to steal the paddle. The paddle release system is usefully simple yet difficult to figure out.

The friendly coastguard officials stamp my passport and we bid our goodbyes. I freestyle a shortcut tributary to the sea but am turned back by Romanian border guards. They are just doing their job, and even give me fried fish and vitamin pills before watching me paddle back the way I'd come. The only way I am allowed to enter Romania is via a very long detour out to sea, and then up the Sulina branch of the Danube delta. The current rips out of here. With an unfavourable wind it would have been an impossible task. And had I succeeded with my earlier shortcut, the cut through back to the Sulina channel would also have been an impossible task, or requiring of a 30 horsepower outboard to overcome the rushing hump of water. It is perplexing that luck always seems to be on my side. Best not to question it. Best to KBO, as Churchill used to say.

Sulina – in Romania – is lovely, and so are its coastguards. This is the EU again. If I do nearly drown tomorrow, at least it will be on home waters.

Ukraine: you have been a fascinating, beautiful, and entirely unexpected highlight of this journey.

A storm fills the sky over the coastline of Ukraine

Danube Delta – Part Two

28-29 May 2019, in part from log entry

Sulina to Delta Coastline

A kayaker arrives from upriver having paddled here from Germany. We exchange notes, and then I depart, despite a wind forecast that should advise more caution. The Sulina branch – up which I had sailed yesterday – opens to the sea after 5 nm. But going with the current I can exit after 3 nm through a leaky side exit. Imagine a pin prick in a pressurised garden hose.

The wind blows onshore and steadily builds. Over the next hour or so, sea conditions that are lively become livelier. Waves in my vicinity increasingly crumble into white water. Occasionally I am caught out and broadsided: my platform is washed away from under my feet to leave me swimming under the sail. This is not wise. In response to the building sea I harden up and head seaward in search of deeper water. The board climbs up and over the oncoming waves and crashes down behind them. The daggerboard takes big gulps of air and the whole dagger assembly creaks in protest. Already I am miles offshore – but truly deep water never comes. The waves and the crumbling white water just get bigger. I estimate wave height at 2.5 metres. There is no safety to be found out here.

The upwind miles and a gentle curving away of the coast mean that it will now be possible to sail in downwind mode. In downwind mode the board will have the speed and agility to escape the breaking waves. My plan is to sprint through to the inside of the break and then sail very close to shore. The line is now good to clear the point of a spit behind which there will be shelter. Such a shallow line would mean shipwreck for a yacht, but for me a fin's depth of water is sufficient.

Fuck! The dagger has jammed. Try as I might the thing will not retract. It will be impossible to charge in through the waves with the dagger down. It really is stuck. I hate making myself a sitting duck for a rogue set, but there is no option other than to turn over the board and climb on the underside and force the thing. I don't care if it breaks. With brute force, clicks and a graunch the dagger retracts into the board. I flip my craft back upright and seconds later am tearing along at between 15 and 20 knots.

It is a crazy ride to shallower water. Waves break with serious menace and the white water reaches halfway up the mast. The sail has the reliable pull of a spinnaker, allowing me to sail deeper when needed to outrun their threat. For 5 or 10 minutes – who knows how long – my focus is intense and absolute. Then I realise that the waves no longer have destructive intent. They roll in tame. Their energy is spent.

The wind howls, and current swirls, at the tip of the point where I haul the board ashore. I am also spent. There is no immediate urgency now. The waves from this distance look tiny.

What a place to have reached! Deposits from the river arrive here. Behind a narrow tongue of sand is a thick soup of sticks and plastic bottles that will eventually become land. Plastic is everywhere. It is sobering and appalling. But perhaps this is also mother nature fighting back. Perhaps in the froth she is evolving bacteria that will consume our waste. Perhaps – as our antibiotics become useless – so too will our plastics. Life will continue to do just fine without us, that is for sure.

A more comfortable shore for camping is nearby: a beach of sand and shells, backed by wetlands and swaying vegetation.

Delta Coastline to Gura Portitei

Wait. Allow time for swell to drop. Enjoy wandering on this deserted shoreline. Choose a shell to take home for my niece, Alba.

Wind good for making miles, but swell builds soon after launch when protection of spit is lost. The landing will be a problem. Important not to sail into late afternoon and failing breeze.

An empty coast. An eco-tourism complex: the first resort seen and a last resort as a landing. Sea defences that offer partial shelter. Head shoreward for a closer look. Find myself committed: within range of bigger sets. Hook onto a swell from 200 metres out and surf at an angle until on my preferred line and it becomes steep. Then set the board straight, with back foot jammed up against the barrel, ready for the break of the wave. Momentum keeps me clear. White water chases the now powerless sail, but there is sufficient breeze to prevent backwinding, which means I can stay sufficiently over the stern to prevent a nosedive. We race shoreward between the twin jaws of concrete tetrahedrons that form an artificial bay. The wave steepens again and then surges up a sharp incline of sand. The fin crash-grounds, and an inelegant gear haul later we reach beach proper – unscathed.

Romania – Southern Part

30 May – 3 June 2019

Romania has a low coastline. A ridge of white sand is topped by coloniser plants and separates the Black Sea from vast tracts of farmland.

The ex-communist countries have not witnessed the sprawl of development typical in countries with more permissive political systems. In the wide open landscapes between towns, nature blossoms and spreads her wings. Delicate flowers bend on the breeze, and Great White Pelicans follow the ocean road.

It is a coastline under attack by the sea. In the north, sediment from the Danube provides a natural defence. South of the delta region, sandy cliffs are either in retreat or protected by an armour of imported rock.

The ports around the city of Constanta are protected by immense moles that run for miles and miles. The moles are made of tens of thousands – maybe hundreds of thousands – of concrete tetrahedrons, piled haphazardly onto the seabed, until they protrude from the surface to the desired height. The part that is seen is just the tip of the iceberg. The cement used in their construction has a huge carbon footprint.

Critical infrastructure has to be protected. But – more generally – I hope we accept that coastlines change. The alternative is that all low coasts become sea wall. China's new "Great Wall" – constructed with concrete – already covers 60 percent of its mainland coastline length. In the US, 14 percent of the coastline is already concrete, and that could rise to one-third by 2100. The loss of natural coastline is devastating for biodiversity, and through various mechanisms leads to higher atmospheric CO_2 levels – which puts further pressure on our coasts, through sea level rise and extreme weather.

The problem is that humanity has invested so much in digging in. We are now reluctant to use the mobility and adaptability – that enabled us – unique amongst primates, and with remarkable speed – to initially colonise and later populate the entire planet. No-one can contemplate moving a city. And we are now so many that we have nowhere to go.

There is time to contemplate when sailing alongside a mole that is 8nm ($\approx$15 km) in length.

***

Protected by the mole is the port city of Constanta. I had enjoyed a brief tour yesterday with Cosmin, a friend of a friend of a friend who had volunteered as a contact. The old town has many elegant buildings, but a notable proportion are in partial disrepair. The overall impression is of a city

Navodari beach with fisherman Ilie (left) and Cosmin (right)

that is struggling. Cosmin explained that there has been mismanagement since the fall of communism, with unresolved ownership disputes about many properties, and a resulting paralysis of investment.

With hindsight, I realise that it is unfair to single out Constanta. The seeming absence of self-care is representative of Romania more generally. Simple things – for example the squalor of the toilets at border crossing facilities – tell a story. Of the countries that I visit, Romania seems lowest on self-esteem.

Romania needs more help and support. It suffered terribly under Ceauşescu – whose totalitarian regime is considered the most repressive of the Eastern Bloc. The country has moved on from then. But abuse leaves scars. History has a long shadow.

For the reader who has travelled with me to this point, it should come as no surprise that the people I meet are caring and capable. Cosmin saw to it that my barrel supplies were topped up. His fisherman friends provided a caravan for the night at their compound on Navodari beach. I drank the minimum of vodka to be polite; and the fish they barbecued and shared, carp, from a canal that cuts back to the Danube, were delicious.

***

The last port in Romania is Mangalia. The next stop will be in Bulgaria. Both Romania and Bulgaria are EU countries, but neither are in the Schengen area – so there is the red tape of the border crossing to contend with. I arrive at Mangalia on a sunny Sunday afternoon. Yachts are racing outside the harbour. Cosmin is aboard one of them.

Inside the harbour there is a ramp to exit the water from. Next to the ramp is a robust, orange-painted search and rescue vessel with the friendliest captain I could hope to find. Iulian has a smile that suggests he knows no other way to be. He offers a spare bunk for the night; and leads me to the relevant border officials.

I follow Iulian from one agency to another. He translates for various low level bureaucrats for whom time has slowed down or is yet to speed up. The processing is done by hand: pen and paper. I am required to return tomorrow, at 7am, before departure.

The sail to Balchik in Bulgaria must be completed as a single passage. It takes 14 hours to cover the 44 nm crow-flies distance. There is a 5 to 20 knot headwind for the first 25 nm. The coastline transitions from beach to rock, and then to high cliffs that eventually double back on themselves at Cape Kaliakra, in Bulgaria. Beyond the cape the wind improves in angle but begins to die away. By 35 nm the wind has essentially stopped. I take the opportunity for coffee from my flask and a much anticipated apple strudel pastry. Tired legs enjoy some minutes dangled in the cool water. Then another 4 nm are scraped with the sail because the sea is still far from being flat. After sunset, the paddle delivers most reward. Balchik harbour – my port of entry – is reached on a glassy sea in the nautical twilight. The sea inside the harbour is flat. No longer is there any urgency. The board is stable. It glides without effort as I go in search of the appropriate place to moor up and turn myself in to the border police.

Arrival at Balchik

Bulgaria – The End of the Voyage

4-9 June 2019, from log entry

After the exertion of reaching Balchik I eat and rest for two days. When the seaside-town restaurant music becomes too grating it is time to sail.

Perhaps these final days afloat will be uneventful: experienced with a sense of "seen it all before" – accumulated fatigue having numbed mind as well as body. I look forward to changing to the bike. The windsurf journey has been shared. Posting updates has been part of the deal. That is not something which I resent but the demands have sometimes been wearing. The bike journey I intend to be a more private affair.

A donation of food has been left on the deck of the board. The customs officers wave when I depart. A paddleboarder glides over to say hello. A big grin identifies him as the food donor.

Light headwinds make for slow progress. The Black Sea has been almost all headwind. Norway and Portugal were almost all following wind. 10 nm is the day's haul. Approaching the city of Varna there are some beaches with arrays of sun loungers, one of which becomes my camp site.

Next day begins with a swim in refreshing and clear water, then repairs to a broken daggerboard hinge plate. The daggerboard itself is also badly cracked, but earlier structural reinforcement prevents it folding. I sail beyond Varna, following near continuous beach on this hilly and pristine coastline. The weather is glorious and the water green. An island of storm cloud provides late afternoon wind. Sailing at its most blissful is like drinking nectar, or inhaling the scent of a dewy rose. If you could drink or inhale forever, you would. And I do – for miles – until the storm fills the sky. A lightning bolt cracks overhead. I scamper to an empty shoreline – now sobered up. Nights are still cold. A campfire provides warmth before I turn in.

I awake in the early hours, alert to activity around me. On the beach are hushed voices, shadows in the dark, and the orange of cigarette ends. A gang of people. Of thieves? Smugglers? So close they might stumble into my sail shelter. A small boat ghosts past, betrayed by the gentle tick of an engine. Fishermen. They work through the night to beyond dawn. Nets are hauled back to the beach. The sun rises from the sea. I count fourteen hooded figures around a bigger, engineless boat now also upon the sand. Their catch is some bullet tuna and two crates of sprats. Enough to eat. Not enough to rejoice over.

A land breeze provides some easy miles in the morning. When it stops I am near to a town. I buy water and a filling brunch. The coastline continues to inspire. Cape Emine is a struggle to pass and is where the dolphins say

The night fishermen stow their nets

their goodbye. Fifty individuals at least – the largest pod I have met on the entire journey – at the very last headland of my voyage. I prefer not to resort to the mystical, but cannot help but wonder. My camera, plunged beneath the surface, records their clicks. "This is the guy your cousins met and piloted through the Gibraltar Strait," says one.

"Same dude we cruised with south of Istanbul," says another.

Light wind and a moderately strong current run away from the cape and resist sailing against. With sunset approaching I complete the rounding by paddle, then stop on a strip of sand to savour a last wild camp under sail.

I resume in the morning by paddle. Then comes a rain shower and two hours of lucky wind. Then a final mile by paddle, until the board glides in and the fin grounds at the port city of Burgas.

There is no fanfare for the conclusion of the voyage. No press to meet. No disturbance to the calming routine of landing. Just time – some precious minutes – to realise that I have finished.

All Change at Burgas

9-12 June 2019

Peter is the safe pair of hands who oversees the transition from board to bike. I had reached out to Surf Shop Burgas last month, having decided upon an onward route. Peter's reply to my email came the next day. It was clear that I had found the right guy.

Burgas is very pleasant. Peter provides a comfortable apartment in the centre of the city. There is tasty food to be enjoyed and the vibe on the streets suggests that it is a good place to live.

According to the track, the board has sailed 8908 nm (≈16,500 km). But the tracker was only taking a position fix every 30 minutes, which smoothed out the zigzags on both upwinds and downwinds. Forced into a guess of the actual sailed distance I would estimate at least 12,000 nm (≈22,200 km). The board has carried the gear like an overladen mule, and it has made a thousand launchings and landings – probably double that – often where rock has crunched into its outer shell. With some TLC Windsurfer *Phantom* would go further, but she owes me nothing. Peter is happy to leave the board on display at Surf Shop Burgas. And I am happy if someone is inspired to adopt her one day for another journey.

My engine – the sail – number three – is still going strong. The rig therefore is sent back to the UK. In case my retirement is not complete.

At Surf Shop Burgas there are two boxes waiting. The larger box has a bike: a Genesis "Croix de Fer" – a gravel-bike made of robust steel. A beautiful machine. The second box has a trailer – a single wheel Topeak "Voyager" – made of aluminium. Bag and barrel go straight from the board into the trailer.

I buy lights, a helmet, and a puncture repair kit. Peter gifts a pair of shoes and an enormous bag of walnuts, and of course a few kilos of honey! The trailer has too much weight and is too top heavy. The resulting stability issues will be resolved in due course. I remember being heavy and unstable at the beginning of the windsurf journey too.

"Good to go!" I report to Peter, hugely grateful for his contribution. We snap a photo for the album. Warm smiles fill the frame. I hop aboard, grip the bars, and pedal round the corner. By the evening I will be 20 nm inland, and my units will have switched to kilometres.

Peter made the transition from board to bike *perfect*

26. Biking from the Black Sea

Northward

12 June – 8 August 2019

This book is about the seas and the voyage round Europe. The return bicycle journey was a hugely interesting and enjoyable adventure in its own right, but the landlocked part is not a nautical story. However, for completeness, some details are provided.

***

"EuroVelo 13 Iron Curtain route" and "EuroVelo 11 East Europe route" provided the outline for navigation. The EuroVelo routes are not well marked – and were not followed religiously – but were a rough guide.

Unintended deviations were plentiful; and several times I deliberately veered off course – often drawn by the pull of water, and sometimes – happily – by the tug of friendship.

The first major detour was southwest, back to the Aegean coast, and some days with Thomas and family at Lake Volvi.

Back underway, I sought mountaintops – for cooler nights; and mountain stream and waterfalls – for the most refreshing showers that money cannot buy.

In Serbia and Romania I linked up again with the River Danube – which underlines that land and sea are intimately connected. Without ocean evaporation there would be no rivers, lakes or streams. Without the land there would be no coastline to navigate. I bathed in the waters of the Danube and felt I knew it like a friend. Unfortunately, I was frequently appalled by the filth left by anglers at their riverbank fishing sites.

Hungary was flat, fast, and full of mosquitoes.

Bike Track
from the Black Sea

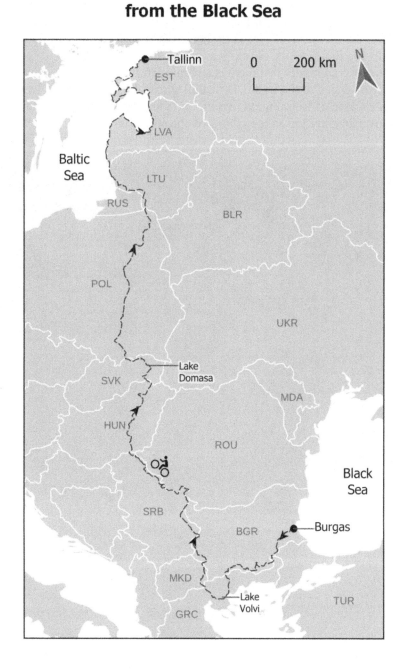

In Slovakia – not flat – I met with Patrik, amongst others from the sailing world, and stayed some days at Lake Domasa. The break was welcome and well timed. I played chess with Patrik's dad, swam in the lake, ate well, received delivery of a tent, and even borrowed a Raceboard setup to test my speed against Patrik, As is habitual he beat me round the course.

Near the Slovak-Polish border is a significant watershed juncture for the continent. To the west of the watershed, rain runs to the North Sea; to its south, drizzle drains to the Black Sea; and to its east, showers settle towards the Baltic. It is a wonder that there is any rain left for Lake Domasa.

I am also headed to the Baltic. Downhill across Poland – yippee! Leave the Russian exclave of Kaliningrad to port, and race for the coast in Lithuania. I cannot overstate my joy at being back by the sea!

Bathing in a ford in Bulgaria

A reunion with the Danube where it forms the Serbia-Romania border

Lake Domasa (Slovakia) with surrounding hills draped in cloud

27. Baltic Sea

The Baltic Sea is nearby for about a month. Good fortune provides the opportunity to sail its waters on several occasions. It was not part of the voyage, but it *was* part of the journey. Consider it, as I did, a bonus sea.

***

On the Atlantic side, the Baltic shares a limit with the Kattegat: that is, at the Sound and Belts. Going eastward from this limit, the remainder of the branch corresponds to the Baltic Sea. Subdivisions of the Baltic Sea are the Gulf of Bothnia, Gulf of Finland, and Gulf of Riga.

The name Baltic became dominant around 1600. Possibly it derives from the German for belt – "*belt*", itself from the Latin *balteus* – and relates to the aforementioned Sound and Belts. Hence the Belt Sea. The term was generalised to cover the entirety of the modern Baltic around 1900.

Germanic languages except English use the name East Sea. Estonia uses the name West Sea and – rather charmingly – Evening Sea, which clearly relates to the position of the setting sun.

Numerous rivers empty into the Baltic. In a geological sense, the Sea occupies a hollow – gouged by glaciation – where rivers once flowed.

After the end of the Last Glacial Period – about 12,000 years ago – the hollow became a freshwater lake. Since that time, bodies of water that correspond to the Baltic have alternated between lake and sea. 9000 years ago the lake had an outlet to the sea between where Stockholm and Gothenburg are now found. The exit closed as post-glacial rebound of Scandinavia outpaced sea-level rise, and the lake filled until overflowing at the Great Belt. The new outlet was more easily eroded, resulting in the lake becoming a sea that resembles today's Baltic.

Average depth is around 50 metres, and salinity is low, particularly in the Gulfs. At the Sound and Belts surface water flows out towards the Atlantic; and a lesser amount of denser, saltier water flows in at greater depth. Winter ice maximums typically cover about 45 percent of the Sea by area. Winds move the ice to create pack ice that may pile up to 15 metres high. Icebreakers keep sea routes open.

Sea life includes freshwater and marine species. Fishing is commercially important. Much of the sprat and herring catch is destined for fishmeal. Bottom trawling for cod and flounder is indiscriminately damaging to the sea floor inhabitants. The European Eel – once abundant – is now critically endangered.

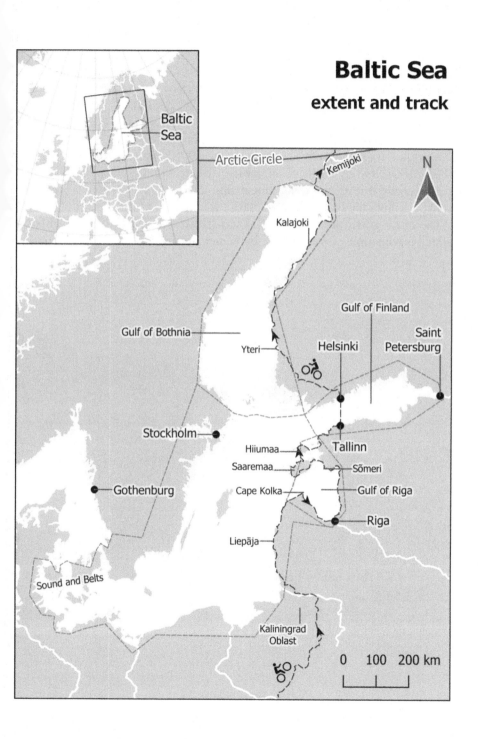

Baltic Sea
extent and track

Excessive nutrient loading from agricultural run-off, sewage, and fossil fuel burning has encouraged summer algal blooms and increased the extent of hypoxic "dead zones" in bottom waters.

Since the Viking Age the Baltic region has been important for trade and notable for conflict. Peter the Great recognised the strategic importance of the Baltic and founded his new capital on its shores. Saint Petersburg today has a population of over 5 million people.

The Nord Stream pipeline – on the seabed of the Baltic – has pumped gas from Russia to Germany since 2011. Nord Stream 2 – unused, and unlikely to be used in any near future – follows a similar route.

Maritime tragedy in the Sea includes the 1945 sinking of the civilian ship *Wilhelm Gustloff* by a Soviet submarine. The death toll – over 9000 people – still exceeds that of any other single ship disaster. In 1994 the MS *Estonia* sunk, claiming the lives of nearly 900.

Though a graveyard, the sea also has treasure – in the form of amber – which is sometimes tossed ashore by winter storms.

A Baltic shoreline near to Liepāja (in Latvia)

The Baltic States

9 - 29 August 2019

Lithuania soon becomes Latvia. The view from the bike is mostly of forests or farmland, but sometimes I head to the beach, and other times even cycle along it on the hard sand by the water's edge. The weather is glorious. The grasses of the sand dunes sway to the gusts of an onshore wind.

In a café in Liepāja I hear my name called. "Hey Jono! I saw your barrel outside!" The faces are familiar but it takes a while to place them. In fact I need to ask for help. Nonetheless is it lovely to cross paths again with Olivier and family – originally met nearly two years ago at Cherbourg. They are on a road trip holiday. Little Juliet – who still has a winning smile – is now four.

First camp in the Gulf of Riga is reached at Cape Kolka – a sandy headland – after 85 km of empty forest road. Riga itself arrives two days later. I have been quite anonymous as a cyclist – without a sail billboard there is little to catch the eye of onlookers – but at Latvia's capital I have two windsurfer contacts: Christian and Dana provide accommodation and a proper bed for the first time since Lake Volvi in Greece; and the following morning there is a most agreeable link-up with Maris.

Estonia is on the north side of the Gulf. The coastline becomes more intricate. Boulders protect it from the waves, and reedbeds flourish in the

A beach camp in the Gulf of Riga (Latvia)

more sheltered parts. Sõmeri Lighthouse becomes a favourite camp spot. There is an abundance of space, and a near absence of people. The onshore wind is understood as the breath of nature.

EuroVelo 11 detours via the islands of Saaremaa and Hiiumaa. These are natural paradises rich in flora and fauna: including bears, elk, and – on rare occasions – people. A confirmed sighting is Eric the cyclist. We strike up a conversation on a ferry crossing. My ignorance is lessened through hearing about Baltic State occupation by Germany then Russia, and eventual restoration of Estonian independence in 1991. Eric explains the three options available to men of his father's generation: Russian army, German army, or Forest Brothers resistance.

I read a little more about Estonia after the encounter, impressed at how modern, tech-savvy, and Nordic-like the country has become. All three Baltic States joined the EU and NATO in 2004. Useful insurance against the whims of Russia's current de facto dictator.

On Hiiumaa, harbourmaster Boris is a registered contact. He is teaching kids to windsurf when I arrive. Triangle sails glide like ducklings on flat water. Classic yacht *Lea Bernice* – cedar and mahogany, 1904 – provides a berth for the night.

When Tallinn arrives, the scrum of the city wears thin within hours. I jump on a ferry to cross the Gulf of Finland.

Saaremaa (Estonia) where I missed the ferry but caught the sunset

Finland

30 August – 15 September 2019

"Welcome Jonathan!" say Juha when I roll up to the family home 20 km outside of Helsinki. The Blinnikas are a Raceboard family through and through. "Make yourself at home, take a sauna. Tomorrow we do the Lauttessauri race. We lend you gear." *Sauri* means island. The Finnish-English pronunciation is like Italian with hiccups in the middle of words.

Lauttassauri is one of the bigger islands of the 330 that comprise the Helsinki archipelago. There is good wind for the circumnavigation race and Juha lends me proper gear, which I sail well enough to snap at his heels and take second place.

Sunday is less windy, and the course around a different *sauri* is longer which allows me to level the series. Next weekend there will be more racing, at Yteri on the Gulf of Bothnia coast. Four days away by bike.

I cut inland, detouring via Janne and Anna's organic farm and woolly hat business – Myssifarmi – "Hat farm". Janne is an ex-professional windsurfer, Anna a designer, and their hats – knitted by a team of local pensioners – are sold worldwide as articles of fashion that – if I have understood correctly – are cool for being not cool but at the same time hot. I cycle off the following morning, after a hearty farmer's breakfast and early farmer's lunch, proud owner of a *myssi*.

My tent at Yteri nestles amongst trees behind a generous sweep of sand. The Finnish Raceboard community welcome me as an honorary competitor at their National Championships. The event begins with good wind and the racing is intense. After seven races Juha has the lead by a single point; and with flat calm on day three that is how the results stay. People return to work and lives elsewhere, and Yteri falls quiet. These days – and the connections forged – are held dear.

The weather deteriorates and temperatures take a dive as progress north is made. The roads are good. There are long stretches with separated cycle lanes. Every now and then there is a bridge over a *joki* – a river. At Kalajoki – fish river – Jarno reaches out to offer support. He arranges a caravan to sleep in, and a friend lends some gear for a sail the next day. My hands suffer from the cold, but the seawater is comparatively warm, and at this latitude it is fresh enough to drink.

The head of the Gulf of Bothnia is a sea of islands. Post-glacial rebound of about 8 millimetres per year reclaims the land, such that Finland grows annually by about 7 square kilometres.

28. Biking to the Barents Sea

Between Seas

16-23 September 2019

I follow the Kemijoki, passing its numerous hydroelectric dams; briefly stop to inspect Santa's wonderland situated close to where the Arctic Circle wanders; and then continue on the only road headed northeast.

The road is long and straight, and although traffic is infrequent, vehicle noise is harder to escape: The sound of tyre on road carries far in the arctic stillness. Occasionally I see reindeer, or even have to steer around them. Elk are shyer, but allow some distant glimpses. The colours are autumnal and occasionally exquisite – particularly when the low sun breaks through.

Morning frosts are severe. In south Finland I bought gloves, gaiters, and waterproof trousers. The isolation between settlements means that bad weather could be dangerous if caught-out unprepared. A sprinkling of snow adds to the sense of bleakness.

The hamlet-town of Inari – on the edge of an expansive lake system – registers as an interesting place. Perhaps it would be possible to SUP paddle to the sea from here. A future adventure is noted. There is also a museum that explains Sámi culture, and the life-sciences of the Arctic.[35] I spend a happy morning inside, and emerge more appreciative and less ignorant of the world around me.

The Finland-Norway border is close now, and the Barents Sea coast Norway-Russia border is two days beyond that. I have some nerves – uncertainty really – about how the journey will end. I would like to cycle the last day with Helene, because it is thanks to her that this journey had the opportunity to begin.

---

[35] The Sámi are the indigenous people of the northern Nordic countries and the Kola peninsula of Russia. Semi-nomadic reindeer herding is still the way of life for some Sámi.

Bike Track
to the Barents Sea

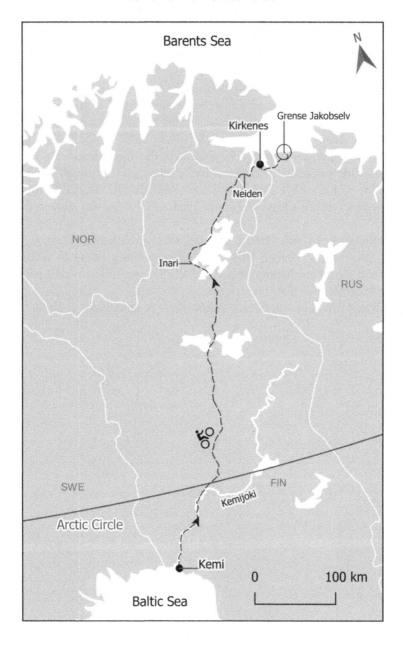

Distances are relative. At a camp close to Näätämö – Neiden, in Norwegian – we rendezvous. Not much has changed. Her hug is not clingy. She brings an axe and knocks up *ventepølse* and eggs for a quick dinner. She fits in a tent better than I do. Other things have changed. Two years have passed. She has skied across Greenland. I have windsurfed to the Black Sea. What else has changed?

She has school lessons next morning. I break camp; cycle across the border into Norway; pass Neiden's waterfalls; and soon after roll down a long hill to the head of Munkefjorden. The low tide has left exposed great piles of seaweed. The salt smell of the shoreline infuses the air. It bathes my senses – activating ancient neural pathways that rely – not on maps and GPS – but on our connection with the natural world. In a distant past we would have navigated by emotion. The sense of "what feels right" would have been our guide. I "follow my nose," and those gulps of salt air tell me that I have come full circle.

I bushwhack my way through vegetation to the shore; leap across rivers in the sand, slide on seaweed covered rocks, and splash through dabby pools until at the water's edge. The tears flow. And slowly the realisation dawns upon me that I needn't leave the shore again: that whatever mission this was, is done.

That afternoon I reach Helene's house, near to Kirkenes. There is a room for me, downstairs. Helene tells me she has a thing going on with a guy somewhere else. I am happy for her and tell her so. This is what I had hoped for, I tell myself. We'll still be friends.

The shared final leg – to Grense Jakobselv – is scheduled for Friday.

The Loop Closed

27 September 2019, from log entry

Helene reschedules some lessons. My trailer rig is loaded with appropriate celebratory supplies.

The last 60 km to Grense Jakobselv are special. The snow will soon arrive, and the road will not be open again until next year. Arctic vegetation struggles to hold on to the 2.6 billion year old rock. That's half the age of the planet. Up here is as close as Europe gets to true wilderness.

The final 10 km are along a gorge, with Russia just a stone's throw away across the river, though stone throwing is explicitly prohibited.

With 5 km to go we pick up some wood for a fire, Helene had pre-arranged the drop. We pile that on the trailer too. The couple who put out the wood invite us inside their cabin for a coffee. Norwegian hospitality is unfailing.

We are nearly there – just 3 km of bouncy track to go – when the trailer gives out. It drags me off the road and now lays there with a busted arm, completely lame. It was asked to carry too many tent pegs, along with all that beer and wood. We sling the gear over our backs and scrape the final miles to the estuary hamlet. My favourite place? A special place certainly.

The sunset is a good one. We camp on a suitably perfect grassy knoll and cook over an open fire: reindeer meat with potatoes in cream. A band of light goes contrary to the direction of the wisps of high cloud. Soon after, the aurora begins and at times the entire sky is painted in strokes of green. The display lasts an hour or so. More than ever, I know this is the end.

The trailer is kaput. After cycling back we recover it the next day by car. The weather has turned rainy and windy. The old rocks are now dusted with snow.

I had been considering cycling back to the UK, making use of the ferry from Esbjerg to Harwich, but learn that this service is discontinued. Helene also asks if I actually *want* to cycle back. The truth is: *no*. Now I would like to go and see my family. I book a flight. Easy as that. And again the tears flow.

Downhill to the sea at Grense Jakobselv.
Photo: Helene Erlandsen

Epilogue

The world has changed a great deal since 2017. Deep concern for the ecological balance of our planet was a minority viewpoint at that time. Fast forward to 2022 and it now the mainstream view that – to mitigate catastrophic outcomes – humanity urgently needs to reign in its impact. This attitude change is encouraging. Just five years ago it would have been edgy to comment on overpopulation. No longer does it feel exposing to say out loud that we are too many.

Covid-19 happened. A "once in a lifetime" event. Maybe. Unfortunately, there are a limitless number of "once in a lifetime" events that are waiting to happen. The next one was Putin's Russia invading Ukraine. A human catastrophe is unfolding there, and an environmental one may follow.

Perhaps we will stabilise the Jenga tower of civilisation, or perhaps it will fall. It really is in the balance. Perhaps that was the purpose of this book: to instil a bit more realism; to encourage us to face the future rather than to look away.

My stated objective was to windsurf from Russia to Russia. That head-in-the-sand optimism was a demonstration of my own naivety. Even at the outset of my journey, the waters bordering Russia in the Black Sea were militarised and not open for me to sail. I also stated and assumed that the journey would be continuous and unbroken. In fact, although the track is continuous, the journey was segmented by a winter break each year. Reality blows with a fierce wind, and we can either sway like a branch or risk being snapped. Pragmatism won through. A reviewer of this manuscript commented that it described an "imperfect journey in an imperfect world", and then outlined my shortcomings as an author, to confirm that it was also "imperfectly told". Nonetheless, I gave it my everything.

Appendix 1 – Thankyous

This endeavour was supported by an enormous number of people and organisations. Thank you to:

The many sailing clubs of the Europe's seas, and occasionally lakes. The coastguards, harbourmasters, rescue services and maritime police encountered, all of whom smiled eventually.

The many for whom I am missing the names, such as those who encouraged me to eat from their table or picnic, and the fishermen who shared their harbours and fish stews. And all those people at the places I didn't stop though the offer was made to do so.

Sponsors who provided gear: Starboard, Severne, Tushingham Watersports Distribution, Stohlquist, Aquapac and the always dependable YB Tracking, who put a dot on the map every 30 minutes. Thanks to YB, people found me where I never expected to be found.

Hurtigruten, who ferried the gear, and me, to the north of Norway. And the Norwegian Army, who dumped us at the border with Russia.

It is the support that came from the heart and from the home that sustained me most and propelled me furthest. I am inspired by them and I hope that you are too.

Thankyou to Ian and Brendan for their encouragement to make this journey happen. Thankyou to Nick for being a (virtual) writing companion during Covid lockdown. And, most important of all, thankyou to my dear mother – Jenefer – because without her this journey would never have become a book.

***

Takk (NO): Helene, Dag, Øystein and Guru from Hurtigruten, Kari Kristian Diego and Captain Lars from MS *Nordlys*, Fernando and Susanna, Marc and Martine, Brona, Torbjørn and Irina, Svein-Harald, Per and Annika, Irene and John, Björn, Layla, Siri, Rob and family, Lena, Håvard, Carlo, Torgeir, Louise Morten Trond and Karin, Dag2 and family, Björn and Lill, Erlend and Harald, Linda, Kjell Heidi and family, Grindøya family, Herbjörn and family, Marit and Avre, Tord, Trond and family, Lorent, Lillejohn, Alex N-22, Surfer group, Ragnar and family, Geir and Bente, Harald-Dag and Marit, Morten's dad and Karin, Egil, Kjell.

Tack (SE): Dag and Maud, Grundsund harbourmaster, Sven, Maritime police guys.

Tak (DK): Ingemar and Elizabeth, Aaron, David, Ole, Klauss Trina and Emil.

Danke (DE): Manuel, Surf Magazin, Sven and family, Per and Steffi, all at Helgoland SC, Phil, Josef and friends.

Bedankt (NL): Rodney and family, Ameland harbourmaster, Ole and Joop, Jens and Dan, lifeguards old and young, Vincent, Emma and Noa, Mimi and family, Bram, Jump Team surf station, Caroline, Zealand Catamaran Club.

Bedankt (BE): Robby and Pascuale, Johan, Kristoff Tania and Jonathan, Thomas.

Merci (FR): Silvain and family, Alba Gregg and Andy, Laurent and Corrine, Fabrice, Stive, Caroline and family, "Poste de secours de saint Laurent sur mer", Olivier Celine and family, Julien and Isabel, Patrick and Anne, Fefe and family, Olivier and Marianne, Charlie and Laser sailor dad, Bruno and Lucie, Dominique and Veronique, Franck and Corrine, Eric, Astrid and Erwan(s), Charlie Annou William and Oliver, Eric and family including Mathieu the Lego engineer, Anne Jean Eloise and Victor, Nicolas and Anne-Sophie, Ian Solenne and Lily-Rose, Jeff-dixsept, Nathalie, Lacanau Surf Club, The wonderful Arcachon family whose names all escape me, Aurelie Loys and Hélia, François Christian and housemates, Odile, Gilles, Pablo and Shona, Renée and Yvves, Joel Laurence and Leo, Nico and Nadine, Fabian, Loïc, Caroline and Jérôme, Hervé Adrian Eloise and Antéa, Ben, FFV.

Gracias (ES): Josema, (Eskerrik asko!) Itziar Iñaki Iker José-Mari and the rest of the family, Alejandro Itzi Miguel and Carmen, Lander, Juanma, Fernando and Helena, Iban, Real Club Náutico de Laredo, Ignacio Ana and Alejandro, Iñaki y Castro Urdiales, Alfonso and Josema and Enqrique, Santi, John ("Q") and Sarah, Montse and Ignagi, Sergio, Pepe, María and family, Marcos and Olga and family, Miguel, Marcos, Caroline and Rufo, David and Pablo, Sam and Mel and Lorena, Tino, Jorge and Pancho and Marcos and Mori and Carlos and Mauro and Carmen and María and Ana and Beatriz, David, Juan, Neli, Tono, Florian and crew, Javi and Sandra and Sara, Ana and Xosé, Juan, Gonzalo, Islas Cies sailors, Fernando, Paco and Miguel, Antonio and María, Karma Surf, CN El Candado, Jose AWA, John and Fatima, La Rabita family, Cisco, Dani Rafa and Nacho, José-María, Frank David Chemi and friends, Nick, Lorenzo, Amadeo, Oropesa marinero, Alan, Bià and Pili, Rita, Till, Inés, Xavi, Ferran Nellie and team, Mingo, Blanes sailors Luis Jordi Kim Jaime Pedro etc., Alberto and Nuría, Club Nàutic Fornells.

Obrigado (PT): André, Rui, Monica, Vasco, Sasha, Hugo Sandra and family, Filipe and family, Aveiro port pilots, Nazaré harbourmaster, Filipe and Manuella, Sarah and Philip, João, Gonçalo Sara and Sergio, CN Fuzeta.

Grazie (IT): Darsenún beach group, Giacomo and Francesco, Marina and Bert, Billabong Beach Café, Alessandro, Matt Helen Florence and Matilda,

Austrian pizza sharers, Chris Sophie Jamie and Edward, Marco Letizia and all at LNI Civitavecchia, Maura Carol Carlotta and all at LNI Ostia, Sabrina and friends, Frank Teresa and friends, Mauro and Silvia, Lido One Fire team, Josep and Maximilian, Ilenia Rodolpho Rachel and Francesca, Manu Lilly Guilia and Georgia, Catamaran sailors Calabria, Bruno and Daniela, Beatriz Francesca and family, Fabrizio and LNI Crotone, Giacomo-Francisco, Franky and Vicenzo, Rocco and sailing club group, Felippo and Basilica Vela, Brunella Cataldo and Guiseppe, Jonathan Seagull and LNI Columena, Gabriele and Gabriele, Andrea.

Faleminderit (AL): Viktor and brother and family, Imar, Mustafa.

Ευχαριστώ (Efcharistó – GR): Yannis and Dimitri, Lazarus, Guy et Justine, Mark Polly Andy Doug Paul and Ocean Elements team, Avner, Angela and Hans, Hans "Zephyr", Victoria and Kurstan, Moira and Zoe, Anonymous local at Limoni, Kevin and Simone, Kate John Matsolas and Maria, Manos, Tasos, Varkiza crowd Hugh Jane Chris Ali Sam Tatyana Pinar Patrik (also Billy Alvaro and Toni), Nikos, Eftychia, Nikos2, Ilias, Dimitris – who introduced me to Ithaka (the poem by Cavafy), Thomas Stavroula Kostas and family and friends, Stonero Surf Club, Odyseas Harris Themelis Yannis Vasilis Giorgos Popi Stelios and many others unmentioned from the Hellenic Rescue Team, Theodore, Paris, Evi Gianni and Evridiki Hotel, all those who donated honey, Thimios and coastguard colleague, Vatopedi monastery, Alexandros, Tasos Eleni and family, Makis Claudia and family, Christos, Christoforos, Nikos, Nasos, Babis, Dimitris.

Teşekkür ederim (TK): Murat, Lipari and Given, Faruc and Sovinc, Memet, Mert, Gem and Evren, all at Mimarsinan Windsurf Club, Edhem and all at Tuzla YC, Sonia Hassan and Ali, Admiral Cem, Selçuk, Sitki, Erdinç DJ-Metin Emin and Sezai, Wiola, Ferruh and family and friends, Taşkin and all at Amasra SC, Erdin, Semih, Cenker Özden and Sinop SC, Gülşah, Furkan Gökhan and Samsun SC, Evren, Hamdi and all at Ordu, Miktat and Ali Ihsan and their oasis of green on Giresun harbour wall, Içime and Mustafa, Onur and students, Idris Caner and Yunus, Seçkin.

მადლობა (Madloba – GE): Vaxo and friends.

Спасибі (Spasybi – UA): Aleksandr, Max, Victoria, Edward and family, the Danube border guards who (briefly) detained but also fed me.

Mulțumiri (RO): Stefan, Cosmin, Gabri and Crocodile Dundee, Iulian.

Благодаря (Blagodarya – BG): Balchik paddleboard guy, Petar, Burgas Surf Shop, George, Vayto.

Благодарам (Blagodaram – MK): North Macedonia was a quiet but enjoyable ride, with memorable mountain-top camping.

Хвала (Hvala – SB): Mountains, natural spaces, roadside fruit, and the family who offered shelter at Sutjeska.

Köszönöm (HU): Decathlon's display tent – for the only night without mosquitos! And a conversation on a riverbank.

Ďakujem (SK): Dusan, Patrik Josef and friends, Domasa Surfclub.

Dziękuję (PO): Krakow bike mechanics, Imielno shower and breakfast, Kielce parish priest, Suwalki bike mechanic, Tomek and family.

Dėkoju (LT): For the peace and quiet!

Paldies (LV): Christian and Dana, Maris.

Aitäh (EE): Eric, Boris, Kärdla Marina.

Kiitos (FI): Juha and Pike, Aleksandra, Jusso, Helsinki SC, Janne Anna and family, Yyteri Surfclub, Barbora Rado and family, Stefan, Johan, Jarno Juha2 and Kalajoki Surf Center.

This list is inevitably incomplete. Thankyou also to those who have been missed.

A memorable welcome from Håvard and Carlo at Trondheimfjord, Norway

Appendix 2 – Data and Track

Duration:

Windsurf journey duration excluding winter breaks: 597 days
Windsurf journey days sailed/paddled: 408
Winter break 2017/8: 85 days
Winter break 2018/9: 71 days
Cycle journey duration: 108 days

Track:

Norway to Georgia track: 8556 nm (15846 km)
Georgia to Ukraine (ferry) track: 569 nm (1053 km)
Ukraine to Bulgaria track: 352 nm (651 km)
Bulgaria to Norway (bicycle) track: 3412 nm (6319 km)
Average distance on a day sailed/paddled: 21.99 nm (40.7 km)
Maximum distance sailed in a day: 97.26 nm (180.13 km)
Note: tracker sampling frequency was set to once every 30 minutes. More frequent sampling would have increased the above numbers.

Overnights:

347 night sleeping "rough" (under sail, in tent, or otherwise outside)
239 nights in a "home" or with "homely lodgings"
62 nights with "rudimentary shelter" (vehicle, shipping container, etc)
32 nights on a boat
25 nights in a hotel

Track of the Journey

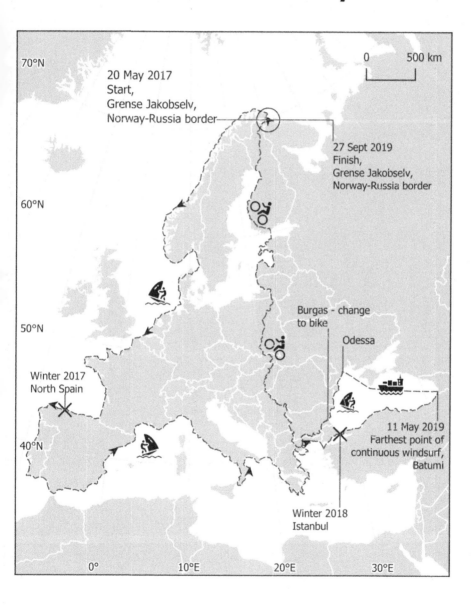

Made in United States
Orlando, FL
13 February 2023

29952178R00221